Binding Men

Binding Men tells stories about men, violence and law in late Victorian England. It does so by focusing upon five important legal cases all of which were binding not only upon the males involved but also upon future courts and the men who appeared before them.

The subject matter of *Prince* (1875), *Coney* (1882), *Dudley and Stephens* (1884), *Clarence* (1888) and *Jackson* (1891) ranged from child abduction, prize-fighting, murder and cannibalism to transmitting gonorrhoea and the capture and imprisonment of a wife by her husband. Each case has its own chapter, depicting the events which led the protagonists into the courtroom, the legal outcome and the judicial pronouncements made to justify this, as well as exploring the broader setting in which the proceedings took place. In doing so, *Binding Men* describes how a particular case can be seen as being a part of attempts to legally limit male behaviour.

This book is essential reading for scholars and students of crime, criminal law, violence and gender. It will be of interest to those working on the use of narrative in academic writing as well as legal methods. *Binding Men's* subject matter and accessible style also make it a must for those with a general interest in crime, history and, in particular, ideas about men.

Lois S. Bibbings is a Senior Lecturer at University of Bristol Law School and an honorary member of the University's Centre for Ethics in Medicine. Her research focuses primarily upon gender and violence.

Binding Men

Stories about violence and law in late Victorian England

Lois S. Bibbings

Routledge
Taylor & Francis Group
LONDON AND NEW YORK

First published 2014
by Routledge
2 Park Square, Milton Park, Abingdon, Oxfordshire OX14 4RN

and by Routledge
711 Third Avenue, New York, NY 10017

First issued in paperback 2015

Routledge is an imprint of the Taylor & Francis Group, an informa business

British Library Cataloguing in Publication Data
A catalogue record for this book is available from the British Library.

Library of Congress Cataloging-in-Publication Data
Bibbings, Lois.
Binding men : stories about violence and law in late Victorian England/
Lois S. Bibbings.
pages cm

ISBN 978-1-904385-41-7 (hardback) – ISBN 978-1-84314-799-2 (ebk)
1. Men–Legal status, laws, etc.–Great Britain–Cases. 2. Men–Legal status, laws, etc.–Great Britain–History–19th century. 3. Masculinity in popular culture–Great Britain–History–19th century. 4. Sociological jurisprudence–Great Britain–History–19th century. 5. Criminal law–Great Britain–History–19th century. 6. Violence–Great Britain–Histor–19th century. I. Title.
KD732.B53 2013
345.42'02509034–dc23
2013014041
A catalog record has been requested for this book.

ISBN 13: 978-1-138-95079-5 (pbk)
ISBN 13: 978-1-904-38541-7 (hbk)

Typeset in Baskerville
by Cenveo Publisher Services

To my father, (John) Graham Bibbings
(3 August 1930 – 16 April 2013)

Contents

Acknowledgements

There are many to thank for their help, support and patience through the sometimes difficult times during which this book was researched and written. The idea for *Binding Men* arose from a conversation with a certain Dave Cowan, who planted the notion that there might be a book in a 2001 'Masticating the Male' paper about the wreck of the *Mignonette* (the paper came to form the basis of Chapter 3 of the present volume). Other colleagues and friends at Bristol have provided invaluable assistance, encouragement and friendship. In particular, the project has benefited from the support of Research Directors, Richard Young and Tonia Novitz, Head of School, Celia Wells, as well as the enthusiasm and faith of Gwen Seabourne and Oliver Quick. Those who have read and commented upon draft chapters deserve special acknowledgement and gratitude: Andrew Charlesworth, Jessica Hambly, Richard Huxtable, Karl Laird, Morag McDermont, Karen Morgan, Tanya Palmer and Gemma Short. It is also worth noting that this research would also not have been possible were it not for the University of Bristol Law School's Research Leave Policy.

Beyond Bristol, Peter Alldridge supplied some references and sparked a search for the precise location of the Clarences' abode (see Chapter 4). The latter led me and a colleague down a number of intriguing tangents that do not feature within these covers but may yet form the basis of further research. In addition, I have given papers on this project at Keele University as well as at my own institution and to groups of school and college students as part of widening participation projects. I am grateful to those who commented, questioned and contributed at these events. And, as usual, the Bristol Widening Participation crew deserve to be bigged-up for their continued backing and sense of fun (you know who you are).

The research that led to this book has been conducted in the British Library at Euston, British Library Newspapers at Colindale and the National Archives at Kew as well as in university libraries. I should like to thank staff for their assistance and for making the process so enjoyable – and especially the University of Bristol Law Library staff for rescuing volumes of nineteenth-century law reports from storage. I am also immensely grateful to the

British Library staff who helped secure the cover image and illustrations, particularly Jaimee McRoberts, who took the effort to search other newspaper archives for the pictures I had selected and Jackie Brown who sorted the permissions. I would also like to thank my publishers and, in particular, Beverley Brown who signed me up when she was working at Cavendish, along with Holly Davis, Melanie Fortmann-Brown, Colin Perrin and Rebekah Jenkins, not least for their forbearance and understanding.

I owe a vast amount to my friends who have been amazing, not least for continuing to put up with my tendencies towards obsessive working and general angst as well as for keeping me going at particularly stressful times. Their backing and (seeming) willingness to listen to me wittering on about, amongst other things, men, crime and violence has been, to say the least, astounding – and is hugely appreciated. Some have already been named but are worth repeating. So the following need to know how especially wonderful I think they are: Andrew Charlesworth, Richard Huxtable, Linda and Alex James, Karen Lance, Genevieve Liveley, Robyn Martin, Morag McDermont, Karen Morgan, Wambui Mwangi, Tanya Palmer, Christina Pantazis, Kathy Pinney, Gemma Short, Caitlin, Ciaran, Petra and Simon Wilson. Special thanks also goes to the people I run with: Karen (again) and (latterly) Celia and Lydia.

My family have supported and lived with this project. So my thanks, love and apologies (not necessarily in that order) go to Graham and Suzanne, as well as Grace, Ian, Louise and Willow.

Doubtless I have unwittingly omitted to mention some of those who helped along the way, so I close with a general vote of thanks and apology to those who do not figure here but should – and, of course, with an acknowledgement that any errors or inadequacies remain my responsibility.

Combe Park
Bath

Postscript

A debt of gratitude is owed to copyeditors, Kathryn Wolfendale and Rebecca Wilson, proofreader, Brian McDowell, and to Michelle Antrobus at Deer Park Productions.

List of illustrations

This is one of a series of three illustrations which tell the story of 'A Clever Deceptive Scoundrel'. Charles Neale, was charged with the theft of a horse and, with a previous felony conviction, this meant that he was liable to be given a substantial term of penal servitude should he be found guilty on this occasion. On the night of his arrest, he seemed to have fallen severely in his cell, injuring his back. Apparently paralysed, he was transferred to the infirmary and given special treatment. When he appeared before the court he was carried in strapped to a pallet, as pictured here. He pleaded guilty and his plight was met with great sympathy from those present, with many a tear reportedly being shed. The judge was amongst those affected and, as a result, the sentence was much more lenient than would ordinarily have been imposed. However, when the convict was removed to jail he was recognized from a previous period of incarceration as an 'old malingerer' and his paralysis was doubted. In order to resolve the matter Neal was wired up to an electric battery. As the power increased, he could not maintain the sham and first his leg moved and then he jumped up. Having recounted these details, the paper speculated as to whether Neale would or could be re-sentenced.

Neale's case does not appear in this book – but the picture seemed appropriate and this version of his story provides a (light-hearted) taste of the (more serious) legal tales which are to be found within these covers.

Table of reported cases

Table of statutes

Introduction

> [H]istory is first and foremost a literary narrative *about* the past, a literary composition of the data into *a* narrative where the historian creates *a* meaning *for* the past.
>
> The past ... is a building site, not a foreign land to be explored.[1]

Binding Men tells stories about men,[2] violence and law in late nineteenth-century England. It does so by focusing upon five important legal cases all of which were binding not only upon the males involved but also upon future courts and the men who would appear before them.[3] The overarching tale told is that in this period anxieties about the behaviour of the male of the species were reflected in judicial efforts (not all of which were successful) to rein men (and, in particular, *English*men[4]) in by creating precedents as to the parameters of unlawful violence.[5] Each of the five chapters below recounts a different version of this 'binding men' narrative by describing how a particular case can be seen as being a part of these attempts to legally limit male behaviour.

Of the cases considered, four involved men charged with criminal offences and took place within the criminal courts, whilst the fifth played out in the civil courts. In *R v Prince* (1875)[6] a man who seduced a girl was prosecuted for child abduction. *R v Coney* (1882)[7] concerned assault charges brought against men who were present at an illegal prize-fight. In *R v Dudley and Stephens* (1884)[8] two sailors who, when shipwrecked, decided to kill (and then ate the flesh of) their cabin boy faced the death sentence if convicted of murder. In *R v Clarence* (1888)[9] a husband who infected his wife with gonorrhoea was prosecuted for offences against the person. *R v Jackson* (1891),[10] the civil case, involved an attempt to free a wife who, having refused to cohabit with her husband, had been seized by him and was being held against her will. *Prince* is portrayed here as being a part of efforts to restrain men's violence in the form of sexual conduct towards girls. *Coney* and *Dudley and Stephens* are narrated as reflecting fears about violence between men in hyper-masculine settings. *Clarence* is depicted in the context of worries about male sexual behaviour towards women both within and outside of marriage, whilst *Jackson* is cast as a case demonstrating concerns about domestic violence committed by husbands upon their wives.

In recounting these tales I draw upon a variety of sources. For example, the five focal cases are each considered in the context of other contemporary litigation, drawn from both civil and criminal law, as well as legislation and a range of nineteenth-century publications which expressed concerns about men or suggested how they should behave. Consequently, the textual notes include references to legal reports of cases, trial transcripts, court records, newspapers, periodicals (including medical and legal journals), parliamentary debates, religious pamphlets, novels, political and scientific writings, sporting manuals and self-help texts.[11] Additionally, *Binding Men* utilizes more recent scholarship about law, gender and history in order to construct its argument, shape its narratives and analyse its texts.[12]

The rest of this introduction forms a brief background to *Binding Men.* It gives an overview of the history of this book, the approaches adopted and the text's theoretical underpinnings. In closing, a few words are directed to this volume's structure.

A history of *Binding Men*

The idea for the book you have before you originated in overlapping interests in law, men, violence, criminalization, the late nineteenth century and narrative. More specifically, it grew out of work on men and violence[13] and develops my narrative approach to historical research and writing. *Binding Men* began with a paper presented at a workshop on gender and crime which was jointly organized by the Law and Criminology Departments at the University of Keele in June 2001. The paper looked at ideas about men in relation to *Dudley and Stephens*, a case which had intrigued me, as it does many law students, from the time it was first mentioned – in a first year undergraduate criminal law lecture, delivered by Peter Alldridge.[14] At that time, as now, I was also inspired by A.W. Brian Simpson's brilliant book, *Cannibalism and the Common Law: The Story of the Tragic Last Voyage of the Mignonette and the Strange Legal Proceedings to Which It Gave Rise*,[15] and the tales it told about the case of *Dudley and Stephens*, which included setting it in a broader legal and socio-cultural context.

After the Keele seminar (and with another of Simpson's books, *Leading Cases in the Common Law*, in mind[16]), I began to wonder if these beginnings might have in them the makings of a book. So, I (re)read huge numbers of cases reported in the law reports[17] as well as newspaper accounts of litigation from the closing decades of the 1800s – this being a period I had been studying for some time. Given that my research centres on male violence, my focus was on cases dealing with this issue. However, I defined violence widely to include, for example, not only physical and sexual violence but emotional and psychological cruelty, property crimes and blackmail. This meant that I was mainly, but by no means entirely, looking at cases that were heard in the criminal courts. I also continued researching contemporary late Victorian thinking about males, as well as studying subsequent scholarship about both gender and law in this period. As a result, I came up with an initial list of cases and a list of the themes concerning men which they raised. It was around this point that I submitted the book proposal and, after a challenging[18] but extremely enjoyable chat with the then commissioning editor for Cavendish, Beverley Brown, was offered a contract for *Binding Men.*

There then followed more research and some writing. This involved shifts in terms of which cases I would include and, indeed, how many cases I could focus on – as well as what would unite them. At first I had a list which included cases that had only been heard by first instance courts[19] as well as some where the initial decisions had subsequently been appealed or reviewed by another court. Gradually it became apparent that a more coherent book would result if the focal cases had all been subject to appeal or review, not least as they would each, therefore, have created precedents which bound future courts deciding similar matters (making *Binding Men* the perfect title). First instance cases, however, would form a part of the context in each chapter.

I finally came up with the five cases that appear here. Then, I came across a paper by Martin J. Wiener entitled 'The Victorian Criminalization of Men',[20] which accorded with my thinking and, as it turned out, the five key cases I selected – although I was looking at litigation involving both criminal and civil law. Wiener explored the 'growing pressure of nineteenth-century institutions of social control upon *men*.'[21] In doing so, he highlighted the way in which law 'increasingly stigmatized and proscribed long accepted modes of *male* behaviour',[22] focusing upon tendencies within the criminal justice system to criminalize different forms of violence committed by men as part of what Norbert Elias had described as a 'civilizing process'.[23] In the course of the paper, Wiener pointed to shifting notions of manliness and indicated how this civilizing process reflected these ideas by criminalizing particular kinds of male violence with the aim, amongst other things, of 'reforming men'[24] and 'rein[ing] in male aggressiveness'.[25] In particular, he identified concerns about sexual violence and statutory reforms which made it easier to prosecute those who preyed upon young girls[26] and argued that legal attitudes to pugilism had also undergone a shift, with an increasing tendency to prosecute participants.[27] Wiener also highlighted the fact that judges and juries 'showed a new interest in prosecuting violence in jurisdictions traditionally outside their sphere, such as among the military and at sea', pointing out that these were both realms which were 'strongholds of aggressive male culture'.[28] Sexual violence towards women[29] along with domestic violence against wives[30] were other areas where he identified change.

By accident rather than design these latter five 'types' of male interpersonal violence are those which are focused on in *Binding Men* and, consequently, Wiener's thesis is to some degree explored and developed here. However, this book differs from the work of Wiener, not least because I have approached the research and writing of this text primarily as a lawyer, focusing first upon law, legal argument and binding cases. So, whilst contemporary thinking, policing and cases in courts of first instance all figure in this text, *Prince*, *Coney*, *Dudley and Stephens*, *Clarence* and *Jackson* (as well as other authoritative cases[31] and statutes) are at its centre.

Binding Men, law, gender and historical studies

Telling tales

As the title of this book (along with the above talk of stories and narrative) might suggest, the idea of *doing* history as involving the conscious construction of tales about the past is central to the approach and methods adopted here, as it was in my previous monograph, *Telling Tales About Men: Conceptions of Conscientious Objectors to Military Service During the First World War*.[32] Mine, then, is an approach to history which entails the adoption of the view that 'things happen *and* they get told' and that these are 'two ontologically distinct categories'; but this is by no means a perspective that denies that '[t]here is at the ground of history that which happened: facts and events that occurred'.[33] Rather, it recognizes that facts and events can be told in different ways. Nor is this a completely nihilistic or relativist position. Instead, it is intensely political – so that within these pages my primary purpose is to focus attention upon the male of the species as well as upon the problems that were associated with men and, in so doing, to deflect attention away from women.[34]

On a more structural level, the weaving of yarns is key to the form which *Binding Men* takes. This reflects the view that stories matter of and in themselves; a perspective which is influenced not only by scholarship on narrative and history such as that just quoted,[35] but also by writings about story and fact construction in law, work which emphasizes the importance of story in narrative ethics and, of course, work on law, narrative and legal stories.[36] So ideas about narrative and history underpin this book and they also constitute a part of its methods.

In terms of tale-telling influences upon *Binding Men*, there are a couple more texts that warrant at least a brief mention. Whilst I was researching this book, two key fictional accounts of actual cases in and around my timescape were published. Both were excellent and informed my approach to storytelling. Kate Summerscale's 2008 *The Suspicions of Mr Whicher or The Murder at Road Hill House*[37] focused upon the killing of a child and traced the resulting investigation and trial. Julian Barnes's *Arthur and George*, published in 2005,[38] retold Arthur Conan Doyle's involvement in the case of George Edalji. The former, in particular, appealed to me greatly, not least because I am a huge fan of textual notes:[39] *Suspicions* includes a generous use of footnotes, allowing Summerscale to cross reference details from the actual murder and its aftermath.[40] The manner of blending multiple sources in *Suspicions* in order to construct a story also recalled in-depth historical, legal and socio-legal (of which, see further below) studies of cases, including the legal-historical work of Simpson,[41] which all resonated with my own approach. At a more general level, of course, Summerscale, Barnes and Simpson's work demonstrated the ways in which real legal cases might be narrated.

Reading cases

Beyond this, traditional legal studies form an important part of *Binding Men*. For example, to some extent, researching and analysing the cases discussed within these pages involved the use of traditional legal methods. The latter include identifying the legal issues to be resolved within a case, locating what was decided in relation to them and then assessing their precedent value; that is, to what extent they will be binding on or may be considered persuasive by future courts.[42] However, cases were not only read, researched and written about with an eye to such legalistic questions. A number of other, not entirely unconnected fields also had an influence upon my approach. Not least amongst these was socio-legal studies.

Socio-legal studies depicts a 'multi or interdisciplinary' field which involves the study of legal phenomena in a way that brings together ideas and methods drawn from a range of disciplines.[43] Within *Binding Men* a socio-legal approach means that, for example, non-legal nineteenth-century sources form a key part of the text. In addition, legal materials are analysed not only using traditional legal methods, but also in the context of understandings and ideas from gender, historical and literary studies.[44]

The cross-disciplinary field of gender studies is also crucial to this book and, in particular, scholarship which focuses on masculinities. Indeed, *Binding Men* takes men (and ideas about maleness) as the *subject* and *object* of study. In this context, Raewyn Connell's work is a key influence – most significantly, *Masculinities*.[45] Although her thesis about hierarchies of masculinities has been variously critiqued and developed, including by Connell herself,[46] for me it remains pivotal (or, perhaps, seminal) in relation to the study of men and inter-male relations. Fundamentally, Connell set up a way of conceptualizing how we think about and study men. In brief, she suggested that one might analyse masculinities by thinking about those clusters of ideas about men and boys which might be said to be hegemonic, marginal and deviant at a particular place and in a specific time.[47] This then facilitates an analysis of the relations *between men* as well as *between men and women*.[48] These ideas form a backdrop to *Binding Men*, with its focus upon violence not only between men but also perpetrated by men against women and girls.

Binding Men is also informed by other scholarship on men and masculinities, particularly in the fields of law and history, and by feminist work which focuses upon women in the late nineteenth century. In addition, a range of other history texts influenced this book. Given the subject matter of *Prince, Coney, Dudley and Stephens, Clarence* and *Jackson*, these include works which consider violence, crime and marriage in the nineteenth century.[49]

Methods of *Binding Men*

Overarchingly, as the above suggests, the methods adopted in researching this book followed traditional legal techniques as well as arts and humanities approaches. This involved reading, thinking, identifying key ideas and themes in materials – and more reading and thinking and identifying as well, of course, as writing. So, broadly speaking, I have used what might be generically referred to as a literary-historical approach to data collection, organization and analysis (as well as text construction).[50] I opted to take this course not only because it seemed most in keeping with the theoretical underpinnings of this project and the range of materials (both nineteenth-century and more recent) which it utilizes, but also as, in doing so, I was following other legal historical work, including that of Simpson.[51]

The chapters

The remainder of this book comprises five chapters, followed by a brief conclusion. The chapters largely stand alone and, consequently, can be read as separate papers – as a result there is a little repetition in what is said by way of exposition (in particular, as to the Court for Crown Cases Reserved in Chapters 1, 2 and 4). There is also some overlap in terms of the ideas about men which are explored. However, I have tried to construct the consideration of this material in such a way as to allow the chapters to be read separately, whilst also allowing the reader who dips into several chapters to get a deeper sense of the various theories, writers and campaigners. So, for example, the influential and popular work of Samuel Smiles is considered at various points in this book but, to some extent, different aspects of it are addressed in each chapter – meaning that those who read *Binding Men* from cover to cover (or consult the index to locate him) can gain a fuller sense of his perspective as to the male of the species – and similarly Muscular Christianity is considered in three of the chapters.[52]

All the chapters take the same basic shape, although, beyond this, there is some variation in terms of their exact content and form. So, for example, Chapter 3 focuses solely upon *Dudley and Stephen*, whereas the other chapters include references to other cases. Also, some chapters delve further into the past, considering developments in the eighteenth century, while others focus largely or solely on the late nineteenth century. All, however, seek briefly to comment upon the current law in relation to their case, if only in the textual notes.

So, in terms of structure, after much agonizing, I decided that each chapter would include two narrations of and about their case. Following a very brief mention of what happened by way of introduction, the first takes the form of a reconstruction of the case, including the events which led to a legal action being brought, what happened in the courts and the decision as to law. This not only serves as a chronicle in itself, but also offers a detailed explanation for readers who are unfamiliar with the litigation, adds to the often limited facts which lawyers generally gather from the law reports and provides a backdrop to the version of the tale which is to come.[53] The second rendering of the story represents a re-narration of the litigation in the context of contemporary nineteenth-century ideas about men and of other cases, as well as legislation in the period. So the tale told at this point takes the form of a story about the case which focuses explicitly upon efforts to legally bind men, whether by attempting to criminalize male behaviour or through trying to legally limit the conduct of men using the civil law – with some of the chapters also including some consideration of resistance to any, let alone legal, limitations being placed upon the male of the species.[54] Each chapter then closes with a few words by way of conclusion.

Notes

1 A. Munslow, Preface to K. Jenkins, *Rethinking History*, London: Routledge, Routledge Classics Edition 2003, pp. xii, xiii (original emphases). In both the quotations Munslow is depicting Jenkins's work.
2 The focus here is upon adult males rather than boys.
3 That is to say, they created precedents as to the boundaries of the various areas of law with which they dealt.
4 Whilst the focus here is upon England and Englishmen, along with ideas about Englishness, I recognize that the terminology is rather slippery – with 'English' and 'British' sometimes being used to mean the same things and on other occasions being used to refer to distinct geographies, identities and ideas.
5 And, of course, in the time period under consideration the pronouncement and making of law, whether by statute or judges were entirely male preserves; so here men were aiming to bind other men.
6 (1875) LR 2 CCR 154; 39 JP 676; 44 LJMC 122; 13 Cox CC 138; 24 WR 76; [1874–80] All ER Rep 881; 32 LT 700.
7 (1882) LR 8 QBD 534; 46 JP 404; 51 LJMC 66; 15 Cox CC 46; 30 WR 678; 46 LT 307.
8 (1884) 14 QBD 273; 49 JP 69; 54 LJMC 32; 15 Cox CC 624; 33 WR 347; [1881–5] All ER Rep 61; 52 LT 107; 1 TLR 118.
9 (1888) 22 QBD 23; 53 JP 149; 58 LJMC 10; 16 Cox CC 511; 37 WR 166; [1886–90] All ER Rep 133; 59 LT 780; 5 TLR 61.
10 [1891–94] All ER Rep 61; [1891] 1 QB 671; 60 LJQB 346; 64 LT 679; 55 JP 246; 7 TLR 382.

11 The nineteenth-century case-related sources utilized in each chapter vary depending, in particular, upon what was recorded at the time and what has survived.

12 Of course, every reflection on the past cannot but be influenced by the knowledges of the particular present in which their author is situated.

13 This work includes the study not only of men (and boys) who use violence but also those who (at least in some contexts) eschew violence. See, for example: 'Boys Will Be Boys: Masculinity and Offences Against the Person', in D. Nicolson and L. Bibbings (eds), *Feminist Perspectives on Criminal Law*, London: Cavendish, 2000, pp. 231–53; 'Images of Manliness: The Portrayal of Soldiers and Conscientious Objectors in the Great War', *Social and Legal Studies*, 12(3), 2003, 335–58; *Telling Tales*; 'Men Refusing to be Violent: Conscientious Objectors to Military Service Then and Now (1916–present day)', in A. Carden-Coyne (ed.), *Gender and Conflict Since 1914: Historical and Interdisciplinary Perspectives*, Basingstoke: Palgrave, 2012, pp. 41–54; 'Conscious Decision', *Socialist Lawyer*, 59, 2011, 34–6.

14 Peter was then a lecturer at what is now Cardiff Law School, Cardiff University and lectured criminal law.

15 Chicago: University of Chicago Press, 1984.

16 Oxford: Oxford University Press, 1995. This focused upon nine cases selected because of their legal significance and ranging from the late sixteenth to late nineteenth century.

17 As the name suggests, a law report is a published account of legal proceedings in a case, generally including a summary of the facts which led the parties to the courtroom and the legal decision as well as the text of the judge's or judges' pronouncements (the judgment(s)). Whilst any court case can be reported in this way, it is mainly appeal or review cases which form the contents of law reports – this is because the reports' purpose is to inform as to law and courts of appeal and review can make authoritative or binding statements on law.

18 Challenging in a good way – this involved an investigation of my knowledge, ideas and thinking.

19 That is, the court where a case commences or a court of trial, as opposed to a court of review or appeal.

20 In P. Spierenburg (ed.), *Men and Violence: Gender, Honor, and Rituals in Modern Europe and America*, Ohio: Ohio State University Press, 1998, pp. 197–212.

21 Ibid., p. 197.

22 Ibid., p. 198.

23 *The Civilizing Process*, trans. E. Jephcott, Oxford: Blackwell, 1982 (this was originally published in German in the 1930s and first published in English translation in the 1960s). Elias's ideas make an interesting comparison with those of Michel Foucault (also an influence upon *Binding Men*), not least his *Discipline and Punish: The Birth of the Prison*, trans. A. Sheridan, London: Allen Lane, 1977 (first published in French in 1975). See further, in particular, Spierenburg's comparison of the two: 'Punishment, Power, and History: Foucault and Elias', *Social Science History*, 28(4), 2004, 607–36. For Wiener's discussion of civilizing see 'The Victorian Criminalisation of Men', especially pp. 200–1.

24 For example, see Wiener, 'The Victorian Criminalisation of Men', p. 207.

25 Ibid., p.208. Others have made similar arguments – and some figure in these pages.

26 Ibid., p. 206.

27 Ibid., p. 204.

28 Ibid., p. 203.

29 Ibid., p. 206.

30 Ibid., pp. 206–8.

31 That is cases which have precedent value or, to put it another way, which are binding on future courts.
32 Manchester: Manchester University Press, 2009.
33 J.E. Young, 'Towards a Received History of the Holocaust', *History and Theory*, 36(4), 1997, 21–43, pp. 37, 34.
34 Or, as Richard Collier has (more elegantly) phrased it, to 'engage with questions of masculinity as part of a discursive attempt to stop the depiction of women as "the problem" and deflect an objectifying gaze from women.' Book review of *Telling Tales About Men: Conceptions of Conscientious Objectors to Military Service During the First World War, Journal of Law and Society*, 37(4), 2010, 678–81, p. 679.
35 Along with other historical scholarship which takes a similarly literary turn, including, in particular, the work of Hayden White. See, for example: 'Historical Emplotment and the Problem of Truth', in S. Friedlander (ed.), *Probing the Limits of Representation: Nazism and the 'Final Solution'*, London: Harvard University Press, 1992; *The Content of Form: Narrative Discourse and Historical Representation*, London: Johns Hopkins University Press, 1987; *Metahistory: The Historical Imagination in Nineteenth-Century Europe*, Baltimore MA: Johns Hopkins University Press, 1973.
36 See, for example: D. Nicolson, 'Truth, Reason and Justice: Epistemology and Politics in Evidence Discourse', *Modern Law Review*, 57(5), 1994, 726–44, pp. 737–9 and 'Telling Tales: Gender Discrimination, Gender Construction and Battered Women Who Kill', *Feminist Legal Studies* 3(2), 1995, 185–206; J. Winter, 'The Truth Will Out? The Role of Judicial Advocacy and Gender in Verdict Construction', *Social and Legal Studies*, 11(3), 2002, 343–67; D. Watkins, 'Recovering the Lost Human Stories of Law: Finding Mrs Burns', *Law and Humanities*, 7(1), 2013, 68–90; *Michigan Law Review* (Special Issue) 87, 1988–9; 'Legal Fictions', *New Formations* (Special Issue), 32, Autumn/Winter 1997; R. Charon and M. Montello (eds), *Stories Matter: The Role of Narrative in Medical Ethics*, London: Routledge, 2002.
37 London: Bloomsbury. Also see *Mrs Robinson's Disgrace: The Private Diary of a Victorian Lady*, London: Bloomsbury, 2012.
38 London: Jonathan Cape.
39 See *Telling Tales*, pp. 19–20, n.8.
40 See Summerscale's explanation (*Suspicions*, p. xiii) and the notes to the book (pp.315–51).
41 Although, in *Cannibalism* and *Leading Cases* he choose not to, to his mind, weigh down the texts with notes. See, for example, his explanation in *Cannibalism*, p. 325.
42 On legal methods see, in particular: J.A. Holland and J.S. Webb, *Learning Legal Rules: A Students' Guide to Legal Method and Reasoning*, 8th edn, Oxford: Oxford University Press, 2013; C.F. Stychin and L. Mulcahy, *Legal Methods and Systems: Text and Materials*, 4th edn, London: Sweet & Maxwell, 2010.
43 On socio-legal studies see, for example, P.A. Thomas, *Socio-Legal Studies*, Aldershot: Dartmouth, 1997. On historical socio-legal scholarship see, in particular, L. Charlesworth, 'On Historical Contextualisation: Some Critical Socio-Legal Reflections', *Crimes and Misdemeanours*, 1(1), 2007, 1–40.
44 In particular, my approach to case analysis here is influenced by work within this genre which explores legal cases. For example, see: D. Cowan, '"Rage at West*sin*ster": Sociolegal reflections on the power of sale', *Social and Legal Studies*, 12(2), 2003, 177–98; J. Winter, *The Use of Gender in the Trials of Myra Hindley and Rose West*, PhD thesis, University of Bristol, 2001; Nicolson, 'Telling Tales'.
45 Cambridge: Polity, 2nd edn, 2005.

46 In particular, see: R.W. Connell and J.W. Messerschmidt, 'Hegemonic Masculinity: Rethinking the Concept', *Gender & Society*, 19(6), 2005, 829–59.

47 See, in particular, *Masculinities*, ch. 3.

48 It, of course, also suggests that we might begin to talk about femininities and look to relations *between women.*

49 Some key scholarship in these vast fields is directly cited within these pages. Of those writers who do not feature, important influences include: C. Emsley, *Hard Men: Violence in England Since 1750*, London: Hambledon and London, 2005; A. McLaren, *The Trials of Masculinity: Policing Sexual Boundaries, 1870–1930*, Chicago: University of Chicago Press, 1997; J.C. Wood, *Violence and Crime in Nineteenth-Century England: The Shadow of Our Refinement*, London: Routledge, 2004; S. D'Cruse, *Everyday Violence in Britain, 1850–1950*, Harlow: Pearson, 2000. In addition, there is, of course, Wiener's *Men of Blood: Violence, Manliness, and Criminal Justice in Victorian England*, Cambridge: Cambridge University Press, 2004.

50 As opposed to methods of data collection, organization and analysis more in keeping with non-law social science research, where software packages such as NVIVO might be utilized.

51 In fact, I did briefly test NVIVO as a possible aid to the research process but found it unhelpful, given the types of materials I was dealing with and my particular take on the processes of research and writing.

52 On Smiles and his writings see, for example, A. Jarvis, *Samuel Smiles and the Construction of Victorian Values*, Stroud: Sutton, 1997; K. Fielden, 'Samuel Smiles and Self-help', *Victorian Studies*, 12, 1968, 155–76. On the Muscular Christianity movement see, for example: D.E. Hall (ed.), *Muscular Christianity: Embodying the Victorian Age*, Cambridge: Cambridge University Press, 1994; N. Vance, *The Sinews of the Spirit: The Ideal of Christian Manliness in Victorian Literature and Religious Thought*, Cambridge: Cambridge University Press, 1985.

53 I decided that this needed to form a separate section, not only as the tale-telling stands alone but also because, after a few early drafts, it became too complex and unwieldy to blend this with the narrative which was to follow.

54 In so doing, I set up a crude dichotomy (for and against binding men), which, of course, over simplifies things rather – for this I hope I will be excused, as this is consciously employed as a story-telling device. This is not, however, the only conscious dichotomy used, as sometimes my consideration of the socio-legal-cultural context of a case somewhat separates the legal from the socio-cultural.

Chapter 1

R v Prince 1875[1]

Constraining carnality

> The act forbidden is wrong in itself, if without lawful cause; I do not say illegal, but wrong ... The statute ... principally aims at seduction for carnal purposes ... Let us remember what is the case supposed by the statute. It supposes that there is a *girl* – it does not say a woman, but a girl – something between a child and a woman; it supposes she is in the *possession* of her father or mother, or other person having lawful *care or charge* of her; and it supposes there is a *taking*, and that that taking is *against the will* of the person in whose possession she is ... I say that done without lawful cause is wrong, and that the legislature meant it should be at the risk of the taker whether or no she was under sixteen.[2]

This chapter takes as its focus the 1875 criminal case of *R v Prince*, which concerned a young man by the name of Henry (or William) Prince[3] and Annie Phillips, a 13-year-old girl. The two went away together, were apprehended and Prince was charged with abducting a girl under the age of 16. His trial took place in March at the Surrey assizes.[4] It looked like he had committed all the elements of the crime – but one question remained uncertain: could or should the fact that Phillips had at some stage told Prince that she was 18 and he had apparently believed her mean that he should be acquitted? In addition, because she had willingly left her parents' home in order to be with him, some did not see the matter as criminal; rather it was conceived of as an elopement.

At the close of Prince's trial Justice Denman directed that the jury find the defendant guilty but reserved the case so that the Court for Crown Cases Reserved (CCCR) could make an authoritative ruling on the law. Beyond its implications for Phillips and Prince, the CCCR'S decision was crucially important in legal terms. It would not merely set the future parameters of the crime with which Prince was charged, it could potentially apply to other sexual offences where the age of the victim was a component of the crime. The majority of the CCCR judges decided to affirm Prince's conviction, thereby signifying that in such cases a belief that a child was of age would not absolve a defendant from liability, regardless of whether that belief was genuinely and reasonably held.

In terms of this book's 'binding men' narrative, the CCCR decision is depicted here as constituting an attempt to legally restrain men's violence in the form of sexual conduct towards girls.[5] As we shall see, a number of efforts were made to address this problem both through statutory reform and court cases during the latter decades of the nineteenth century. This legal activity reflected broader societal anxieties and, in this context, *Prince* can be seen as being a part of the contemporary sense of alarm about men's immoral conduct when it came to girls as well as young women below the age of majority (which was then 21),[6] although the focus in this chapter is upon cases involving under-16s (following the parameters of the offence in *Prince* and given the continued significance of this age). Whilst such concerns extended to both Englishmen and foreigners, in keeping with this book's subject, this chapter considers only the former.[7] Additionally, the majority's ruling in *Prince* is also conceived of here as being a response to worries about a tendency, alluded to already and evident both in courtrooms and in wider society, not to view such conduct as occurred between Phillips and Prince as criminal.

The chapter begins by exploring *Prince*, looking at what happened – and it does this in more depth than in previous writings about the case, which have, for the most part, included only relatively fleetingly references to it.[8] The decision is then placed within a broader legal and socio-cultural background, which includes other cases and legislation, with the text tracing some of the attempts to address male sexual conduct towards girls from the 1860s until the close of the nineteenth century. Whilst the focus in all this is upon efforts to rein in and penalize men's violence in the form of sexual conduct towards girls, along the way resistance to this trend is also considered, including judges and juries who demonstrated a reluctance to see (all) men who had sexual relations with girls as being (equally) blameworthy.

Prince

The account of the events both before and during the trial reconstructed below is largely drawn from the press coverage of the case.[9] The law reports give little by way of information about the circumstances beyond that which was deemed necessary for the CCCR decision and surviving court records do not offer much by way of assistance.[10] Nevertheless, a good deal of back story can be added to the meagre details familiar to students and scholars of criminal law.

The seduction and abduction

Annie Phillips, who was proved by her father to be 13 at the time of the alleged offence,[11] lived with her parents in Kingston upon Thames. She revealed that she had known Henry Prince, who was described in the press as a 'well-dressed young man',[12] for five weeks prior to their departure and that during this period she had met him without the knowledge of her parents, their liaisons taking place behind the Fighting Cocks public house.[13] In giving evidence she recalled his constant appeals to her to go away with him and his promise of marriage should she do so.[14] Initially, she said that she had refused to comply but in the end had altered her view. Indeed, her evidence was that when they left she went not merely willingly but enthusiastically. Under cross-examination by the defence and in response to the judge's questions she added to this, admitting that before they had gone she had told him she wanted to go away and had complained to him of her mother's and father's behaviour.[15]

On the evening of Sunday 3 January 1875, at some time between five and six, Phillips left her parents' house and met Prince as they had previously arranged. He drove them away in a horse and cart, heading first for Reading. They stopped on the road that night, staying in a country public house where they slept together. They arrived at Reading late on Monday. There Prince bought Phillips a ring, saying that he would marry her 'in a day or two' and they again took a room. The next day they headed for Oxford where they found lodgings and lived as man and wife. Later that month they were located by friends of the Phillips family and the girl's father was sent for. Upon his arrival, despite the pleadings of Prince's friends to the effect that he abandon the matter in return for payment, he decided to pursue it. Prince was arrested by a police detective on 18 January and charged with the offence of abduction – no charges were brought in relation to the sexual contact which they appear to have had, as Phillips was above the then age of consent (12)[16] and was apparently consenting. Both he and the girl were returned to Kingston by train.[17]

As to what she had said to Prince regarding her age, at trial Phillips gave evidence that he had asked her about this and that she had told him she was not sure but thought she was 18. There was some dispute as to when the latter occurred, however, with both defence counsel and the judge questioning her version of events, not least as there was some uncertainty over whether she had changed her initial account regarding this detail.[18] This meant that it was not clear whether the question was asked and answered before or after Prince and Phillips left Kingston. However, under re-examination by the prosecution, Phillips added the claim that during their journey back to Kingston Prince had promised to marry her if she gave evidence that she had told him she was 18 before their departure for Reading.[19]

The trial

On 24 March 1875 Henry Prince appeared before the Surrey assizes in Kingston upon Thames charged with the offence of 'unlawfully' taking an unmarried girl under the age of 16 'out of the possession and against the will of her father or mother, or of any other person having the lawful care or charge of her' under section 55 of the Offences Against the Person Act 1861 (a misdemeanour[20] which carried a possible maximum penalty of two years' imprisonment with or without hard labour). At this time the offence of 'abduction' applied only to girls but could be committed by a male or a female. Whilst it appeared in the list of sexual offences against girls and women in the 1861 Act, sexual activity was not required in order for there to be a conviction. However, as the epigraph to this chapter suggests, a central purpose of the section was undoubtedly to penalize those (and, in particular, men) who had sexual motives in mind when they enticed girls to leave their parents.

The trial was presided over by Justice Denman, with Mr Lilley appearing for the prosecution and Mr Straight for Prince. Evidence was given by Phillips, who was noted by reports of the case to look older than her years, along with her father, Philip Phillips, a 'general dealer', and Charles Clayton, the police detective who had arrested the defendant. Lilley, for the prosecution, opened the case by characterizing it as being of 'considerable social importance' and, in so doing, emphasized the weightiness of the jury's task. He presented the offence charged as one committed by a man against the girl's parents (or, more often, their fathers),[21] rather than against the girl – this meant that he could argue that Phillips's role in the taking away (that is, the fact that she had apparently consented or was keen to go with him) was irrelevant. In this view the only legal question was whether Prince's belief as to her age could in some way negate his liability for the offence. For the prosecution this too was immaterial as Lilley constructed section 55 as a strict liability offence, meaning that no particular criminal state of mind or *mens rea* was required on the part of the defendant; he merely needed to have done the deed for a conviction. Consequently, the only question to be answered was whether she had reached the age of 16 by the date of the taking away – if she had not, Prince was guilty.[22]

At the close of prosecution evidence, on Prince's behalf, Straight moved to have the matter dropped, claiming that there was no case to put to the jury because there was no proof that his client had knowingly or wilfully taken Phillips away believing she was under 16.[23] This request was not treated sympathetically. The judge noted he was aware of previous cases where the fact that a girl appeared to be older had not prevented a conviction and this was suggestive that any mistake as to the age was not relevant to the offence, so a guilty verdict should be returned in the present case. However, as this particular set of facts had not to his knowledge been presented to a court before, the law was uncertain. Consequently, if the jury found that Phillips had told Prince that she was 18 before they left and that the defendant had believed her, Denman intended to refer the case to the CCCR for a decision as to the law. Significantly, in so saying, the judge seemed to be indicating that the jury would not be given the opportunity to acquit the defendant – because in his view even if they found in Prince's favour in terms of the facts, this would entail a conviction and a reservation.

The defence consisted of Straight's cross-examination of Phillips and his address to the jury. Despite Denman's view as to the law, the main line of argument was that Prince had genuinely believed that Phillips was 18 and that this belief was reasonable not only because she looked older, but also because she had told him this. Thus Straight argued that, although he could not 'justify [Prince's] conduct in a moral view', because the defendant had truly believed Phillips to be over 16 he had done nothing legally wrong and could not, therefore, be guilty of the offence.[24] In his cross examination of Phillips he also managed to highlight her willingness to leave and the fact that she remained with Prince despite being offered assistance to return home whilst they were in Reading.[25] All this was presumably intended to encourage the jury to think that Prince was not entirely to blame for the taking away and to suggest the possibility of an acquittal. The lawyer's efforts were, however, to be of no avail.

In bringing the trial to a close, Denman effectively ensured that the case would be dealt with as he had already indicated. Aside from the fundamental matter of whether they found that Prince had taken Phillips away from her parents against their will (which they answered in the affirmative), Denman put two crucial questions to the jury. He asked them whether they thought that Prince believed Phillips to be over 16 when he took her away from Kingston and whether she had told him she was over 18 at that time. Accepting the view most favourable to the defendant as regards the age issue, they answered yes to both these queries, so Prince's belief was found to be genuine and reasonable at the point of the taking.[26] The judge then 'directed that a verdict of guilty be entered'.[27] In doing so (and it seems from the various reports that he pressed this upon the jury), Denman ensured not only a conviction, but also that he could reserve the point of law as to the age issue – because, as we shall see, referrals to the CCCR could only be made following a conviction. Judgment was, therefore, respited and Prince was released on bail pending the CCCR's decision.

The review

The CCCR had been created in 1848 by the Crown Cases Act. It was a court of review rather than of appeal – in fact, there was no court of criminal appeal until one was created by the 1907 Criminal Appeal Act, which in turn brought the CCCR to an end. The CCCR consisted of all the common law judges who went on circuit, presiding over the assizes around the country (the exact number of judges increased during its lifespan). In the normal course, cases sent for review were heard by a panel of five of the judges; however, where the five were divided and/or felt the matter to be of sufficient importance or controversy, it could be considered by all the judges. The CCCR could only hear cases which had resulted in a conviction and was empowered to consider only matters referred or reserved to it by a judge. Neither the defence nor the prosecution had any say in whether a case should be reserved, although lawyers could ask for this to be considered. Generally, if the decision was taken to do so, sentencing would either be respited or, once sentence was passed, a convicted person would be released on bail, whilst the legal questions and their consequences were resolved.

On the day the case came before the CCCR for consideration, a statement of the facts decided by the jury as well as the legal questions to be resolved would be provided by the judge who had presided over the trial.[28] Where the referring judge was himself a member of the court, he could again sit in judgment of the case (as happened in *Prince*). Matters would then be argued by prosecution counsel (assuming there was one) and, if a defendant was represented, their lawyer, with the judges often interjecting repeatedly. The CCCR could only rule upon the matters of law reserved for its consideration – and they were left to accept the findings of the jury as to the facts of the case. The effect of their decision would be either to quash or to affirm a conviction – and, if the latter course was decided upon, the 'prisoner' or 'defendant' would be recalled to the trial court, so that the sentence could be either confirmed or pronounced ('appellant' was not the correct term as this was no appeal – and 'prisoner' was often used regardless of whether the person was in custody). Where the result was an acquittal this would be noted at the next sitting of the trial court and the defendants would be formally discharged.[29]

Prince first came before the CCCR on 25 April 1875. The five judges sitting on that day were Lord Chief Justice Cockburn, Barons Bramwell and Pollock, along with Justices Mellor and Brett.[30] However, they felt that the matters to be addressed were of very great significance and, therefore, decided that consideration of the case should be delayed so that it could be ruled upon by the full court. On Saturday 29 May the case was argued before 16 of what was at that time a potential pool of 18 judges (Cockburn, Kelly, Chief Baron of the Exchequer, Barons Bramwell, Cleasby, Pollock and Amphlett, Justices Blackburn, Mellor, Lush, Brett, Grove, Quain, Denman, Archibald, Field and Lindley).[31] Mr Lilley again put the prosecution arguments, whilst Prince was unrepresented.

The question (or questions) for the Court was whether the finding that Prince genuinely believed that Phillips was over 16 and that he had reasonable grounds for this belief constituted a defence to section 55 or, to phrase it slightly differently, whether these facts meant that he did not possess the required *mens rea* or 'criminal state of mind'[32] for this offence. The latter issue was of crucial import not only for Prince, but also for the future of the offence as, if the prosecution arguments carried the day, the result would be that the section 55 offence would be cast as one of strict liability, at least as regards the age issue – making a defendant's inadvertence as to this element of the offence no bar to a conviction. Additionally, this approach might have subsequently been found to have a wider application in relation to other sexual offences which specified the age of a victim.

In arguing for the conviction to be confirmed, Lilley maintained that the approach adopted in previous cases where similar facts were at issue should be followed. According to him, this meant that anyone who took a young female from the lawful possession of another did so at their own risk and must face the consequences if she was actually under age. However, as we shall see, past cases did not all support affirming the present conviction. In particular, a recent CCCR case suggested that Prince should be acquitted and was raised in the courtroom discussions between the judges (there being no defence counsel to put arguments in the prisoner's favour). In response, Lilley disputed both the correctness of this approach and its extension to *Prince* as he maintained that a different issue was at stake.

At the close of arguments in May *The Times* reported that 'there being, apparently, a difference of opinion on the bench,' the CCCR judges adjourned to discuss the case and 'were absent some time'. Upon their return, it was announced that they would deliver judgment in two weeks time. In fact this was delayed until Saturday 26 June.[33]

The decision

In the end the decision of the CCCR was split. All except one of the 16 came to the conclusion that the conviction should stand. However, the 15 in the majority did not entirely agree as to the reasoning by which they came to this result. Consequently, in total four judgments were delivered: three affirming the conviction and one taking the opposite view. In the majority were: Bramwell[34] (Kelly, Cleasby, Pollock, Amphlett, Grove, Quain and Denman concurring); Blackburn[35] (Cockburn, Mellor, Lush, Quain, Denman, Archibald, Field, Lindley and Pollock concurring); and Denman (the trial judge) who, despite agreeing with the judgments of both Bramwell and Blackburn, felt the need to add his own brief adjunct to them.[36] Brett dissented – and it was he who gave the lengthiest pronouncement on the case.[37] Underpinning all three of the majority judgments was the idea that section 55 aimed to safeguard the parent or guardian's right of possession of a girl under 16 and a key consideration for all three judges was the need to convict men such as Prince. In contrast, the sole dissenter argued that because Prince's belief was both reasonable and genuine he could not be convicted.

There, then, the matter rested, the majority of the Court having ruled that the fact that a man who genuinely and reasonably believed a girl to be 18 provided neither a defence to section 55 nor meant that there was an absence of the necessary *mens rea*. The conviction was duly affirmed – and this was reported around the country.[38] As for Prince, he returned to the assizes in Kingston, where he was sentenced to six months' imprisonment with hard labour.[39]

Binding men and policing male sexuality

All this serves to give a sense that *Prince* was seen as being of considerable legal significance. However, *Prince*'s importance also lay in its concern with male behaviour – and, in particular, men's violence in the form of sexual conduct towards girls as well as closely related ideas about male (im)morality. Before this particular version of the binding men narrative is explored in relation to the case, however, the contemporary context needs to be sketched in order to provide a backdrop to what unfolded in 1875.

The pre-*Prince* context

Victorian ideals of male behaviour, particularly when it came to Englishmen, along with shifting conceptions of children, meant that those who mistreated the young tended to be seen as grotesque abominations and degenerate types. In this lexicon of manliness, whatever his class, the male of the species was supposed to be gentlemanly, courageous and chivalrous, not least towards the opposite sex – and he was expected to exercise self-control when it came to matters of sex. Moreover, his relationship with the young, given the romantic concept of childhood which was prevalent at the time, was to be as a protector and guide.

In terms of ideas about men, a particular influence in the years prior to *Prince* was Samuel Smiles. In a range of books, including the immensely popular *Self-Help: With Illustrations of Conduct and Perseverance* (1859),[40] he put forward ideas as to how people and, in particular, how men should behave, emphasizing the need for qualities including restraint, not least in matters sexual, as well as depicting a domesticated version of Christian manhood.[41] A not dissimilar stance was espoused by others who addressed the question of male conduct – and sexual morality along with self-control were, unsurprisingly, deemed to be particularly important within such thinking. For example, amongst advocates of Muscular Christianity, Charles Kingsley called upon men to live healthily and direct their attention away from thoughts of immorality by focusing upon exercise.[42] More specifically, such notions of manliness tended to stress the role of the male as father, nurturer and protector of his family as well as emphasizing the need for men to defend and shelter the weak – including animals, women and children.[43]

In stark contrast to these idealized images of manliness, lurked the figure of the degenerate, whose animalistic, savage and barbaric behaviour was a matter of concern – and one aspect of such ideas related to worries about unbridled and unnatural sexuality. In the context of such fears, men who behaved in ways that were deemed sexually unacceptable were depicted in monstrous terms and seen as something less than human.[44]

Alongside these ideas about men, conceptions of children and of childhood were changing, with the young being viewed increasingly as innocents. Indeed, both girls and boys tended to be seen in quixotic terms.[45] Girls, in particular, were regarded as being in need of protection from the ills of the world and, as the nineteenth century drew towards its close, efforts to target what were perceived to be different forms of child cruelty increased.[46] Anxieties about non-sexual abuse were, for example, reflected in discussions concerning the enactment of section 1 of the Aggravated Assaults Act 1853, which allowed magistrates to sentence men and women convicted for assaulting any female (and boys under the age of 14) more severely where bodily harm was caused. Here, a particular focus was upon men's treatment of the young[47] and especially of girls, who were seen as being not only most vulnerable but also most at risk – as to the measure's most fervent supporters assaults by men (or 'degraded ruffian[s]') upon 'beings weaker than themselves', were a 'monstrous and growing evil', 'a national disgrace' and warranted nothing short of corporal punishment.[48]

In the context of such thinking, it was not surprising that worries about men's sexual conduct and immorality were a common theme, not least when it came to young females. This unease in relation to girls tended to focus on what were perceived to be particular problems. So recurrent, often overlapping, themes included: fears about girls being lured, tricked or forced into prostitution; anxieties about working-class innocents preyed upon by wicked wealthy men; worries about men who sought to exploit the well-off, with the aim of securing property and money through abduction followed by marriage; and apprehensions regarding the presumed immoral sexual habits of the lower classes and the supposed impact of crowded city living upon morality – with incest being a not infrequent subject of debate. Cases of seduction and abduction where a girl was argued to have consented to the sexual activity or (as in *Prince*) agreed to an elopement were also a matter of specific concern. Indeed, as we shall see, the issue of supposed consent was a significant focus in relation to sexual offences involving young female victims.

Such disquiet about men who sexually exploited girls was being expressed in a variety of quarters in the latter half of the nineteenth century. Thus, there was, as Louise Jackson has demonstrated, not only often a feeling of hatred towards men who sexually abused girls (particularly where the victim was especially young), but also a degree of popular feeling in favour of harshly punishing them – and sometimes people would take matters into their own hands rather than leaving them to the criminal justice system.[49] For example, she recounted a case reported in the *Illustrated Police News* in 1870, which involved 'a mob' turning up outside Marylebone Police Court to greet a man accused of raping a four-year-old girl. They 'gave him some rough handling' but he was protected from suffering any great harm by the police who guarded him.[50]

In addition, a range of commentators, campaigners and preachers highlighted the problem of child sexual abuse and worked to reform both male behaviour and the law. Amongst their ranks were socialists, individuals who worked for women's rights and people with morality and religion in mind – although, these were by no means entirely separate perspectives. Whilst interest in these issues probably became more widespread from the 1880s, there was evidence of campaigning before this, not least in relation to girls and prostitution (the 'social evil'). Indeed, opposition to the oppressive regime imposed upon women believed to be prostitutes under the Contagious Diseases Acts (CDAs) of the 1860s often also addressed the issue of how the young were drawn into selling sex.[51] For example, the Associate Institute for Informing and Enforcing the Law for the Protection of Women focused attention upon the problem of girls being lured into prostitution at a young age. In 1863, in a public lecture on behalf of the Institute, Mr Harding discussed this problem and talked about efforts to ensure that those 'monsters who had outraged propriety in the ruin of children' were punished.[52] In 1871 one of the most prominent critics of the CDAs, Josephine E. Butler, expressed not only concerns about those 'poor girl[s] introduced by their seduction into paths of vice' but also supported calls for existing sexual offences regarding girls to be reformed. Thus, she backed CCCR judge Justice Willes's recent support for the raising of the age of consent for girls from 12 to 14. Moreover, Butler saw seduction as a particular concern, highlighting the fact that in such cases men were abusing girls when they should be acting as their protectors.[53]

As the above reference to Willes suggests, these anxieties about male immorality towards girls, including in relation to seduction, were very much in evidence in legal spheres in the years prior to *Prince*, especially when it came to criminal law. Attempts at statutory reform during the period provide a good illustration of this trend. For example, Samuel Wilberforce, a Church of England Bishop, championed the cause of protecting young girls (and women) from the sexual immorality of men – and he too felt that one solution was to raise the age of consent. As part of his efforts, in 1861 he introduced the Protection of Female Children Bill. Whilst this measure failed to pass, it was by no means unsupported[54] and it raised issues which were shortly to be addressed in the 1861 Offences Against the Person Act. Indeed, although this was largely a consolidating measure, its sex-related provisions were said to have been influenced by the concerns raised by Wilberforce and by the contents of his Bill.[55]

Sections 48–55 of the 1861 Act, which were headed 'Rape, Abduction, and Defilement of Women', were seen as being intended to protect against and punish the wickedness of men, including instances where girls had apparently been or were argued to have been consenting parties to sexual activity or abduction.[56] For example, aside from section 55 of the 1861 Act (the offence charged in *Prince*), section 53 provided another route whereby seducers could be convicted and punished. It applied to the situation where a young female who was wealthy or stood to inherit in the future was fraudulently lured away or abducted from 'Motives of Lucre' and against her parents' or guardians' wishes for the purpose of marriage or carnal knowledge.[57] The crime could be committed in relation to girls and women who were not yet 21. As well as the punishment which would result if a person was convicted of this offence, the offender would also be prevented from making any financial gain from his actions.

Following the passing of the 1861 Act, concerns about men's immorality towards girls, whether in the form of forced sexual relations or purportedly consensual activities brought about as a result of (what would in twenty-first century terminology be described as) 'grooming' and trickery, continued. In particular, worries about abduction and seduction were reflected in efforts to extend the reach of existing legislation. In 1873, just two years prior to *Prince*, a Private Members' Bill entitled the Seduction Laws Amendment Bill was proposed.[58] The Bill included a number of changes to tackle what was then conceived of as a pressing social problem. It would, for example, have extended the section 55 abduction offence to girls aged 16 and over but under 21 and sought to effectively raise the age of consent by amending section 51 of the 1861 Act.

Debate of these proposals in the House of Commons focused upon targeting male seducers as well as protecting the young and their parents' interests. Indeed, a good deal of this discussion was directed at castigating such men. For example, speaking for the Bill in the House of Commons, Mr Charley MP argued that 'if a man betrayed the confidence of these young creatures, let him do it at his peril.'[59] Mr Newdegate MP maintained that the 'manly view' was that the seduction of children was 'in every sense a gratuitous offence' committed by 'vile seducers' who should face punishment. Similarly focusing upon male behaviour towards girls, Mr Mundella MP expressed consternation that 'a fearful amount of seduction was going on daily' and that young girls were 'seduced by men of double their years and in a better position of life'.[60] Despite these pronouncements, however, the Seduction Laws Amendment Bill did not pass into law.

A tendency towards castigating and criminalizing men who sexually abused girls can also be seen in the courts in the years leading up to *Prince*. Perhaps the most significant illustrations of this trend were provided by instances where the girl involved was argued by the defence to be consenting. Two CCCR cases, for example, give a strong sense that the views of at least some of the common law judges were firmly against men who had or attempted to have sexual relations with the young. In *R v Beale* (1865),[61] the Court had rejected out of hand the suggestion that the youngest of girls could consent to serious sexual offences. Here the crimes concerned were unlawful carnal knowledge of a girl under the age of 10 (section 50 of the Offences Against the Person Act) and an attempt to commit that offence. The case involved nine-year-old Mary Jane Catherine Green, who had been abused by Frederick Beale, a lodger in her parents' house. Beale had directed the girl not to tell her mother what had happened, but the crime was revealed when she was subsequently diagnosed with gonorrhoea (although no charges were brought in relation to this). The defendant's counsel maintained that Green had consented and, therefore, no crime had been committed; what is more he cited authority for this version of the law. The judge had effectively accepted this view by directing that if the jury found she had consented, they should acquit the defendant. Beale, however, was convicted. The case was then reserved for the consideration of the CCCR (presumably because the judge's interpretation of the law had been ignored).

In the CCCR there were early indications from the bench of some strength of opinion against the notion of the girl's possible consent being of any relevance to the offence. Justice Willes (who was subsequently to support the raising of the age of consent), for example, rejected both the argument made on behalf of Beale on this matter and the legal authority on which it was said to be based, stating that 'I can hardly believe that it is correctly reported.'[62] In the end, the five judges were as one in their judgment confirming Beale's conviction. Chief Baron of the Exchequer Pollock (who went on to sit in judgment in *Prince* and was on the side of the majority) delivered the very brief decision on behalf of the court, stating in no uncertain terms that the trial judge's view as to the law had been 'utterly unfounded' as this was a crime where consent was 'immaterial'; the authorities cited in support of an acquittal were, therefore, dismissed.[63]

R v Barratt (1873)[64] was unanimously decided by five judges, four of whom would also soon affirm Prince's conviction.[65] In this case, short shrift was given to the contention that Mary Redman aged 14-and-a-half, who was referred to as an 'imbecile', might have been capable of consenting to penetrative vaginal sexual intercourse. Following previous cases involving vulnerable girls over the age of consent but not yet women, for Justice Honyman, 'it would be monstrous to say that the man would not be guilty of rape'.[66]

Legal cases resulting from claims of the seduction and the luring away of girls and young women also reflected anxiety at men's conduct and demonstrated a feeling that the perpetrators needed to be reined in. Whilst this was most in evidence in the criminal sphere, a tendency towards condemnation could also be detected in the context of civil litigation – although here the purpose was to provide compensation. For example, where a seduced and/or abducted young female had previously worked for the family business or where her wages had formed a part of the shared income it was not uncommon for relatives to seek financial recompense for such economic loss, often on the girl's behalf if not their own – and such an action could be brought in relation to young women up until they were 21.

Pitt v Physic (1871)[67] involved the stepfather (who was also the uncle) of a 20-year-old woman claiming damages against her seducer. His stepdaughter/niece had become pregnant and could no longer work for the family business, so the stepfather sought remuneration. The tone of the court discussion was clear: whilst the young woman was described as 'innocent', with not even 'the slightest imputation' cast against her, the defendant had taken 'liberties' with her when they were engaged and had then reneged on his promise of marriage. From the judge's perspective the only matter that needed to be considered in a case such as this was the amount of damages to be awarded (at the close of proceedings the figure of £150 was fixed upon).[68]

In the criminal law sphere, the need to protect young females and their families from the dangers of seduction and abduction was a recurrent theme, with men prosecuted and convicted for abductions where the 'victim' seemed to be a willing co-conspirator. Indeed, worries about male exploitation and abuse of girls were in evidence in some of the trials under section 55 which were held around the country in the years leading up to *Prince*. For example, the cases of *R v Olifier* (1866),[69] *R v Mycock* (1871)[70] and *R v Booth* (1872),[71] which were to be cited in *Prince* in support of a conviction, reflected this. Whilst these were all decided by trial courts and, therefore, only represented the views of a single judge, as we shall see, this did not mean that they would not be followed.[72]

In *Olifier*, *Mycock* and *Booth*, men who took apparently consenting girls under the age of 16 from the lawful possession of another were deemed to have done so at their own risk. They, therefore, had to face the consequences of their actions when it transpired that the girls were actually under age. The immorality of these men and their actions, as well as the harm caused to the girls and the need to criminalize them were evident in each of these cases. For example, in *Olifier* it was decided that if a man at some point encouraged a girl to leave home without her parents' consent and she subsequently did so, he was guilty of abduction, regardless of whether by this time he had in fact changed his view as to her leaving. (Bramwell was the judge in *Olifier* and Quain presided in *Booth* – both of whom were to sit in the CCCR in *Prince* and sided with the majority.)

Having said this, as the arguments regarding the relevance of a girl's supposed consent by the defence counsel and trial judge in *Beale* suggest, not all criminal cases in the years leading up to *Prince* reflected the view that men and, in particular, male abductors should be criminalized for their sexual advances and activities towards young girls. Instead some demonstrated a hesitancy to penalize men and a fear of putting males at risk of conviction. In cases of abduction this took the form of a reluctance to convict where the defendant thought a girl to be older than she was, where there was no suspicion that she had parents or guardians whose charge she was in or where she was deemed to have acted of her own volition. For instance, such tendencies were evident in the CCCR case of *R v Hibbert* (1869),[73] along with the trials of *R v Green and Bates* (1862)[74] and *R v Tinkler* (1859)[75] (which were all to be cited in *Prince* in support of quashing the conviction). In *Hibbert* and *Green* it was decided that ignorance on the part of the accused as to the fact that the girl in question was in anyone's 'possession' would absolve him of liability, whilst in *Tinkler*, it was ruled that if a jury found the defendant 'honestly believed that he had a right to the custody of the child' he should be acquitted. Indeed, these cases taken alongside those of *Olifier*, *Mycock* and *Booth* can be said to demonstrate that there was a division of opinion and some uncertainty prior to *Prince* (with some judges seemingly changing their views) as to how far the criminalization of abduction should extend. (Lush was the trial judge in *Hibbert* and had supported his conviction but reported a change of mind when he revisited the case in the in the CCCR and Cockburn had presided in *Tinkler* – both were subsequently to sit in judgment of *Prince* and to support the conviction.)

A reluctance, or outright refusal, to prosecute or convict men who were found to have honestly mistaken a girl's age or familial situation, as well as cases where a girl willingly went with a man, can also be seen in other trials of the period. For example, in a case of abduction heard at the Central Criminal Court in 1870 the judge, (again) Lush, directed that the question for the jury was whether 14-year-old Mary Ann Doyley Case had gone away with 29-year-old Archibald Kennedy Johnson (or Johnstone) 'of her own accord, and of her own free will', rather than 'at the instigation of the prisoner'.[76] If she had chosen to go, then there could be no taking away under section 55 and, therefore, there should be an acquittal. The jury found that Doyley had herself decided to go with Johnson and returned a not guilty verdict, despite the fact that the evidence showed that an 'improper intimacy' had previously developed between Doyley and Johnson, that they had discussed her following him when he left her mother's employ and that on the day she left, he met her and took her to live with him as his wife.

Another notable instance of this tendency not to criminalize men under section 55 was provided by the January 1875 case of Jeremiah Moorcroft.[77] According to press reports, 25-year-old Moorcroft had formed a relationship with Fanny Corner, who was 15 at the time. When he went away, despite her father's efforts to prevent her, she followed him. They lived together for a few days until they were discovered, Corner then being returned to her father and Moorcroft taken into custody. According to the *Nottinghamshire Guardian*, having heard the evidence, the magistrate dismissed the case as he felt that it was difficult to determine who was most to blame. Consequently, the *York Herald* reported that the magistrate was of the view that the prisoner 'had been guilty of very immoral conduct', but because of the evidence 'he was sure no jury would convict.' So, instead of facing a trial, the prisoner was discharged 'after he *and* the girl had received a severe rebuke for their conduct' (emphasis added).

Juries too could show a reluctance to convict abductors, as was demonstrated by a case that came before the courts just days before Denman directed Prince's conviction at trial. On 2 March 1875 William Timms appeared before Justice Quain (again, one of the CCCR judges who was soon to decide *Prince*). The case was reported in the press, including in *The Times*.[78] According to that paper, it was a prosecution that 'excited great interest' and the court was 'densely crowded'. Timms was 60 years old and insolvent, whilst Annie Turner was at the time of the relevant events not yet 16 and stood to become a woman of means in later life. An intimacy formed between them and the girl left her home to be with Timms and subsequently married him. Following their apprehension, he was tried for abduction under section 53 of the 1861 Act rather than section 55 because of the financial motives which were believed to lie behind the case. The defence argued that there had been no taking away in fact because Turner had left her father's house willingly. However, in summing up to the jury Quain rejected this, emphasizing that legally Turner had been in the possession of her parents and that her consent was irrelevant in terms of the law. By way of underlying the need to convict the defendant he explained that section 53 'was designed for the protection of young girls under 16, even when they had been consenting parties to their own elopement.'[79] However, he had, of course, to leave the ultimate decision in the case to the jury – and he did not attempt any strategy such as Denman was soon to use in *Prince* in order to ensure what was to him the legally correct outcome. As a result and despite what looked like a very strong indication that a conviction would be the legally correct outcome, the jury 'almost immediately' acquitted Timms. Moreover, this was reported by *The Times* to have been greeted with 'a strong manifestation of approval by the public' and Timms was 'loudly cheered as he left the precincts of the Court' with his wife; so, those in the public gallery seemed to have shared the jury's rather than the judge's view.

Prince

Given existing anxieties about male sexual exploitation of girls, as well as cases such as *Beale* (where the defendant's lawyer and the trial judge seemed to accept that a nine-year-old girl's consent could defeat a charge of unlawful carnal knowledge) and *Timms* (where, just days before the *Prince* trial, the jury seemingly refused to see the defendant's behaviour as criminal), Lilley's characterization of *Prince* from the outset as being of 'considerable social importance' was understandable. More importantly, Denman's carefully contrived guilty verdict, allowing him to reserve *Prince* to the CCCR, seemed to be an attempt not merely to allow the legal position in relation to a new set of facts to be considered (where an abducted girl had lied about her age and this had been genuinely and reasonably believed by the defendant), but it also offered an opportunity to provide a firm, clear, authoritative and public statement about the moral and legal position of men who took away girls under the age of 16.

Beyond this, concerns about men's sexual conduct towards girls permeated *Prince.* It was, for example, in both the prosecution and defence cases at trial – indeed, as we have seen, even Prince's lawyer admitted that he could not justify the conduct morally, it was just, according to his argument, not illegal. Such issues were, however, most evident when the case reached the CCCR – both in the arguments of Lilley for the prosecution and in what the majority judges said. Thus, on 29 May 1875, when *Prince* was argued before the CCCR,[80] Lilley's contentions included a conception of the case as being about the need to penalize the evil acts of men who lured young girls away for the purposes of seduction. In his view, removing a girl from her parents against their will, whether by force or enticement, in this way was something that was '*malum in se*' – wrong or evil in itself. Consequently, men such as Prince should be found to fall within section 55 regardless of a 'mere belief in the prisoner's mind' about a girl's age or circumstances. Indeed, he argued that men were required by both law and morality to uphold high standards in their dealings with young girls. Thus he maintained that, a man 'was bound to ascertain [a girl's age], and must take the consequences if the girl turned out to be under the age.'[81] Also, as to whether a girl was in someone's lawful possession '[t]he man is bound to know and must find out at his peril.'

What then of the judges? Whilst some of the judicial panel's involvement in previous cases might have suggested their leanings in *Prince*, the interjections at the hearing of the case in the CCCR on 29 May gave little indication of the likely outcome or of the different judges' views – apart from suggesting that Brett seemed to be against upholding the conviction and Bramwell seemed in favour of affirming it. The latter, indeed, appears to have come to a view at this stage and one seemingly informed by moral considerations. For example, in an implicit condemnation of Prince's actions, he stated that the taking away of a girl aged over 16 would also be 'contrary to law' because 'to induce a woman of any age to leave her father's house' is 'intrinsically wrong because it is contrary to morality'. In so saying, he was to prefigure the kinds of views expressed in the judgments delivered on behalf of the majority in the CCCR – and it was in these texts, which were read out in the courtroom on 26 June, that the strongest sense of the need to bind men such as Prince was evident. Thus, it is to the judicial pronouncements of Bramwell, Blackburn and Denman that we now turn.

All three of the judgments made on behalf of the majority focused upon the rights of parents and, in particular, the rights of fathers to their daughters' custody. Their words also reflected concern as to the victims of men's sexual abuse. Most significantly for present purposes, however, they were critical of men who behaved as Prince had done and there was evidence of a determination to affirm the defendant's conviction and, in so doing, ensure that others who committed sexual crimes against young girls could not use their beliefs as to a child's age, however reasonable or genuine these might be, to avoid the full force of the criminal law. However, they each took slightly different routes to their decision.

Baron Bramwell's view was that the case rested entirely upon the purpose and interpretation of section 55 and, as a consequence, his judgment included no consideration of past cases. As the quotation which opened this chapter illustrates, the Baron made it abundantly clear that, despite the fact that both men and women could commit the offence, men's sexual behaviour was the primary problem which section 55 sought to address. Indeed, in his view the Act 'principally aims at seduction for carnal purposes'.[82] So, in order to give effect to this purpose, the section should be interpreted to mean that a taking away was done 'at the risk of the girl turning out to be under sixteen' – and if a man chose to take this risk he had to face the legal consequences of his actions.[83]

The wider subject of men's sexual exploitation of girls was also highlighted in Bramwell's consideration of other sections of the 1861 Act. For example, he dismissed the idea that a man who was charged under section 50 with the felony of unlawful carnal knowledge of a girl under the age of 10, or under section 51 with the misdemeanour of unlawful carnal knowledge of a girl between the ages of 10 and 12, could escape liability for the more serious or even for both of the offences by claiming that he thought that a girl was older than she in fact was. As with section 55, he felt that in such cases 'the act is intrinsically wrong' and should result in a conviction – and that '[i]t would be mischievous to hold otherwise'.[84] So, in this view, men who took away, seduced or had 'carnal knowledge' of a girl were so morally reprehensible as to be entitled to no legal latitude in relation to their beliefs as to their victim's age.

Overall, Bramwell seemed to demonstrate a lack of patience with the arguments presented against conviction and a linked hatred for the behaviour of men such as Prince. Most obviously, he repeatedly emphasized the wrongness of the abduction of a girl under 16-years-of-age, stating that '[t]he act forbidden is wrong in itself', 'I do not say illegal, but wrong', 'the act forbidden is wrong', 'done without lawful cause [a taking] is wrong', 'what I say is wrong'[85] and he made similar comments in relation to sections 50 and 51.[86] However, the Baron did not go so far as to say that a man charged with a section 55 abduction would have no possibility of escaping conviction as a result of his beliefs as to the circumstances – he was of the opinion that if an abductor wrongly thought he had the parent or guardian's consent, or if he or she did not know the girl was in anyone's possession, care or charge, 'he would have no mens rea.'[87]

Blackburn also looked to the 1861 Act, finding that the part of the statute which contained the offence in *Prince* was aimed at 'forming a code for the protection of women, and the guardians of young women'.[88] More specifically, his view was that the legislature's intention in relation to section 55 was clear and that was to 'protect this legal right to the possession'[89] and 'punish the abductor' unless the girl was actually 16 or older[90] – and he followed the prosecution's lead by referring to the approach taken in *Olifier*, *Mycock* and *Booth* as supporting a conviction, maintaining that, whilst there was 'not much authority on the subject', that which existed was 'all in favour of this view.'[91] Like Bramwell, he looked to sections 50 and 51, finding that the legislature's purpose in relation to these provisions was 'to punish those who had connection with young girls, though with their consent, unless the girl was in fact old enough to give a valid consent.'[92] What is more, it would be 'impossible to suppose that the intention of the legislature in those two sections could have been to make the crime depend upon the knowledge of the prisoner of the girl's actual age.' Indeed, the latter view, if applied, would 'produce the monstrous result' that a man who had sexual intercourse with a girl under the age of 10 but who he reasonably believed to be over that age would escape conviction.'[93] He reinforced this, stating that it would be unsupportable to allow a defence in such circumstances as '[t]he man who has connection with a child, relying on her consent, does it at his peril, if she is below the statutable age.'[94] There was a sense of revulsion here in his phrasing and, in particular, in his choice of the word 'monstrous' – a strong term for a judge of this court in this period, although, as we shall see, such language was by no means unheard of.

So, underpinning both Bramwell and Blackburn's judgments were concerns about men's sexual exploitation of girls. In their view a man acted at his own risk if he took away or had sexual intercourse with a young female. Or, to put it another way, in the context of sexual offences committed against girls, the onus to find out the actual age of a girl was placed firmly upon the potential abductor or seducer.

Whilst the original trial judge Denman's lone judgment referred to Bramwell and Blackburn's decisions with approval, he emphasized that what was key for him was that Prince had 'wrongfully' and 'knowingly' violated 'the father's rights against the father's will'.[95] So here the abductor's actions were largely conceived of as being wrong because they violated male authority. Consequently, this need to regulate relations between men was the focus of Denman's concerns in deciding that males who acted as Prince had done should be brought within the ambit of the criminal law. Moreover, this judge seemed to want to extend the boundaries of the law still further as he argued that a father (or a guardian appointed by him) had the right to a girl's 'personal custody' up to the age of 21.[96] As a result, to his mind Prince's belief that she was 18 was of no consequence, as 'by taking her, even with her own consent, he must at least have been guilty of aiding and abetting her in doing an unlawful act', namely of 'escaping against the will of her natural guardian from his lawful care and charge.'[97] So, according to Denman, Prince had committed a wrong without lawful excuse and his conviction (which had, of course, resulted from his own careful engineering of the jury decision at trial) was, therefore, correct.[98]

In the context of such strength of opinion against the prisoner, Brett's dissenting judgment stood very much alone. According to this judge, following *Hibbert*, *Green* and *Tinkler*, Prince's genuine and reasonable mistake as to Phillip's age meant that his conviction should be quashed. Thus, he embraced an advertent approach, prioritizing the defendant's view of a potentially criminal act rather than what had actually transpired – although he was clear that a defendant's ignorance of the law would provide no excuse.[99] Indeed, here he viewed the situation where a man did not know that a girl was in the possession of another in the same way as a man who thought a girl was older than she in fact was.[100] In addition, in the text of his judgment he made repeated references to the law in England, suggesting that he felt it would be unEnglish to extend the law so that it criminalized men who acted on the basis of a genuine and reasonable factual mistake. So for Brett, it was the decision of the majority that went against notions of Englishness rather than what Prince had done.

The effect of Brett's words, had his view carried the day, would have been to reduce the scope of section 55, making it less likely that an abductor would be convicted. As the judicial references to sections 50 and 51 of the 1861 Act suggested, it would also most probably have had a similar effect upon other age-specific sexual offences. Thus, in stark contrast to the other judges' focus upon binding men, he seems to have been concerned to safeguard what he saw as the rights of blameless men who should not be penalized for what they mistakenly thought. However, for the majority in *Prince*, the need to criminalize men in order to police male sexual morality in relation to girls was a key consideration in interpreting the statutory abduction provision and applying what had been decided in past cases.

Post *Prince*

Although most commentators seemed to support the CCCR decision in *Prince*, reaction was divided as in some quarters there was at least a degree of hesitation or a little unease at the outcome of the case. For example, the *Law Journal* strongly supported the majority, reflecting contemporary concerns about sexual immorality. Consequently, there was criticism of Brett for opting to stand alone:

> ... judicial unanimity is most desirable upon points of criminal law, not only because this part of the law directly affects the life and liberty of the subject, but also because the moral force of a legal prohibition is seriously diminished by the dissent of any part of the bench. Especially does this remark hold good where the law is framed to curb the sexual passions, and where lawlessness clutches eagerly at any excuse in favour of licence.

Moreover, the majority's interpretation of section 55 reflected both 'wisdom and necessity', whilst, had Brett's view carried the day, the *Journal* felt sure that Parliament would have swiftly intervened in order to 'mend the gap so made in the fence by which young girls are supposed to be protected.'[101] As to less welcoming responses to *Prince*, the comments in the *Pall Mall Gazette* are perhaps most worthy of note, particularly (as we shall see) given what was to transpire in relation to that paper a decade later. The *Gazette* expressed a fear that the majority had gone too far in affirming the conviction and felt that this might be an instance of 'judicial legislation', rather than mere interpretation of Parliament's intention in creating the abduction offence. In addition, the CCCR decision was a matter of concern as it meant that section 55 had effectively become a strict liability offence.[102]

Despite such unease, in the decades following *Prince*, worries about men who sexually abused girls, along with the trend towards criminalization continued. Indeed, not long after the CCCR had delivered its decision, statute again addressed the issue. An amendment was introduced into law by the Offences Against the Person Act 1875, which received royal assent and came into force on 13 August (the decision in *Prince* having been handed down in June of that year). Sections 50 and 51 of the 1861 Act were repealed and replaced by sections 3 and 4 of the new measure. Section 3 made it a felony to carnally know and abuse a girl under the age of 12, raising the relevant age for this offence by two years. Section 4 made it a misdemeanour to carnally know and abuse a girl of 12 years of age, whereas previously the equivalent offence had related to girls aged 10 and 11; in so doing, the age of consent to sex was effectively raised to 13 for girls.

Such moves to criminalize men who behaved sexually towards girls can, to some degree, be depicted as continuing through the 1880s and 1890s and, indeed, into the early years of the twentieth century.[103] In the 1880s the focus was in the Parliamentary sphere, with the key development during this decade being the Criminal Law Amendment Act 1885.[104] The attempts to pass this measure began in 1881 and its provisions emerged from a House of Lords Select Committee Report into the issues of child prostitution and what we would now refer to as the trafficking of girls for the purposes of prostitution. The Report suggested that vice was rife, not least in the capital, and it made a series of recommendations as to how the law should be altered in order to address this problem.[105] However, despite continued discussions, the reform proposals kept foundering. In 1885 a Bill was reintroduced but its entry onto the statute books was still by no means a certainty. Its eventual enactment was probably greatly assisted by the 'Maiden Tribute' revelations, which stirred up existing feeling against men who preyed upon and exploited innocent girls.[106] The latter and their legal ramifications were so important that it is worth pausing at this point to describe what happened.

'The Maiden Tribute of Modern Babylon' was the title given to a series of four articles written by the editor of the *Pall Mall Gazette*, William Thomas

Stead, and published in that paper during the summer of 1885.[107] These purported to evidence the fact that sexually innocent young girls were being sold to older wealthy men and it did so in sensationalist terms. The articles had been researched by Stead, along with a number of campaigners who wanted the laws relating to prostitution to be reformed. Investigations included, for example, women posing as prostitutes and infiltrating brothels in order to gather information, as well as attempts to purchase children for the purposes of prostitution. However, it was felt by Stead that something more concrete and, perhaps, more dramatic was needed. He decided to buy a girl from her parents and create the impression that he had had sexual relations with her in order to add weight not only to efforts regarding prostitution law, but also to his case for legal reform and societal action to protect

Figure 1 Eliza Armstrong, the girl at the centre of the 'Maiden Tribute' revelations and trial.

The Illustrated Police News, 5 September 1885, p. 1.

young females. Eliza Armstrong, who features in one of the illustrations to this book (see Figure 1), was 13 when she was purchased from her mother at Stead's behest. The parent was told that Armstrong would be going into service as a maid but it was assumed she was aware that prostitution was the real purpose. Stead had the girl's virginity confirmed by a midwife and she was then taken to a brothel, where she was drugged and placed in a bedroom. There Stead created the impression that the girl had been acquired for him and that sexual activity had occurred. This story was then published as part of the 'Maiden Tribute' articles, with the details changed so that Armstrong was given a pseudonym and Stead's identity as the man for whom she was bought was hidden.[108] The reaction to the articles was considerable in terms of the general public, but they also had the effect of cohering the diverse groups who were already campaigning around the linked issues of child prostitution, the protection of girls from male sexual exploitation and the age of consent for females.[109]

As noted above, it was probably as a consequence of the breadth and strength of feeling which the *Pall Mall Gazette* had occasioned that the Criminal Law Amendment Act at last passed in August 1885.[110] Amongst other things, section 5(1) of this measure effectively raised the legal age of consent for a girl to 16. The offence here was that of unlawfully and carnally knowing or attempting to have unlawful carnal knowledge of a girl of or above the age of 13 and under 16. The Act also created a new abduction offence in section 7. This prohibited the 'abduction of a girl under the age of 18' where there was 'intent to have carnal knowledge.'

Significantly for present purposes, the 'Maiden Tribute' articles resulted in another legal development relating to the crime of abduction. The story of a young girl's purchase raised concerns about the morality of those who orchestrated her ordeal and worries about the 13-year-old herself. Investigations led to Eliza Armstrong and a trial ensued, with Stead and a number of others charged with various crimes relating to their behaviour towards the girl.[111] The alleged offences included the taking away of a girl under the age of 16 without the consent of her parents (the same offence of abduction under section 55 which had been the subject of *Prince*). Significantly, Armstrong's father had not been consulted when she was taken away and there was no proof as to the exact nature of the bargain which had apparently been struck between the girl's mother and Stead's agent. As a result, Stead was convicted of abduction (and of aiding and abetting an indecent assault[112]) and was sentenced to three months' imprisonment without hard labour.

The reaction to Stead's role in the affair by those who failed to see what he did as being justified by its purpose was at least critical, if not condemnatory in the extreme. In this view, he, like other men who bought or abused girls, was monstrous and immoral and deserved to be categorized as a criminal. For example, in the words of the trial judge, Justice Lopes, he had 'dragged' Armstrong 'through the dirt' by causing her to be treated in abominable ways, wrought an 'irreparable injury' upon her parents and 'deluged ... the whole country with ... filth'. In consequence, the judge concluded: 'I cannot pass anything but a substantial sentence.'[113] *The Times*, a rival publication to Stead's *Pall Mall Gazette*, had pursued the investigation into Armstrong and, unsurprisingly, took an especially harsh view of its editor. Thus, upon his conviction and sentencing, its editorial described what had happened to Armstrong as a 'revolting drama' of which Stead was the 'Chief Director'.[114]

Moving forward in time, during the 1890s a continuing focus on criminalizing men who sexually exploited girls can be depicted through a number of sexual offence cases which were reserved for the consideration of the CCCR, although these were not abduction cases – and, noticeably, in this period there seems to have been a tendency to be more vocal in the condemnation of defendants meted out in CCCR judgments than was reflected in the earlier case law. *R v Marsden* (1891)[115] was a particularly important case – not for what it decided but rather because of the reasons for its reservation to the CCCR. It involved the prosecution of James Marsden for having carnal connection with a girl under the age of 13, contrary to section 4 of the Criminal Law Amendment Act 1885. Marsden was convicted at trial on the basis of Justice Wright's direction to the jury that it was not necessary to prove emission for the offence to be established, as penetration was sufficient. In unanimously affirming the conviction, the CCCR confirmed that the trial judge's interpretation of the law was correct. Significantly, the case involved no resolution of a tricky legal point but merely a restatement of the established law in the face of courts' failure to apply it. Indeed, the reservation was done with this purpose in mind and was approved by Lord Chief Justice Coleridge, who delivered the judgment. In his very brief pronouncement he made a point of noting that single judges around the country had been incorrectly taking the opposite view and emphasized that 'we none of us entertain the slightest doubt that the conviction is correct, and must be sustained.'[116]

Not long after *Marsden*, in *R v Tyrrell* (1893)[117] Coleridge, along with Justices Mathew, Grantham, Lawrence and Henn Collins, swiftly dismissed the argument that a girl aged between 13 and 16 could be found to have assisted, encouraged or provoked a sexual offence perpetrated against her. Jane Tyrrell had been convicted of aiding and abetting, soliciting and inciting Thomas Ford to commit the crime of unlawful carnal knowledge upon her.[118] Quashing the conviction, Coleridge took the view that one of the Act's central objects was 'to protect girls against themselves', so the argument that it should be 'construed so as to render a girl against whom an offence is committed equally liable with the man by whom the offence is committed' was totally untenable.[119] So, this was conceived of as a matter of criminalizing men rather than penalizing girls – and so the conduct of the girl was irrelevant.

Efforts to legally restrain men who behaved sexually towards girls can also be seen in the field of evidence law. Towards the end of the century, *R v Lillyman* (1896)[120] involved a conviction for an attempt to have carnal knowledge of Florence Sevestre Green, a girl aged between 13 and 16. The CCCR ruled that a statement made by the girl to her mistress shortly after the attack was admissible into evidence and, in so doing, affirmed the conviction. *Lillyman* was subsequently applied and extended in *R v Osborne* (1905),[121] as the CCCR was in its twilight years. Here William Henry Osborne's conviction for the indecent assault of 12-year-old Keziah Parkes was affirmed following a ruling that evidence of what she had said to her 11-year-old friend, Mary Moule, immediately after the incident was admissible.

Even in CCCR cases that did not go so favourably in terms of criminalizing men, there could be indications of judicial concern at the way in which some of their gender were behaving and at the inadequacies of law in addressing such conduct. Notably, Justice Hawkins in *R v Paul* (1890)[122] found himself unable to affirm a man's conviction for an indecent assault committed on Frances Coles, a girl who was stated to be under the age of 13. The problem here lay in the fact that there was no provision allowing for unsworn evidence to be admissible in relation to a charge of indecent assault under the 1861 Act,[123] although, as a result of sections 4 and 9 of the Criminal Law Amendment Act 1885, unsworn evidence was admissible in relation to other sexual offences involving children.[124] In delivering the judgment of the Court, Hawkins took time to consider the 'unsatisfactory state'[125] of statute law which led to this, to his mind, inconsistent result, observing along the way that one key purpose of the recent legislative change was to 'afford greater protection to young female children of tender years' from 'wickedly lustful men, who desired carnal knowledge of their bodies'.[126] Moreover, he expressed his lack of comprehension as to why the legislature had not in 1885 allowed unsworn evidence in relation to all sexual offences committed against 'little children',[127] pointing out that, as a result of this apparent oversight, abusers 'were frequently enabled to carry out their criminal desires with impunity.'[128]

In the trial courts around the country there was also evidence of continuing efforts to castigate, criminalize and punish men who preyed upon girls. For example, take the case of Edward George Smith who was charged and convicted of what was described as 'having, on the 20 April, 1876, and on divers other days ... attempted and endeavoured feloniously to carnally know and abuse' eight-year-old Elizabeth Ann Duckworth.[129] Smith had on a number of occasions enticed Duckworth to accompany him into his residence, giving her gifts to ensure both her compliance and her silence – and he seemed also to have cultivated some of her friends. At trial the prosecution presented the facts along with the law, dismissing the idea that the girl might have been consenting, as the law 'forbade' so young a girl to consent. Amongst other things, even the defence admitted the 'revolting nature' of the charge, whilst noting also that Smith, a respectable tradesman, faced it at a point when 'crimes of this sort were occupying the public mind more than at any other time' and, in so doing, the continuing prominence given to the problem of men's sexual abuse of girls was acknowledged.

When the case was given to them the jury delivered a guilty verdict almost immediately and it was left to the judge to pass both comment and sentence upon the defendant. Smith had, he said, committed an 'abominable' crime, by attempting to satisfy 'the wretched impulse of his brute passions' in attacking a girl's innocence 'in the most beastly and disreputable manner'. In short, the convicted man had been 'brutal, cowardly, unmanly' and 'there was no sort of conduct so low and despicable as that of which the prisoner was guilty'. Smith was duly sentenced to two years' imprisonment with hard labour – this being deemed 'the extreme sentence'.

However, despite trials such as that of *Smith*, along with the CCCR's development of precedents and the legislative attempts to ensure that men who sexually exploited girls were more likely to be convicted and suitably punished for their conduct, not all legal developments were in this direction. For instance, the changes introduced by the Criminal Law Amendment Act were mixed. In particular, both sections 5 and 7 (which respectively prohibited unlawful carnal knowledge or attempting to have unlawful carnal knowledge of a girl of or above the age of 13 and under the age of 16 and the abduction of a girl aged under 18 where there was intent to have carnal knowledge) provided a defence if a defendant was found to have had 'reasonable cause to believe that the girl was of or above the age' of 16 or 18 respectively. So *Prince* did not apply to these offences. However, the 1875 decision still potentially applied to some sexual offences involving young female victims (indeed, it has only recently been called into question)[130] – and, in particular, it continued in relation to section 55 of the 1861 Act, which remained on the statute books (and was not replaced until the middle of the twentieth century).[131]

In the courts around the country too there was evidence that sometimes men who sexually abused girls were treated with sympathy and understanding, rather than being unequivocally branded as criminals and harshly punished. For instance, in 1891 the prosecution of one such man received a great deal of attention in the press. 'The Strand Abduction Case' took place at the Central Criminal Court in September of that year.[132] Edward Arthur Callender Newton, a 39-year-old journalist who was married but separated from his wife, was charged with a number of offences in relation to 15-year-old Lucy Edith Pearman (see Figures 2 and 3, which depict the man and girl in court). Pearman's father ran a tobacconist on The Strand and it was as a customer frequenting this establishment that Newton had come to know her family several years earlier. As they had become better acquainted, he had taken to eating with the family at their home every Sunday and the children had become accustomed to referring to him as 'uncle'. Subsequently, it became clear that Newton had struck up a particular relationship with Pearman. Discovering this, her mother forbade her from seeing him and Newton was told not to come to the home or have any contact with the girl. The two then disappeared on 21 July 1891. A warrant was issued for Newton's arrest and placards requesting information as to the whereabouts

Figure 2 Edward Arthur Callender Newton, defendant in 'The Strand Abduction Case'. *Hampshire Telegraph and Sussex Chronicle,* 22 August 1891, p. 2.

of the man and child were issued by the police. On 8 August Pearman turned 16. Newton and the girl were found in Hastings on Tuesday 18 August by her father and a detective-sergeant with the Metropolitan Police. There Newton had taken rooms under an assumed name, with Pearman posing as his daughter but sharing his bedroom.

Newton appeared before a crowded Bow Street Police Court on the Wednesday, initially only facing a charge of abduction. His request for bail having been rejected, he was taken from the dock, at which stage he was reported to have exchanged sympathetic glances with Pearman – as the two apparently did at various points during the legal proceedings. In arguing that he should face trial, the prosecution portrayed an exploitative relationship between the man and the girl, with Newton preying upon and, in modern parlance, 'grooming' Pearman. The evidence was argued to demonstrate that

Figure 3 Lucy Edith Pearman, the young victim in 'The Strand Abduction Case'.
Hampshire Telegraph and Sussex Chronicle, 22 August 1891, p. 2.

the 'inducement' used by Newton, along with his 'great influence and power' had resulted in his 'getting over this girl'. It was maintained that Newton had first met Pearman at the age of 10 or 11, when she was playing with her brothers and sisters and that he then sought out her company by calling upon her father's shop and getting to know the family. Moreover, the prosecution version of the case portrayed a 'criminal intimacy' which had existed between Newton and Pearman since she was 14 but that he had actually begun to 'take liberties' with her when she was aged 11. At the same time, evidence that Pearman was very much attached to Newton and had requested that he take her away from her parents was submitted by the defence.[133]

Newton was committed for trial for charges of abducting a girl under the age of 16 with intent to have carnal knowledge (under section 7 of the 1885

Act) and of having unlawful carnal knowledge of a girl of or above the age of 13 but below the age of 16 (under section 5 of the 1885 Act). When he appeared at the Old Bailey on Friday 18 September the court was crowded. Newton pleaded guilty to both charges. However, in his own and his counsel's statements in mitigation to the court much was made of his affection for the girl and her family and the age at which sexual intimacy had begun was called into doubt – although it was accepted that she was under 16 at the time.

Piecing together the various accounts of the judge's (who was the Recorder of London) comments in passing sentence, it seems clear that some understanding was shown for Newton. The account of his words which was most sympathetic to the prisoner appeared in the *Morning Post*.[134] This paper had the Recorder noting that the girl was 'extremely attached' to Newton and that he had taken her away 'at the girl's request'. The Recorder then focused upon what he seemed to see as Newton's sorry plight, saying that he was 'extremely sorry that Newton was in his present position' – adding that it was, however, 'no excuse that, being separated from his wife, he should give way to temptation'.[135] Moreover, he (the Recorder) 'could not help thinking there was something to be said for him [Newton]' and '[t]aking everything into consideration, one could hardly consider that the offence was so bad as, under ordinary circumstances, it might have been.' In addition, the judge noted both that the section 7 abduction offence would not have been committed if Pearman had been slightly older (her 16th birthday having occurred whilst she was in Hastings with Newton) and that the offence of unlawful carnal knowledge had only been a crime since the age of consent was raised in 1885 – and would also not have been committed had she been a few months older, as it applied only to those under 16 (here the Recorder seems to have accepted Newton's assurance as to the time when sexual intimacy commenced, with the long history of abuse depicted by the prosecution seemingly either dismissed or forgotten).

From the various reports of the case, the Recorder had nothing to say about Pearman or her family and of the effects of what happened upon them. Also absent was any indication that he was aware of the battles that led to the passing of the 1885 Act and, in particular, the wider societal and legal concerns about men which had been reflected in legislative efforts and in the case law of the CCCR in the last few decades. Indeed, the only signal that Newton had done anything wrong was an acknowledgement that the law had technically been breached and the fact that a sentence of six months' imprisonment was handed down. However, as the 1885 Act offences each carried a maximum penalty of two years' imprisonment with or without hard labour, this seemed lenient.

Reaction to *Newton* reflected conflicting perspectives. The *Daily News*'s view was that, whilst Newton was a sinner, he had not behaved as badly as might have first appeared from the prosecution evidence.[136] In accepting the defence's account of the matter, the paper saw Newton and Pearman as 'lovers' who were 'sincerely attached to one another' and rejected the view that the convict was 'a singularly calculating, cold-blooded villain.' Consequently, the Recorder's 'merciful view' was 'justified'. In contrast, the *Pall Mall Gazette*, with its interest in the protection of girls and the criminalization of the men who preyed upon them, unsurprisingly, took a very different view.[137] The paper was critical of what it described as the 'general feeling' that Newton had 'got enough' in terms of the sentence and recounted the prosecution evidence that indecent behaviour had begun when Pearman was 11.

The *British Medical Journal*'s response to the case revealed an extra element. A short article under the heading 'Public Health' criticized the fact that assault charges were not brought in the offence, as Pearman had apparently contracted venereal disease from Newton.[138] In doing so, it drew attention to the links between concerns about men's sexual abuse of girls and worries about the spread of venereal disease. The latter is an issue which will be revisited in relation to adult women in Chapter 4. For the moment, however, the matter uncomfortably rests.

Conclusion

This chapter began by focusing upon *Prince*, depicting not only the decision but also the happenings which led to the prosecution and the resulting courtroom proceedings. It then cast the case as a part of contemporary attempts to rein in men who behaved sexually towards girls. In so doing, the narrative in the second part of this chapter has traced efforts to enact statutory reforms, particularly in the 1870s and 1880s, as well as telling the tales of cases which involved efforts to castigate and convict men.

This is not to say that all decisions were as radical as they might have been in setting the borders of criminal liability for those who sexually exploited girls, nor was the CCCR always unreservedly in favour of convicting abusers. In addition, there were cases during the period which demonstrated that not all magistrates, judges, juries, let alone all sections of the public, were minded towards binding men in relation to their sexual behaviour with girls. For example, Brett in *Prince* was undoubtedly worried about what he saw as the unjustified expansion of the criminal law so as to criminalize inadvertent wrongdoing in cases involving section 55, as well as, should the principle be upheld more generally, in other age-specific sexual offences. Indeed, far from expressing concern at the behaviour of men such as Prince, Brett felt it would be unEnglish to criminalize their conduct – and *The Times* has him as describing such a prospect (rather than Prince's behaviour) as 'monstrous'.[139] In addition, there were sub-currents in his judgment suggesting fears of female untruthfulness – and that men may be deliberately duped by girls. Brett, however, was by no means alone in expressing such worries in the context of sex and girls. Indeed, amongst upper class men in particular, there was a tendency to assume male sexual licence as of right – thus, for some discussions about the 1885 Act were concerned with the need 'to protect men from immoral girls and women'[140] and to ensure that the age of consent was not raised (or was not raised unduly), lest 'they and their sons might be threatened by the new legislation.'[141]

This sense of anxiety at potentially leaving men open to untruthful or malicious allegations of sexual wrongdoing – or, perhaps, of curtailing male freedoms – is a theme that will be returned to in relation to sexual crimes committed against women in Chapter 4's narrations of *Clarence* (1888).[142] Before that, however, the next two chapters consider examples of attempts to bind men in relation to instances of inter-male violence, turning first to efforts to ban prize-fighting.

Notes

1 (1875) LR 2 CCR 154; 39 JP 676; 44 LJMC 122; 13 Cox CC 138; 24 WR 76; [1874–80] All ER Rep 881; 32 LT 700. These references refer to the different law reports in which the case was reported. Unless otherwise stated, the references to the Court for Crown Cases Reserved judgment in this chapter are from (1875) LR 2 CCR 154, although the other reports of the case were consulted in constructing this chapter. As the name suggests, a law report is a published account of courtroom proceedings in a case. It is produced for lawyers and generally includes a summary of the facts which led the parties to come to court and the legal decision as well as the text of the judge's or judges' pronouncements on the law.

2 Baron Bramwell in *Prince* at 174–5 (original emphases).

3 The CCCR records along with different reports of the case reveal some disagreement as to the defendant's name – different sources have him as Henry Price, Henry Prince or William Prince (see, in particular, The National Archives (TNA): PRO KB 30/3, on the front of which 'Henry Price' is crossed out and 'William Prince' written in, although the text itself names him as 'Henry Prince'. Most sources, however, have his surname as 'Prince'.

4 The assizes heard the most serious of criminal cases and were essentially a forerunner of the Crown Court. Circuit judges travelled the country, presiding over cases. On the assizes see further, for example, J.H. Baker, *An Introduction to English Legal History*, 4th edn, London: Butterworths, 2002, pp. 20–2.

5 The focus here is upon sexual crimes against girls rather than against children as any sexual activity between males (including consenting adults) was, of course, at the time considered to be immoral and unnatural – making the issues very different from those relating to men's sexual abuse of girls (and women). Sex crimes committed against women are the focus of Chapter 4.

6 Of course, the legal implications of full adulthood for women at this time were a very different thing than the age of majority for men, with females having limited legal rights and independence.

7 For example, on white slavery and the enticement and detention of English girls by foreigners see: A. Dyer, *The European Slave Trade in English Girls: A Narrative of Facts*, London: Dye Brothers, 1880.

8 The case has figured to a greater or lesser degree in articles and textbooks but has rarely been subjected to detailed investigation and analysis. A notable exception being Rupert Cross's 'Centenary Reflections on Prince's Case', *Law Quarterly Review*, 91, 1975, 540–54.

9 The stories drawn upon here are: *The Times*, 25 March 1875, p. 12; *Daily News*, 25 March 1875, p. 4; *Morning Post*, 25 March, p. 7; *Newspaper*, 28 March 1875, p. 6; *Era*, 28 March 1875, p. 9; *Standard*, 25 March 1875, pp. 4, 6; *Lloyd's Weekly Newspaper*, 28 March 1875, p. 2. These papers agree as to the details, although some give additional facts.

10 TNA: PRO ASSI 31/38 (Records of Justices of Assize, Gaol Delivery, Oyer and Terminer, and Nisi Prius, South-Eastern Circuit, Kingston-Upon Thames Assize Records) and KB 30/3 (CCCR, Pleadings).

11 At the trial her father testified that she would be 14 on 6 April 1875 (*Prince* at 155).

12 For example, see *Daily News*, 25 March, p. 3. I have not been able to establish Prince's exact age.

13 For example, see *Reynolds's Newspaper*, 28 March 1875, p. 6 and *The Times*, 25 March 1875, p. 12.

14 In theory children could marry at a very young age at this time, although a marriage could be found to be invalid where a boy was under the age of 14 and a girl under the age of 12 – however, parents could challenge a union where their child was under the age of 21. The minimum age of 16 was not introduced until the Age of Marriage Act 1929.

15 For example, see *Daily News*, 25 March 1875, p. 3.

16 See further below and section 51 of the 1861 Act.

17 For example, see *Lloyd's Weekly Newspaper*, 28 March 1875, p. 2.

18 For example, see *Lloyd's Weekly Newspaper*, 28 March 1875, p. 2 and *Reynolds's Newspaper*, 28 March 1875, p. 6.

19 For example, see *Daily News*, 25 March 1875, p. 3.

20 At that time offences were divided into misdemeanours and felonies, the former being the less serious of the two.

21 Parental rights then were usually seen as resting in the father. On the legal position regarding legitimate children at the time see, for example, Richard Collier's discussion of the 1883 case of *Agar-Ellis v Lascelles* [1883] 24 ChD 317 in *Masculinity, Law and The Family*, London: Routledge, 1995, pp. 186–7.

22 For example, see *Daily News*, 25 March 1875, p. 3.

23 For example, see *Lloyd's Weekly Newspaper*, 28 March 1875, p. 2.

24 For example, see *Morning Post*, 25 March, p. 7.

25 For example, see ibid.

26 Some reports had the jury taking a view that Phillips looked to be 16 rather than 14. See, for example, *Era*, 28 March 1875, p. 9.

27 This wording is taken from the *Daily News*, 25 March 1875, p. 4.

28 Some of these documents, signed by the judges concerned, are preserved in TNA: PRO KB 30 (CCCR, Pleadings) – the (rather grubby) statement of the case in *Prince* is in KB 30/3.

29 On the CCCR see further: J.F. Stephen, *A History of the Criminal Law of England*, London: Macmillan, 1883, vol. I, pp. 311–13; P. Handler, 'The Court for Crown Cases Reserved, 1848–1908', *Law and History Review*, 29(1), 2011, 259–88, pp. 263–4.

30 See *Prince* at 155 and *The Times*, 26 April 1875, p. 13.

31 See *Prince* at 155 and *The Times* report of the arguments (31 May 1875, p. 13). The account of the court proceedings on 29 May given here is largely drawn from the latter source.

32 Brett dissenting used this phrase in *Prince* at 160.

33 In *The Times* Law Notices, the case was scheduled for judgment at 10.30 (26 June 1875, p. 13).

34 *Prince* at 173–7.

35 Ibid., at 170–3.
36 Ibid., at 177–9.
37 Ibid., at 155–70.
38 For example, see: *The Times*, 28 June 1875, p. 6; *Daily News*, 28 June 1875, p. 2; *York Herald*, 28 June 1875, p. 5; *Hull Packet and East Riding Times*, 2 July 1875, p. 3; *Sheffield & Rotherham Independent*, 29 June 1875, p. 6; *Jackson's Oxford Journal*, 3 July 1875, p. 7; *Lancaster Gazette*, 3 July 1875, p. 6.
39 See the commentary on the case from *All ER Annual Review 2000, Criminal Law*, pp. 1–2.
40 London: John Murray.
41 In particular, see *Character*, London: John Murray, 1871, pp. 299–342.
42 For example, see 'The Science of Health' in *Health and Education*, London: Isbister, 1874.
43 On these ideas see further, for example: John Tosh, 'Domesticity and Manliness in the Victorian Middle Class: The Family of Edward White Benson', in M. Roper and J. Tosh (eds), *Manful Assertions: Masculinities in Britain since 1800*, London: Routledge, 1991, ch. 3; L. Davidoff and C. Hall, *Family Fortunes*, revised edition, London: Routledge, 2002, ch. 7. 3 HL 161, col. 179, 8 February 1861.
44 On degeneracy see, for example: W. Greenslade, *Degeneration, Culture and the Novel 1880–1940*, Cambridge: Cambridge University Press, 1994.
45 On shifting ideas regarding children and childhood in this period see, for example: P. Coveney, *The Image of Childhood. The Individual and Society: A Study of the Theme in English Literature*, Harmondsworth: Penguin, 1967; C. Steedman, *Strange Dislocations: Childhood and the Idea of Human Interiority 1780–1930*, London: Virago, 1995.
46 On shifting ideas relating to child cruelty, including sexual abuse, during the nineteenth century see, for example: M. Flegel, *Conceptualizing Cruelty to Children in Nineteenth-Century England: Literature, Representation, and the NSPCC*, Aldershot: Ashgate, 2009; G.K. Behlmer, *Child Abuse and Moral Reform in England, 1870–1908*, Stanford: Stanford University Press, 1982.
47 For example, see the comments of Mr Phinn MP, reported in the *Daily News*, 7 April 1853, p. 2. However, at this time it was, of course, accepted that adults had a (not unlimited) right to physically chastise children who were in their care or charge.
48 Mr Phinn MP reported in *The Times*, 7 April 1853, p. 4.
49 On masculinity and child sexual abuse in the period see further, in particular, Louise A. Jackson, *Child Sexual Abuse in Victorian England*, London: Routledge, 2000, ch. 6.
50 Ibid., p. 39.
51 As to the Acts, see further Chapter 4. D. Gorham discusses the development of such campaigns from the late 1870s in 'The "Maiden Tribute of Modern Babylon" Re-Examined: Child Prostitution and the Idea of Childhood in Late-Victorian England', *Victorian Studies*, 21(3), 1978, 353–79.
52 *Bury and Norwich Post and Suffolk Herald*, 24 March 1863, p. 5.
53 See *The Constitution Violated. An Essay [Advocating the Repeal of the Contagious Diseases Acts 1866, 1868 and 1869]*, Edinburgh: Edmonston and Douglas, 1871, pp. 68 and 137, 139–41.
54 See further: *Daily News*, 9 February 1861, p. 2 and 27 February 1861, p. 2; *Lloyd's Weekly Newspaper*, 3 March 1861, p. 2; 3 HL 161, col. 179, 8 February 1861; 3 HC 161, cols 930–1, 26 February 1861.
55 For example, see *The Times*, 5 March 1875, p. 11.
56 Justice Quain took this line and made specific reference to the Bishop's efforts and influence on the 1861 provisions in the 1875 *Timms* case, which is discussed below; ibid.

57 'Carnal knowledge' was defined in section 63 of the 1861 Act as requiring 'Proof of Penetration only.'
58 For discussions of the Bill and its contents see 3 HC 215, cols 468–88, 2 April 1873.
59 3 HC 215, cols 470–1, 2 April 1873. Charley was moving the second reading of the Bill.
60 Ibid., col. 476.
61 (1865) LR 1 CCR 10; 35 LJMC 60; 10 Cox CC 157; 12 Jur NS 12; 14 WR 57; 13 LT 335.
62 (1865) LR 1 CCR 10 at 11.
63 Ibid., at 11–12.
64 (1873) LR 2 CCR 81; 43 LJMC 7; 12 Cox CC 498; 22 WR 136; [1861–73] All ER Rep 792; 29 LT 409.
65 The four were Kelly, Blackburn, Lush and Pollock. The fifth judge was Justice Honyman, who had reserved *Barratt* from Leeds assizes.
66 [1861–73] All ER at 794. Here the judge was quoting Lord Campbell from *Fletcher* (1859) 8 Cox CC 131; 15 Digest (Repl) 1009, 9941.
67 *The Times*, 28 January 1861, p. 9.
68 Other examples of such cases for damages are provided by: *Terry v Hutchinson* (1868) LR 3 QB 599; *Berry v Da Costa* (1866) LR 1 CP 331; 35 LJCP 191; Har & Ruth 291; 12 Jur NS 588; 14 WR 279.
69 (1866) 10 Cox CC 402; 15 Digest (Repl) 1030, 10,116.
70 (1871) 12 Cox CC 28; 15 Digest (Repl) 1031, 10,127.
71 (1872) 12 Cox CC 231; 15 Digest (Repl) 1032, 10,136.
72 Whilst by today's standards their precedent value would be extremely low, their significance was arguably greater in the nineteenth century, depending upon the stature of the particular judges involved. See, for example, Lord Chief Justice Coleridge's comments a few years later in *R v Coney* (1882) LR 8 QBD 534 at 569.
73 (1869) LR 1 CCR 184; 38 LJMC 61; 19 LT 799; 33 JP 243; 17 WR 384; 11 Cox CC 246, CCR; 15 Digest (Repl) 1031, 10,131.
74 (1862) 3 F & F 274; 176 ER 123.
75 (1859) 1 F & F 513; 175 ER 832.
76 For reports of the case see, for example: *Reynolds's Newspaper*, 25 September 1870, p. 5; *Pall Mall Gazette*, 28 October 1870, p. 6; *Morning Post*, 28 October 1870, p. 7 (the quotations by Lush are taken from the latter). See also *Old Bailey Proceedings Online* (*OBP*) (http://www.oldbaileyonline.org, version 7.0, accessed 30 March 2013), October 1870, trial of Archibald Johnstone (29) (t18701024-844).
77 See: *York Herald*, 20 January 1875, p. 6; *Nottinghamshire Guardian*, 22 January 1875, p. 2.
78 5 March 1875, p. 11. See also, for example: *Pall Mall Gazette*, 3 March 1875, p. 6; *Standard*, 3 March 1875, p. 4; *Jackson's Oxford Journal*, 6 March 1875, p. 6. The account given here is based upon the story in *The Times*.
79 Prior to the trial Quain had made a similarly strong direction to the grand jury (who were charged with deciding whether the prosecution should proceed). *The Morning Post*, 2 March 1875, p. 6.
80 The information about and quotations from this hearing that are given here are taken from *The Times*, 31 May 1875, p. 13. Other papers covered the proceedings – see, for example, *Morning Post*, 31 May 1875, p. 2.
81 Here he referred to Willes in *Mycock*.
82 *Prince* at 174.
83 Ibid., at 175.
84 Ibid., at 176.
85 Ibid., at 174–5.

86 Ibid., at 176.
87 Ibid., at 175.
88 Ibid., at 171.
89 Ibid., at 172.
90 *Prince* [1874–80] All ER Rep 881 at 886. His exact words vary in different reports. For example, they are given as 'punish the abduction' in LR 2 CCR 154 at 171.
91 *Prince* at 172.
92 Ibid., at 171–2.
93 Ibid., at 171.
94 Ibid., at 172.
95 Ibid., at 179.
96 Ibid., at 178–9.
97 Ibid., at 179.
98 Ibid.
99 Consequently, according to Brett, where, for example, a man did not know of the section 55 offence or thought the relevant age to be 12 he should be convicted.
100 Ibid., at 168.
101 3 July 1875, p. 412.
102 30 June 1875, p. 10.
103 In particular, concerns about incest resulted in the 1908 Punishment of Incest Act. See V. Bailey and S. Blackburn, 'The Punishment of Incest Act 1908: A Study in Law Creation', *Criminal Law Review*, 1979, 708–18.
104 In contrast to the narrative here, Carol Smart's analysis of the Act situates it as one of a number of late nineteenth-century measures which aimed at regulating female reproduction and sexuality. See 'Disruptive Bodies and Unruly Sex: The Regulation of Reproduction and Sexuality in the Nineteenth Century', in C. Smart (ed.), *Regulating Womanhood: Historical Essays on Marriage, Motherhood and Sexuality*, London: Routledge, 1992, pp. 7–32.
105 On the attempts to pass the Act and the work of the Committee see further, for example, Gorham, 'The "Maiden Tribute of Modern Babylon"', pp. 358–60.
106 For example, this argument is addressed by Judith R. Walkowitz in *Prostitution and Victorian Society: Women, Class and the State*, Cambridge: Cambridge University Press, 1980, pp. 246–50 and in Gorham, 'The "Maiden Tribute of Modern Babylon"'.
107 These were published in the paper on: 6 July 1885, pp. 1–6; 7 July 1885, pp. 1–6; 8 July1885, pp. 1–5; 10 July 1885, pp. 1–6.
108 The coverage of these events is deliberately very partial here. Other scholarship adopts a range of perspectives and gives far more in-depth and nuanced accounts of 'The Maiden Tribute'. See further: Gorham, 'The "Maiden Tribute of Modern Babylon"'; J.R. Walkowitz, *City of Dreadful Delight: Narratives of Sexual Danger in Late-Victorian London*, Chicago: University of Chicago Press, 1992, chs 3, 4.
109 See further, Gorham, 'The "Maiden Tribute of Modern Babylon"', p. 361.
110 See further, ibid.
111 The brief account of the abduction trial given here is drawn from newspaper reports and the *OBP*. For reports of the legal proceedings (which involved not only the initial hearing in Bow Street Magistrates' Court but also two Old Bailey trials) see, in particular: *The Times*, 9 September 1885, p. 8, 14 September 1885, p. 4, 15 September 1885, p. 3, 28 September 1885, p. 13, 24 October 1885, p. 3, 26 October 1885, p. 3, 28 October 1885, p. 13, 29 October 1885, p. 3, 30 October 1885, p. 3, 3 November 1885, p. 3, 4 November 1885, p. 3, 5 November 1885,

p. 3, 9 November 1885, p. 3, 11 November 1885, pp. 3–4; *OBP* (http://www.oldbaileyonline.org, version 7.0, accessed 30 March 2013), October 1885, trial of Rebecca Jarrett, William Thomas Stead, Sampson Jacques, William Bramwell Booth, Elizabeth Combe (t18851019-1031) and October 1885, trial of Rebecca Jarrett, William Thomas Stead, Sampson Jacques, Louisa Mourez (t18851019-1032). On the trial see further, Walkowitz, *City of Dreadful Delight*, pp. 106–15.

112 This seems to have related to the midwife's testing of Armstrong's virginity at Stead's direction. Such activity might now constitute assault by penetration (section 2, Sexual Offences Act 2003).

113 See, for example, *The Times*, 11 November 1885, p. 4.

114 Ibid., p. 9.

115 [1891] 2 QB 149; 60 LJMC 171; 17 Cox CC 297; 39 WR 703.

116 [1891] 2 Q.B. 149 at 150.

117 [1894] 1 QB 710; 63 LJMC 58; 17 Cox CC 716; 10 R 82; 42 WR 255; [1891–4] All ER Rep 1215; 38 Sol Jo 130; 70 LT 41; 10 TLR 167.

118 Under section 5 of the Criminal Law Amendment Act 1885.

119 [1891–94] All ER Rep 1215 at 1215–16. On the 'Tyrrell principle' in the twenty-first century see, for example, M. Bohlander, 'The Sexual Offences Act 2003 and the Tyrrell principle – criminalising the victims?', *Criminal Law Review*, September 2005, 701–13.

120 [1896] 2 QB 167; 65 LJMC 195; 74 LT 730; 60 JP 536; 44 WR 654; 12 TLR 473; 40 Sol Jo 584; 18 Cox CC 346; [1895–99] All ER Rep 586.

121 [1905] 1 KB 551; 69 JP 189; 74 LJKB 311; 53 WR 494; 92 LT 393; 21 TLR 288; [1904–7] All ER Rep 54.

122 (1890) 25 QBD 202; 54 JP 677; 59 LJMC 138; 17 Cox CC 111; 38 WR 704; 62 LT 845.

123 The offence of indecent assault upon a female was contained in section 52 of the Act.

124 This had recently been ruled upon by the CCCR in *R v Wealand* (1888) 20 QBD 827; 52 JP 582; 57 LJMC 44; 16 Cox CC 402; 36 WR 576; 58 LT 782; 4 TLR 483, in which Hawkins had also had a part. See further Hawkins in *Paul* (1890) 25 QBD 202 at 212–13.

125 Ibid., at 213.

126 Hawkins in *R v Paul* (1890) 25 QBD 202 at 206. The full citation for the case is 25 QBD 202; 54 JP 677; 59 LJMC 138; 17 Cox CC 111; 38 WR 704; 62 LT 845.

127 Ibid., at 208.

128 Hawkins in *R v Paul* (1890) 25 QBD 202 at 206. The full citation for the case is 25 QBD 202; 54 JP 677; 59 LJMC 138; 17 Cox CC 111; 38 WR 704; 62 LT 845.

129 The account given here is taken from: *Preston Guardian*, 20 May 1876. p. 3; *Lancaster Gazette*, 24 May 1876, p. 1.

130 See *B (a minor) v DPP* [2000] 2 A.C. 428; [2000] 2 W.L.R. 452; [2000] 1 All E.R. 833; [2000] 2 Cr. App. R. 65 and *R v K* [2001] UKHL 41; [2002] 1 A.C. 462; [2001] 3 W.L.R. 471; [2001] 3 All E.R. 897; [2002] 1 Cr. App. R. 13. See further, for example, L. Toczek, 'Mistake and Age-based Sexual Offences', *New Law Journal*, 151, 2001, 1328.

131 Section 55 was repealed and replaced by section 20 of the Sexual Offences Act 1956. Today the offence of child abduction by a non-parent is contained in section 2 of the Child Abduction Act 1984 and, whilst child sexual abuse is obviously a concern in the context of the offence, its purpose still relates to the removal of a child (female or male) from their parents or legal guardian without their consent. The 2013 case of Jeremy Forrest provides a good illustration of the application of the current law and raises some unnerving parallels with

the cases considered here, not least in terms of responses to the defendant. Forrest, a teacher, was convicted of the abduction of one of his 15-year-old-pupils. See, for example: http://www.cps.gov.uk/news/latest_news/jeremy_forrest_convicted_of_child_abduction/; http://www.guardian.co.uk/uk/2013/jun/21/jeremy-forrest-jailed-pupil-sex-abduction?INTCMP=SRCH; http://www.guardian.co.uk/commentisfree/2013/jun/25/jeremy-forrest-no-romeo-pervert?INTCMP=SRCH; http://www.thesun.co.uk/sol/homepage/news/4990403/Abducted-schoolgirl-tells-The-Sun-I-groomed-my-teacher.html (accessed 5 July 2013).

132 The account of the case along with the events which led to it which is given here is reconstructed from various newspaper reports. See especially: *Daily News*, 20 August 1891, p. 7, 27 August 1891, p. 7, 3 September 1891, p. 2; *The Times*, 20 August 1891, p. 11; *Standard*, 20 August 1891, p. 2; *Lloyd's Weekly Newspaper*, 23 August 1891, p. 4; *Pall Mall Gazette*, 27 August 1891, p. 7, 18 September 1891 (4th edn), p. 4; *Morning Post*, 19 September 1891, p. 8.

133 By the time of the trial, Pearman, it was said, took her parents' view of the matter, although descriptions of her demeanour towards Newton in court do not all entirely accord with this. *Daily News*, 3 September 1891, p. 2.

134 *Morning Post*, 19 September 1891, p. 2.

135 However, it was emphasized that temptation provided no excuse as 'it was his duty to resist.' *Lloyd's Weekly Newspaper*, 27 September 1891, p. 5.

136 *Daily News*, 19 September 1891, p. 5.

137 *Pall Mall Gazette*, 19 September 1891, p. 2.

138 2(1605), 3 October 1891, 776.

139 28 June 1875, p. 6.

140 K. Stevenson, 'Observations on the Law Relating to Sexual Offences: The Historic Scandal of Women's Silence', *Web Journal of Current Legal Issues*, 19, 1999.

141 J. Weeks, *Sex, Politics, and Society: The Regulation of Sexuality Since 1800*, London: Longman, 1981, p. 88.

142 (1889) LR 22 QBD 23; 58 LJMC 10; 59 LT 780; 53 JP 149; 37 WR 166; 5 TLR 61; 16 Cox CC 511; [1886–90] All ER Rep 133.

Chapter 2

R v Coney, Gilliam and Tully 1881–2[1]

Civilizing combatants and limiting lawlessness

> [T]he injuries given and received in prize-fights are injurious to the public, both because it is against the public interest that the lives and the health of the combatants should be endangered by blows, and because prize-fights are disorderly exhibitions, mischievous on many obvious grounds.[2]
>
> ... there is a class of persons to whom prize-fights are attractive, and ... pugilists fight in public for the gratification of those persons, and ... the chief incentive to the wretched combatants to fight on until (as happens too often) dreadful injuries have been inflicted and life endangered or sacrificed, is the presence of spectators watching with keen interest every incident of the fight.[3]

The case of *R v Coney and Others* originated in what was apparently an organized fight between two men, which drew a large crowd. These events became the subject of a jury trial at the Berkshire quarter sessions. There, a number of men were found guilty of assault either as combatants or because they were deemed to be in some way liable as accessories to the assaults committed by the fighters. The case against three of the defendants (John Coney, William Gilliam and Thomas Tully) proved controversial as there was no evidence against them, excepting they were amongst the gathering. The central issue in terms of the law was, therefore, whether they had done enough to be convicted of aiding and abetting the assaults. This question was reserved to the Court for Crown Cases Reserved (CCCR) for an authoritative legal statement.

The CCCR unanimously affirmed the (il)legal status of 'prize-fights' and other non-sporting combat but were split as to the boundaries of liability for aiding and abetting criminal conduct.[4] Consequently, Coney, Gilliam and Tully's convictions were quashed because it was deemed that they had not done anything to assist the assaults. However, the case did reaffirm that some of those present at a prize-fight could be liable as accessories if, for example, they helped with its organization or actively did something to encourage the fighters.

Coney was (and remains) an important legal authority and so it is not surprising that a number of (largely legal) scholars have written about the case. At times this attention has been fleeting, taking the form, for example, of a statement as to the facts and decision, along with consideration of how the case has subsequently been applied in the courts. Occasionally it has involved exploration of the legal and more broadly socio-cultural history and implications of the case. Work has considered the decision in the context of developments regarding the regulation of boxing, including the introduction of the Marquis of Queensberry's Rules. Also, in reflecting on sport, sex, violence and law, scholarship has briefly looked at issues of gender and sexuality in relation to the case. At the same time, much has been written about male violence and the history of fighting and some of this has included (often brief) reference to *Coney*.[5] This chapter is informed by and utilizes the work of these writers but does so in order to explore the case in more detail than previously and then to tell a particular tale about it, focusing upon the male of the species.

Aside from the very obvious fact that *Coney* and, indeed, all the cases considered in this chapter involved only men (whether as fighters, fight organizers, seconds, spectators, defendants, victims, lawyers, judges or juries), the areas of law considered, along with the issues at stake in decision-making, were very much concerned with males and male behaviour. Moreover, read in the context of late nineteenth-century thinking about males, *Coney* can be viewed as having a wider significance. In terms of this book's 'binding men' narrative, it seemed to embody the contemporary sense of unease about men and can be portrayed as forming a part of efforts – both legal and more broadly societal – to delimit appropriate conduct and (re)enforce these standards in relation to all Englishmen. More specifically, in this chapter *Coney* is depicted as being part of a tendency to try to rein in unacceptable instances of inter-male violence. In this context, the overarching aim of all the CCCR judges was the eradication of prize-fighting, not only in order to prevent the combatants trading blows, but also to bring an end to the sometimes vast, often unruly and largely male crowds who were drawn to watch such contests. However, only the three minority judges went so far as to seek to achieve this by criminalizing even those who were merely present at a contest.

This chapter starts with a retelling of *Coney*, which offers more detail than is provided either in the law reports of the case or in previous academic writings about it. This reconstructs what led Coney, Gilliam and Tully into court and considers the legal proceedings and decision. *Coney* is then placed within a wider legal and socio-cultural background. Here the story told about the case traces some of the worries about and efforts to restrain male violence in the form of prize-fights, focusing upon the latter decades of the 1800s, but drawing upon a longer history of anxiety. In doing so, consideration is given to the qualities and behaviour which were viewed as being desirable in men as well as the distinctions drawn between male criminal violence and manly sport during the period.

Coney, Gilliam and Tully

The following account draws on the law reports of the case and on a number of other sources. Newspaper stories of the fight, the resulting legal proceedings and the subsequent CCCR review give more information as to the events.[6] Surviving court and other records are also utilized here but add little that is additional in this first tale-telling about *Coney*.[7]

The prize-fight

On Thursday 16 June 1881, following the Ascot horse races, a crowd gathered in a privately owned field next to the Ascot to Maidstone highway. Amidst the assembly and a few yards from the road a ring had been created using four blue stakes and some rope. Soon the fighters, John Burke and Charles Mitchell, having removed their upper garments, entered the enclosure. They were accompanied by six others – two as seconds and one in each corner – and the contest began. Their combat was reported to have lasted between 45 minutes and an hour and was estimated to have been watched by a crowd of 100 to 150 people (the identity of the audience is not mentioned but the vast majority of spectators at such events were male – see further below). Apparently, some of this number made bets on the fight. However, there was no evidence that this was a contest for money on the part of the fighters, making it uncertain whether it should be defined as a *prize*-fight.[8] Nor was it clear whether Burke and Mitchell were wearing gloves – prize-fights being bare-knuckle tournaments.[9]

John Coney, William Gilliam (the various reports of the case carry a number of different versions of his surname, including Gillum and Gilham, but I have opted to use the one which is favoured in the law reports) and Thomas Tully were in the crowd. How they came to be there and what their purpose was remains a matter of some conjecture because different accounts of their story were to be presented during the case's progress through the courts. So, for example, it seems to have been argued in defence of the three that they were either labourers working near the field or were on their way home from the races, had seen the crowd and gone to investigate.[10] It was also suggested that they had joined the spectators because they had been curious to see what was rumoured to be a naked race between two men and had then found themselves watching something of an entirely different character.[11] However, it is worth noting that, despite differing explanations as to the men's presence and of their intentions, at no point during *Coney* was it suggested that the three were fight-followers, nor was it argued that they had planned their presence at the contest.

As to the contest itself, the police turned up and seem to have attempted to stop the combat and break up the crowd but were resisted and a number of men found themselves under arrest. Matters then paused and it was not until late summer that a prosecution was brought against not only the combatants and those men who in some way actively assisted in the fight, but also some who had merely watched. A total of ten men were summonsed to appear before the Maidenhead County Magistrates' Court on Tuesday 13 September, charged with public order or 'affray' offences (as they were described in some of the press coverage) and assault. Five attended and were named in the press as Burke (one of the combatants), Thomas Simmonds or Symonds (who was one of the men in the ring), Robert Parker (who was alleged to have offered a police constable £5 not to intervene), James Goode (who was said to have been present) and Gilliam. All were committed for trial at the quarter sessions and bailed.[12] The remaining men were to be dealt with at the Magistrates' Court's next sitting. Four of them appeared before the Maidenhead bench on Tuesday 27 September. These were Tully, Hezekiah Webb, Mitchell (the other pugilist) and Coney. However, as no evidence was offered in relation to Webb, he was discharged. The other three were sent for trial and bailed.[13] Following this, Coney, Gilliam and Tully, along with the five others (the combatants, Burke and Mitchell, as well as Goode, Symonds and Parker) found themselves charged with 'affray' offences and common assault.[14]

The trial

On Friday 18 October 1881 the eight men were tried at the quarter sessions in Reading.[15] The court was packed, with 'a large number of sporting men being present', who were presumably keen to see the result and were likely to be rooting for acquittals.[16] Burke, Tully, Parker and Coney had legal representation. Although all the men had initially been charged with 'affray' and common assault, at this stage, according to law reports of the CCCR decision, only the assault charges were pursued.[17] For the pugilists there was one charge apiece – Burke was charged with assault upon Mitchell and Mitchell with assault upon Burke. The other defendants were charged with assaults in relation to both Burke and Mitchell on the basis that by assisting with or watching the fight they had aided and abetted the fighters and, therefore, would be liable as if they had committed the full offence.

At this stage, the prosecution case was that prize-fights were illegal, that this had been just such a happening, that all the men were implicated in this illegality and that, therefore, they were guilty of assault. A farmer by the name of Druce was one of the two prosecution witnesses.[18] He gave evidence that he had been returning from the races on 16 June when he saw what he thought was a prize-fight, with a crowd surrounding a ring in which two men were fighting. Druce reported that he 'heard betting going on' and 'shouting'. In court he identified the fighters as Burke and Mitchell and attested to all the other defendants being present, saving Gilliam and Goode. Of the four non-combatants he had seen, he said that all but Symonds were outside the ring. The second prosecution witness, Police Constable Staples, stated that he had arrived on the scene towards the end of the fight. He identified the pugilists, along with Symonds (who he too saw in the ring), Gilliam, Coney and Tully.[19] So of the eight defendants only Goode's presence was not attested to at trial.

In terms of the defence it was urged on behalf of all the defendants that they should be acquitted as there was no proof that this was a prize-fight and, therefore, no evidence to suggest that what took place was an illegal contest. In addition, it was argued that Parker, Symonds, Gilliam, Coney and Tully had not personally assaulted either Burke or Mitchell and that, in the case of the three spectators, there was nothing to show that they had countenanced the fight, or aided, abetted or encouraged the combatants in any way.[20] Indeed, the evidence relating to Coney, Gilliam and Tully was said to demonstrate that they were merely watching proceedings. Thus, it was reported that '[t]hey were not speaking, and were not seen to be betting or taking any part in the fight, or doing anything.'[21] Further, Coney was described in one of the witnesses' accounts as having been 'hemmed in' and, therefore, unable to leave his position in the throng.[22] The implication in favour of this defendant was, therefore, that he may have stumbled upon the crowd, walked into their midst in order to satisfy his curiosity and then been unable to quit the proceedings.

At the close of the trial, the chairman of the quarter sessions, Mr Benyon, explained the relevant law as he saw it to the jury. He told them that they first had to decide if the fight was a prize-fight, explaining that:

> There is no doubt that prize-fights are illegal, indeed, just as much so as that persons should go out to fight with deadly weapons, and it is not at all material which party strikes the first blow; and all persons who go to a prize-fight to see the combatants strike each other, and who are present when they do so, are, in point of law, guilty of an assault.[23]

In so saying, he relied upon the words of Justice Littledale in another prize-fighting case, *R v Murphy* (1833).[24] Murphy had been either a second or a spectator at a contest and was convicted of aiding and abetting the manslaughter of one of the combatants. At the close of his trial in his summing up to the jury, Littledale opined that '[i]f [the defendant] was not casually passing by, but stayed at the place, [he] encouraged it by [his] presence, although [he] did not say or do anything.'[25] Thus, the judge had apparently laid down that any degree of lingering to see what was going on would amount to assisting the fight and, therefore, would constitute aiding and abetting any offences committed in the course of the competition.

Benyon, having quoted Littledale, then left the fate of Burke, Coney, Gilliam, Goode, Mitchell, Parker, Symonds and Tully in the hands of the panel of 12 men.

After a short discussion, the jury found Goode not guilty, there being no evidence that he was present, they convicted Burke and Mitchell of assault as combatants and found Symonds and Parker guilty as accessories. In the cases of Coney, Gilliam and Tully the jury also returned guilty verdicts but added a perplexing qualifier: they found that they had not actually been aiding or abetting the assaults.[26] This seemed to be a contradictory decision as, although there was a conviction, it looked as if the jury were also saying that the men were innocent.[27]

Goode was discharged[28] and Benyon proceeded to sentencing. Burke, Mitchell, Symonds and Parker received six weeks' imprisonment with hard labour. Coney, Gilliam and Tully were given only three weeks with hard labour.[29] At the same time, counsel for the defendants requested that Benyon reserve the case to the CCCR, so that the legal direction could be considered and authoritatively ruled upon.[30] The chairman opted to do this and Coney, Gilliam and Tully were released on bail and told to appear again at the Christmas sessions, it being assumed that the CCCR would have both considered and ruled on the case by that time, allowing the trial court to bring the matter to a close.[31]

The review

The CCCR had been created in 1848 by the Crown Cases Act. It was a court of review rather than a court of appeal – in fact, there was no court of criminal appeal until one was created by the 1907 Criminal Appeal Act, which in turn brought the CCCR to an end. The CCCR consisted of all the common law judges who went on circuit, presiding over the assizes around the country (the exact number of judges increased during its lifespan).[32] In the normal course, cases were heard by a panel of five. However, where the five were divided and/or felt the matter to be of sufficient importance or controversy, it could be considered by all the judges (as happened in the present case). The CCCR could only hear cases which had resulted in a conviction and was only empowered to consider matters referred to it by the trial judge. Neither the defence nor the prosecution had any say in whether a case should be referred, although lawyers could, as happened in *Coney*, ask for this to be considered. Generally, if the decision was taken to reserve a case to the CCCR, sentencing would either be respited or, once sentence was passed, a convicted person would be released on bail, whilst the legal questions and their consequences were resolved.

When a case came before the CCCR for consideration, the judge who had presided over the trial would state or present the basic facts (on paper and sometimes also appearing in person), as well as the legal questions to be resolved, to the judges. Matters would then be argued by prosecution counsel (assuming there was one) and, if a defendant was represented, their lawyer, with the judges often interjecting repeatedly. The CCCR could only rule upon the matters of law reserved for its consideration – and they were left to accept the findings of the jury as to the facts of the case. The effect of their decision would be either to quash or to affirm a conviction. If the latter course was decided upon, the 'prisoner' or 'defendant' would be recalled to the trial court, so that either the sentence could be confirmed or pronounced ('appellant' was not the correct term as this was no appeal – and 'prisoner' was often used regardless of whether the person was in custody). Where the result was an acquittal, this would be noted at the next sitting of the trial court and the defendants would be formally discharged.[33]

The CCCR's task in *Coney* was to rule upon whether the chairman's expression of the law given in guidance to the jury was correct. Thus, the issues they were called upon to consider related to the parameters of criminal liability for aiding and abetting a prize-fight, but it was likely that in doing so they would also comment upon the legal status of such fighting. The question about accomplice liability had a huge significance because the decision would potentially apply to all instances where the charge was one of aiding and abetting an unlawful act and the alleged assisting involved the prisoner merely 'looking at anything unlawful'.[34]

The case first came before the CCCR on Saturday 10 December 1881.[35] At this point the arguments were heard and discussed by five judges: Lord Chief Justice Coleridge and Justices, Denman, Field, Stephen and Cave. On that day, of the defendants only Coney was represented, although most of what was said on his behalf also applied to Gilliam and Tully. The defence's attempts to speak, however, seem to have been met with repeated interjections by the CCCR judges. This led to the discussions rather going round in circles, as Coney's representative attempted to field and respond to their various observations and questions. Amongst other things, the lawyer contended that if the three were guilty of any offence it was riot, affray or unlawful assembly because of their presence in the crowd – but this was speedily rejected by Coleridge, these charges not having been proceeded with. Next, the defence asserted that the three had not taken part in the assaults and, therefore, could not be convicted – highlighting, in particular, the fact that Coney was trapped within the throng. It was further maintained that none of the men had gone to the field with the purpose of seeing the fight, that it had been rumoured a race was about to take place and that those on the outskirts of the crowd could not tell that this was not the case.

The case for the defence also focused upon the trial direction concerning what was necessary in order to find that the men aided and abetted the fight. Here it was argued that participation needed to be proved and this required some evidence of assistance, as mere presence was insufficient to establish guilt. Consequently, the question put to the jury should have been whether the men's presence in the crowd amounted to encouragement or was for the purpose of encouragement. If the law was otherwise, Coney's lawyer argued, anyone who was present at a fight, including a police officer who was in attendance for lawful reasons, would be guilty of the offence. Moreover, this issue was a question of fact not law and, therefore, should have rested with the jury.[36] On the latter basis it was maintained by the defence that the jury direction was wrong and the conviction could not stand. In addition, in the midst of his submissions and the various judicial utterances, Coney's lawyer attempted to suggest that a blow which was delivered within a prize-fight was no assault as the parties were consenting – so the three prisoners could not be guilty of aiding and abetting something that did not in itself constitute an offence.

In contrast, the prosecution case was that mere presence was sufficient to prove aiding and abetting in relation to the assaults. This was argued to be because of the nature of the crowds who went to prize-fights, which were characterized as being 'idle' and 'disorderly'.[37] Given the latter, according to the prosecution, just being there could be seen to constitute encouragement.

According to the report in *The Times*, at the close of this first hearing four of the five judges were 'prepared to give judgment in favour of the prisoners, and, indeed, Mr. Justice Cave had begun to do so', however, Coleridge appeared even at this stage to have taken a different view as he 'interposed and desired another argument'.[38] A conference was said to have then taken place between the five judges. Following their discussion, it was decided that the issue was of sufficient importance for the whole court to be involved.[39]

Coney came before the CCCR again on Wednesday 21 December 1881 and this time the arguments were presented to 11 judges: Coleridge; Barons Huddleston and Pollock; along with Justices Cave, Mathew, Stephen, Lopes, North, Hawkins, Manisty and Denman.[40] As before, of the defendants, Coney alone was represented. The discussions seem to have been broadly similar to those made at the first CCCR hearing, although this time the defence chose to argue that the jury decision actually amounted to an acquittal because they had found that there was no assistance given to the fighters.[41] Beyond this, there was more debate as to the nature of the combat which had taken place between Burke and Mitchell and whether it was, in fact, illegal.

At the close of the submissions the judges retired to discuss their judgment. Coleridge then came back into the courtroom to announce that 'some of his brethren thought the case of so much importance that they desired to put their judgments into writing', suggesting that again a difference of opinion existed on the bench. Consequently, the court's ruling was further delayed.

The decision

The decision was at last given on Saturday 18 March 1882.[42] Whilst all 11 of the judges were of a mind in confirming the long-standing illegality of 'prize-fighting', there was disagreement as to the issue of law which it fell to them to consider, with the court splitting 8:3 in favour of quashing the conviction because they felt that something more than mere presence was needed to establish a charge of aiding and abetting an assault. Those who carried the day were Denman, Huddleston, Manisty, Hawkins, Lopes, Stephen, Cave and North. The dissenters, therefore, were Coleridge, Pollock and Mathew. Unusually, all but one of the judges elected to give their own separate pronouncements, some of which were lengthy, suggesting again that *Coney* occasioned strong feelings amongst those charged with deciding the case (the exception being North who merely concurred with Lopes).[43]

Binding men and curbing lawless, unmanly diversions

In terms of this book's 'binding men' narrative, *Coney* had a wider significance than merely confirming the law on fighting and assault and delineating the boundaries of accessorial liability. Indeed, viewed in relation to contemporary ideas about men, the case resonated with a number of often contradictory but, nevertheless, co-existing notions about the male of the species. Thus, *Coney* can be conceived of as being a part of wider efforts to tame some of the perceived excesses of masculinity. The concerns about men reflected in the case related to some, but by no means all, forms of inter-male violence – and, in particular, what was perceived to be the extreme brutality of prize-fighting. Lurking behind the judicial pronouncements there was also perhaps a linked sense of unease about the large unruly gatherings of lower class men who watched prize-fights – although the latter was more in evidence in other cases arising out of such contests.

In order to tell this story, the text below begins by looking to the nature of prize-fighting as distinct from other forms of combat. It then traces a history of shifting attitudes towards such contests and the men who took part, organized and watched them. Following this, the focus turns to the legal sphere and the attempts to end prize-fighting, of which *Coney* was a part. The three minority judges' decisions are then considered in the light of this background. In this context, some of the words of the majority are also shown to reflect similar ideas about the distinction between legitimate and unlawful male violence. The chapter then looks to developments in the years following *Coney* and concludes by briefly reflecting upon the legal limits upon male behaviour in the context of fighting.

The pre-*Coney* context

A 'prize-fight' was a contest fought by two combatants in front of an audience. Such events were planned and supported by those who made the arrangements, seconded and backed the pugilists. They sometimes arose as a means of settling a quarrel but often involved experienced and extremely well-known fighters. As the name suggests, the combatants often fought for a purse, which would either be awarded to the victor or be divided between the winner and loser in unequal parts. Bets tended to be placed upon the competition.[44]

From the middle of the eighteenth century, prize-fighting's rules were based upon those recorded by celebrated boxer Jack Broughton in 1743. These were gradually developed into the London Prize Ring Rules in 1838 and the Revised London Prize Ring Rules, which were issued in 1853.[45] Amongst other things, the latter stated that breaks between rounds (of which there could be well over 100) were to last no more than 60 seconds – any longer and the fight was forfeit; the vast number of rounds was a result of the fact that each one ended when a man fell or was thrown to the ground. The combat itself involved wrestling and grappling, as well as punching. It was conducted without gloves, padding or knuckle strapping and was, consequently, referred to as bare-knuckle boxing or fisticuffs. Clashes could last for hours and were often particularly bloody tournaments, sometimes proving fatal to one, or even both, of the men involved.[46] Unless stopped by the authorities, bouts were concluded either by one party admitting defeat or being unable to continue the conflict.

From contemporary reports, prize-fights were overwhelmingly male affairs in terms of the fighters, organizers and spectators,[47] although women did sometimes attend[48] and there were very rare incidents of female fights – but these seem to have largely been viewed as something of a salacious novelty.[49] Up until the early decades of the nineteenth century, whilst the fighters tended to originate in the labouring classes, organizers and spectators included not only members of the lower orders, but also far more lofty figures and even royalty.[50] This perhaps meant that, although, as we shall see, such events were potentially illegal, seeking to break up fights and to prosecute those involved was often not a course that was adopted because of the stature and influence of wealthy backers and enthusiasts.

Whilst prize-fighting was by no means either uncommon or unpopular in the earlier part of the eighteenth century, the golden age of the prize-fight is often said to have begun in the mid-1780s and to have ended sometime in the nineteenth century, with writers giving 1822, 1860, the 1880s or even the 1890s as its finish.[51] Certainly during the late eighteenth and for much of the nineteenth century, competitions frequently drew vast crowds of spectators – at the biggest fights, there could reportedly be hundreds, thousands or tens of thousands present[52] and men travelled to the field of action in vast convoys, on special trains or, for fights next to rivers, in flotillas of different sizes and shapes of vessel in a variety of states of sea-worthiness.[53] In addition, the most well-known pugilists were viewed as heroes and celebrities amongst followers of such fighting,[54] who were known as 'the fancy'.[55]

How then was prize-fighting seen in terms of ideas about men during these golden days? Amongst those who followed it, such tournaments were often cast as particularly manly endeavours. Thus, such things as chivalry, honour and patriotism were linked with both the combat and the combatants and texts that extolled the wonders of bare-fist fighting portrayed a strong sense of the perceived simple honesty in such fights – unaided by any weapon or gloves, men fought in a fair and straightforward way. There may have been few rules but this too suggested the natural manliness of what took place within the ring: men could punch, wrestle, push and throw – as long as all they used were their own bodies.[56] Moreover, fighting with fists was held up to be a quintessentially English activity – and one that demonstrated the pre-eminence of the race over others. For example, in sportswriter Pierce Egan's classic early nineteenth-century text on bare-knuckle prize-fighting, *Boxiana*, such combat was conceived of as something that Englishmen (of all classes) had a natural propensity for as '[p]ugilism is in perfect unison with the feelings of the Englishmen'. It also provided benefits for the race: 'the manly art of Boxing has infused that true heroic courage, blended with humanity, into the hearts of Britons, which have made them so renowned, terrific and triumphant in all parts of the world.' Additionally, Egan argued that all Englishmen needed to preserve some natural roughness and, in doing so, display 'those strong and *national* traits so congenial to the soil of liberty'; in his view fighting with fists was the means by which to achieve this.[57] Indeed, it was the fact that an Englishman would not settle disputes by way of the stiletto, duelling or assassination but would rather 'rise or fall but by his *fist*' and then – when '[t]he battle's o'er – all make amends/ [b]y shaking hands, becoming friends', which set him apart from other races.[58]

However, these views about manliness, Englishness and bare-knuckle bouts were by no means shared by all even during their heyday. Indeed, expressions of concern about such contests were being made in the eighteenth century and, as the nineteenth century progressed, the feeling against such fighting gradually gathered momentum. This shift in attitudes led not only to a change in relation to the class of those who attended prize-fights, as they came to be seen as less respectable events, but also to repeated attempts to eradicate these contests. The latter included legal efforts to produce change, one of which was the CCCR decision in *Coney* – but this is rather jumping ahead. First let us consider the revision of ideas about prize-fights and then turn to the treatment of such events within legal spheres during the decades running up to *Coney*.

Changes in attitudes to prize-fighting in the 1700s and 1800s were closely entwined with shifting ideas about men and, more specifically, male violence. As Robert Shoemaker has argued, violence in a variety of forms (including duelling, chance quarrels or planned fights) had been thought to be a key facet of male behaviour in the early eighteenth century but, as time passed, conceptions of masculinity changed and the use of aggression and force was less likely to be accepted, at least by those in authority.[59] In the nineteenth century thinking about how the modern male of the species should behave continued to evolve and Victorian Englishmen, whatever their class, came increasingly to be expected to be civilized, chivalrous, gentlemanly, stoic, respectable and domesticated, reining in their supposedly baser and more primitive urges to violence (although there were, of course, variations in terms of what was to be expected of the different ranks). For example, Samuel Smiles's self-help books were hugely influential during the latter part of the nineteenth century and described how men should behave. In works which included *Self-Help: With Illustrations of Conduct and Perseverance* (1859), and *Character* (1871),[60] he championed such qualities as duty, honour, courage and courtesy. In this context, the comparative disorder and brutality of bare-knuckle fighting as well as the unruliness of the crowd who watched, unsurprisingly, had no place. Indeed, the activity appeared distinctly unmanly.[61] However, the use of force was by no means entirely eschewed by Smiles – as long as it was justifiable, proportionate and orderly. Indeed, he often gave as his exemplars military men who carried themselves and fought in a civilized and gentlemanly way.[62]

Prize-fighting was at odds with other ideas developing in the mid to late Victorian period. For instance, in terms of evolutionary thinking it seemed to be something which owed more to less sophisticated times and places and the savage peoples of Empire, than to the superiority of the English race and, in particular, Englishmen in the latter part of the nineteenth century.[63] In this context it was not only the pugilists and the combat that were deemed to be a problem, as those who helped and watched were also a cause of anxiety. Indeed, the spectre of the crowd was closely linked to fears of degeneration, with various commentators viewing large gatherings as a site of regression and atavistic tendencies, including criminality[64] – and such ideas were to become increasingly prevalent as the nineteenth century moved towards its close. Linked to this, large unruly groups of lower class men also triggered fears of revolution.[65] So, far from Egan's conception of such competitions as quintessentially English, they were increasingly being seen as unEnglish, if not foreign, as well as anachronistic and barbaric – and this suggested the urgent need to bring prize-fighting to an end.

In this same timescape there was also a recognition and promotion of the value of sport for men – but supposedly manly, civilized and organized forms of sport. Thus, healthy modern games and exercise were being advocated as a means of instilling a sense of discipline into men and, in relation to working-class men in particular, of keeping them away from other supposedly less desirable activities, such as crime, disorder, immorality, unionizing, street football and, of course, prize-fighting – and unruly places, including the public house.[66] In addition, prominent figures were advocating the need for all men (and boys) to be channelled into healthy ordered exercise in order to ensure that their masculinity developed properly and was maintained, lest evolution moved in the wrong direction with degeneration the result (or where it was feared that this had already happened, it was hoped that physical activity might remedy the situation). For example, the religious, social and literary Muscular Christianity movement played a prominent part in developing such thinking from the middle of the century.[67] The movement focused upon concerns about the physical and moral (un)fitness of the English race, advocating sport and physical education by way of a solution. The manly ideal which it embraced was associated most with Thomas Hughes and Charles Kingsley who emphasized the value of maintaining fitness and vigour, adopting stoicism and aggressive spirituality, whilst denying the aesthetic and emotional. Indeed, Hughes, author of the *Tom Brown* books, was one of the most prominent advocates of these ideas and his enthusiasm for fighting – or rather, properly organized and refereed sparring and boxing with gloves – was part of this.[68] Prize-fighting, however, did not fit this model of manly, healthy and potentially spiritually uplifting activity.

In the context of these concerns about manliness and prize-fights, along with the promotion of the benefits of sport, there were heightened attempts to discourage and rein in those who participated in, organized and watched bare-knuckle combat and to distinguish these contests from boxing and sparring. In doing so, the aim was not only to bring prize-fighting to an end, but also to expand the progressively more regulated and, it was felt, more civilized, beneficial and legitimate pastime of boxing.

Labours to differentiate the two forms of fighting and bring about prize-fighting's demise included a new set of rules for boxing. These were devised in the 1850s and, following revisions, became what were to be referred to as the Marquis of Queensberry's Rules.[69] Amongst other things, the Rules required that gloves should be worn and they changed the way in which rounds were defined, as well as how the winner was decided upon. In doing so, they were intended to reduce the levels of brutality involved in fighting, shorten the bouts, lessen the chances of death or serious injury occurring (it being assumed, in particular, that fighting with gloves was safer) and to formalize the contests to such an extent that fights could not take place in fields but instead needed to be held in more easily policed settings with a proper umpire. The Rules did not, however, outlaw betting or stop the provision of a prize for the victor – meaning that close similarities between prize-fighting and boxing remained[70] – but they did allow boxing to be portrayed as a modern, noble, thoroughly English and indisputably manly art associated with the kinds of qualities and benefits espoused by the likes of Smiles, Kingsley and Hughes. There was also a sense of continuance here, as much – but by no means all – of what Egan had said about the manliness and Englishness of bare-knuckle contests could also be adapted and applied to regulated boxing.

The worries about and shifts in socio-cultural attitudes to prize-fighting, as well as the attempts to replace such contests with the more tightly regulated sport of boxing, were reflected in legal spheres. Here too, such efforts focused very much upon concerns about the male of the species. This was most evident in the context of the criminal justice system and criminal law; however, it is worth noting that by the nineteenth century in instances where prize-fights were the subject of proceedings before the civil courts, judges were also inclined to view them in negative terms. For instance, in *Burn v Taylor* (1823) the plaintiff, a pugilist, sought to recover the stakes for a prize-fight between himself and a third party, the money having been entrusted to the defendant. Lord Chief Justice Abbott stopped the proceedings on the basis that it was contrary to the interests of society that 'a Court of Justice should countenance public exhibitions of such immoral and pernicious tendency' by enquiring into contractual interests relating to them.[71]

In the context of policing and criminal law, anxieties about prize-fighting focused upon the consequences of a fight for the pugilists as well as the nature of both the combat and the men who gathered to watch. Thus, concerns tended to relate to the sometimes serious injuries and deaths which could result from a contest, not least because this meant the incapacitation or loss of the fittest of men, the often brutal and bloody nature of the proceedings and what were perceived to be the sometimes unruly and potentially dangerous spectators. In relation to each of these concerns, however, fighting as legitimate sport tended to be distinguished from bare-knuckle contests and other illegal encounters, like ordinary fights and duelling.

By the early nineteenth century there were clear authorities on the illegality of prize-fights and, although these offered slightly different explanations as to the basis upon which the criminality of such contests was founded, they often reflected preoccupations with men. Thus, in 1792 Sir Michael Foster's *Crown Law* had drawn a line between conduct which was lawful and activities that were illegal, contrasting 'manly diversions' with 'prize-fighting and … other exertions of courage, strength and activity … which are exhibited for lucre, and can serve no valuable purpose, but on the contrary encourage a spirit of idleness and debauchery.'[72] A few years later, *East's Pleas of the Crown* (1803) stated that there was distinction between 'manly sports and exercises which tend to give strength, activity, and skill in the use of arms, and are entered into merely as private recreations among friends', which were not unlawful, and 'prize fights … which are exhibited for the sake of lucre, and are calculated to draw together a number of idle disorderly people' and 'have a strong tendency in their nature to a breach of the peace'. As a consequence, 'persons', or rather men, 'playing by consent at cudgels, or foils, or wrestling' were deemed to be involved in 'innocent and allowable' sports, so that if the activity resulted in a death, that would amount to 'excusable homicide', but 'if the sport be unlawful in itself, or productive of danger, riot, or disorder, from the occasion, so as to endanger the peace, and death ensue; the party killing is guilty of manslaughter.' Moreover, for East, although 'it cannot be said that [manly sports and exercises] are altogether free from danger; yet are they very rarely attended with fatal consequences; and each party has friendly warning to be on his guard'. Significantly, the text went on to point out that 'if the possibility of danger were the criterion by which the lawfulness of sports and recreations were to be decided, many exercises must be proscribed which are in common use, and were never heretofore deemed unlawful'. Nevertheless, according to this treatise, 'the latitude given to manly exercises' should not be extended to prize-fighting and the like.[73]

So, in the cases of both Foster and East, the illegality of prize-fighting was founded upon both the unmanly and uncivilized nature of the relatively unregulated bouts and the disorderly and potentially threatening crowds who attended them. In addition, in East at least, the distinction between legal and illegal combat meant the difference between lawful killing and manslaughter, should a combatant die during or as a result of a fight.

On the basis of these views and as the mood towards prize-fighting changed along with the identity and perception of attendees (with a not unrelated decline in their status and in attitudes towards their respectability) over the course of the early to mid-nineteenth century, there were more frequent attempts by the police to stop prize-fights taking place. In addition, an increasing number of fighters, along with those who helped organize and assisted at fights, were successfully prosecuted for public order offences (riot, rout, affray and unlawful assembly) and offences against the person, including assaults and homicide. Indeed, regional and national papers regularly reported law enforcers' actions when a combat was rumoured to be planned or was discovered to be taking place and the trials of men involved in fights also received widespread coverage in the press, not least cases where one or more of the pugilists died. This publicity, of course, meant that the technical illegality of prize-fighting would have been widely known by the 1880s.

Most of the nineteenth-century criminal cases concerning prize-fighting prior to *Coney*, however, had not been referred for review, so only involved the pronouncements of single judges in trial courts, rather than the more weighty (in precedent terms) findings of a judicial panel. Nevertheless, given the then practice of reporting some of the latter class of cases, a number of them figured within the volumes of law reports, so there were plenty of previous cases to be drawn upon by the time *Coney* came before the courts – and, indeed, some of these were cited both in argument and by the CCCR judges. Moreover, the fact that most of the earlier cases involved lone judicial statements did not mean they would be dismissed – a point made by Coleridge, who reminded his brethren that 'the criminal law is built up of the dicta of single judges'.[74] Beyond this, some of these judges in the trial courts were extremely well-regarded and also sat in the CCCR or, prior to the creation of that court, had reviewed assize decisions at Searjeant's Inn,[75] so, if their words were questioned, it was likely to be with some reluctance.

One such past case which was subsequently to be relied upon in *Coney* was the trial of James Hargrave in 1831.[76] Drawing on a number of different sources it is possible to reconstruct the facts of the case.[77] A particularly brutal and bloody fight between James Cox and Richard Dodd, who were both shoemakers, took place in London on Monday 22 August of that year, having been arranged previously. The victor was to receive two sovereigns. On the allotted day the two dined together and proceeded with a group of their supporters to the agreed fight location,[78] where they went 17 rounds before the police intervened. The pugilists, along with Hargrave and four others, made off and were conveyed by a waterman to the Isle of Dogs. At this point, Cox and Dodds wanted to stop the fight but were forced on by the stakeholder and the others present. The contest recommenced and a further 14 rounds were fought. Hargrave held Dodd's clothes and picked him up when he fell, urging him to continue until the death if need be: he had wagered money upon Dodd winning and was loath to lose it. When the fight came to a halt Dodd was taken aboard a hospital ship stationed on the Thames, where he soon died of head injuries occasioned in the battle. Cox also perished soon thereafter. Hargrave was charged as an accessory to the manslaughter of Dodd because he was present and his actions were conceived of as aiding and abetting Cox. He was tried at Maidstone assizes in the December, was convicted and sentenced to 14 years' transportation, with the judge forcefully criticizing both Hargrave's conduct and the brutality of prize-fights – and, in so doing, emphasizing their undoubted illegality.

Further efforts to stop prize-fighting were on display in the 1841 case of *R v Brown*.[79] Here a police constable, Daniel Herbert, had received information as to a planned prize-fight which he managed to locate. About 400 spectators were said to be present and men were fighting in a makeshift ring. Desiring to bring it to an end, he attempted to arrest the combatants but was prevented from doing so. Still determined to bring matters under control, he approached Brown who was seated on top of a carriage and four and asked for his assistance. Brown said he could not do so as he had the horses to mind. He was subsequently charged with 'refusing to aid and assist a constable in the execution of his duty in quelling a riot'. Baron Alderson's summing up to the jury recorded the status of such events in no uncertain terms. He said that 'it is clear that all prize-fights are illegal, and that all persons engaging in them are punishable by law.' What is more, he went on to explain that in itself a fight constituted a breach of the peace and if a constable saw such a thing he was bound to prevent it. However, if he was not able to do so unaided, he could ask for help which should not be refused without 'physical impossibility or lawful excuse' and regardless of whether the assistance 'would have proved sufficient or useful'. Indeed, the Baron's view was that where a prize-fight was taking place '[e]very man is bound to set a good example to others by doing his duty in preserving the public peace.'[80] According to Alderson, instead of watching proceedings, a man's duty, should he find himself in the environs of such of contest, was to try to bring it to an end (at least when a law officer requested that he did so) – Brown was convicted.

Beyond this, as the minority in *Coney* were to note, the idea that, at least in some circumstances, those merely watching a prize-fight might be found to have committed crimes, whether as principles, or as accessories to offences committed by the combatants, was by no means entirely new by the early 1880s. This was demonstrated by Littledale's comments in *R v Murphy* in 1833, which were to be relied upon by Benyon and the minority in the CCCR in *Coney*. It was also evident in the earlier cases of *R v Billingham Savage, and Skinner* (1825)[81] and *R v Perkins and Others* (1831)[82]. By way of reminder, in *Murphy*, Littledale's pronouncements had suggested that it was not merely those who directly assisted in a fight who might be liable for offences committed by the pugilists, as all 'persons' who were present at such a fight would be guilty of manslaughter if they stayed watching and 'encouraged it by their presence'.[83]

Billingham, Savage and Skinner (1825) was a trial for riot and assaulting a magistrate in the execution of his duty. The latter, Daniel Rogers, had been attempting with some constables to prevent a prize-fight which had been arranged between Billingham and Savage. The pugilists along with around 1,000 spectators had gathered near Hagley in Worcestershire. When Rogers had told those involved that there would be no fight, the third defendant, Skinner, assured him that the contest would go ahead and the two were involved in a 'scuffle'. This led to 'a general tumult on the part of the mob.' At trial the men were convicted with the judge, Justice Burrough, making it clear that such fights were illegal as 'no consent can make them legal, and all the country being present would not make them less an offence' because they were 'unlawful assemblies'. Reflecting worries about the dangers they presented and the need to eradicate them, he advised law enforcers who became aware of a planned fight 'to secure the combatants beforehand, and take them to a magistrate, who ought to compel them to enter into securities to keep the peace' and if they would not do so to imprison them, as '[i]n this way the mischief would be prevented, and the fights put a stop to.'[84] Indeed, to Burrough, the main problem with prize-fights and the reason for their illegality was the often vast crowds of men (including, it seemed by implication, those of the most disreputable persuasion) who gathered to watch the contests; the throng in itself constituted an unlawful gathering and he was clearly also worried about the possibility of violence breaking out beyond the confines of the prize-ring, as had happened in the case before him. In consequence, in his view 'every one going to [such competitions] is guilty of an offence.' To this observation he added a warning, emphasizing that the knowledge of their illegality 'ought to make persons very careful.'[85]

Perkins arose out of a prize-fight between the prisoner, Perkins, and Robert Coates which 'many hundred persons' attended. Perkins, along with his second, the man who collected money for the prize and another who walked around the ring holding the crowd at bay, were charged with riot and assault in relation to the combat. They were all convicted of the former offence but acquitted of the latter. In directing the jury, however, Justice Patteson drew the boundaries of accessorial liability widely in relation to such events and, in doing so, seemed to be suggesting that the assault charge was also sustainable. To his mind all 'persons' who 'went out to see these men strike each other, and were present when they did so' were 'in point of law, guilty of an assault'. Indeed, he felt that there was 'no distinction between those who concur in the act and those who fight.[86] Of course, the 'persons' referred to here, as in *Murphy* and *Billingham*, were, like the fighters themselves, overwhelmingly male – so all three cases effectively served as a warning to men who in any way involved themselves in a prize-fight.

The idea that prize-fighting was illegal because of worries about men and, more specifically, both the brutality of the combat and the numbers, character and likely behaviour of the spectators was, therefore, firmly established long before *Coney*; prize-fighting, however, continued. Indeed, far from stopping the contests, legal interventions appear to have turned fights into ever more clandestine affairs, with organizers selecting their locations carefully and passing on information about venues and times by word of mouth.[87] Moreover, police attempts to halt proceedings arguably often had the effect of increasing the rowdiness of proceedings, as spectators could become involved in what was essentially a mass brawl,[88] heightening fears about lower class men and violence. Thus, the efforts of the criminal justice system appeared to be counterproductive: the policing and criminalization of fights may have actually amplified the amount of criminality they involved. Indeed, legal interventions could well have added to the allure of contests, making them more attractive to the very class of men which concerns about unmanliness, disorder and criminality focused most upon.

A growing perception that, thus far, legal efforts were failing to bring prize-fighting to an end and that, far from being on the wane, their popularity seemed to be increasing, appears to have prompted some disquiet on the part of both lawmakers and those charged with the oversight of criminal justice in the late 1870s and early 1880s. For example, in 1879 there was an attempt to criminalize prize-fights through legislation, rather than relying on the authority of past cases. Clause 98 of the Criminal Code (Indictable Offences) Bill[89] included the offence of taking part in or promoting a prize-fight. As was noted at the time, this provision would have provided a firmer basis for law enforcement to target events before, during and after they took place – and might have assisted in bringing prosecutions by making the law clearer.[90] The creation of specific statutory offences could perhaps also have been helpful in more widely publicizing and emphasizing the criminality of such activities, although whether this would actually decrease their incidence was doubtful. This attempt to produce a partial criminal code did not pass, however – and so clause 98 did not become law.[91]

Concerns were also expressed about men and prize-fighting by the Director of Criminal Investigation in 1880, when the latter sought an opinion from the Home Office as to the legality of different forms of combat. This request was triggered by a particular fight held at Chelsea Swimming Baths. The Director's view was that there should be a means of preventing such events because of their violence and the potential rowdiness of the men who attended. More particularly, he wanted action taken against those involved in the Chelsea contest.[92]

Coney

Given this background, it is perhaps not surprising that the post-Ascot encounter between Burke and Mitchell in June 1881 drew some very specific attention from those charged with the oversight of criminal justice. Following a summer when fights and their aftermath were regularly reported with some degree of alarm in the press, with a number of pugilists dying as a result of their injuries,[93] on Tuesday 13 September the initial Magistrates' Court hearing took place. The following day, it was widely reported that there had been an intervention in the case from on high. The *Standard* stated that '[i]t was understood that the proceedings had been taken by the chief constable of the county, Colonel Blandy, at the insistence of the Home Secretary'.[94] Indeed, the latter, Sir William Harcourt, had written to the Director of Public Prosecutions on 13 September supporting the prosecution.[95] In this context, it seems that there was at least encouragement to proceed. What is more, it is possible that the Berkshire fight was being seen as a test case which would emphasize the (il)legal status of prize-fighting and might clearly establish that men who merely watched such a contest, as well as those who actively helped or encouraged, would be categorized as criminals. This possibility is lent more credence by press reports that on Wednesday 5 October the Home Secretary issued a general circular to all chairmen of the quarter sessions, directing that they pay special attention to the recent 'epidemic of prize fighting'.[96] However, no such document appears in the bound volume of Home Office circulars for the period, suggesting such stories may perhaps not have been entirely accurate – indeed, they might have been a product of the furore about such contests (or of newspapers sensationalizing the situation).[97] However, that said, the possibility of continued involvement from those charged with the administration of the nation's criminal justice system cannot be entirely ruled out.

As the above suggests, at the same time as this action was playing out within legal spheres, discussions about prize-fighting were taking place in the press. Indeed, worries about contests and the inter-male violence and disorder they involved (and threatened) seemed to be increasing by the autumn of 1881, with the papers identifying an apparent revival of the pastime and repeatedly describing the then state of affairs as constituting an 'epidemic'.[98] This meant that, all in all, there was a general sense of unease at a preceived growth in violence both in and around contests, along with on-going anxieties about the fact that the eradication of illegal fighting (and thereby the reining in of the lower class men who fought and attended them) seemed to be beyond the abilities of the criminal justice system.

On 18 October the trial of Coney and the other men took place in Reading. It can only be supposed that the legal players, including Benyon, approached the case with some care, given the Home Office's seeming interest in prize-fighting in general and in the matter before them, in particular. Also, they can hardly have been unaware of the worries about an epidemic as well as the particular attention which the case they had before them was drawing from the press and the views that had been expressed about it in the papers. In this regard the mood, at least in some quarters, seemed to be firmly in favour of convicting all of the defendants. For example, commenting on the initial magistrates' hearings in *Coney*, the *Penny Illustrated Paper and Illustrated Times* closed its report by opining that '[t]here are quite sufficient brutes at large without breeding any more of the ruffian crew.'[99] Other sources expressed similar sentiments calling for harsh punishments for all involved in such fights, again reflecting worries about the male violence on display in the combat and the potential dangers presented by the type of men who were supposed to be in attendance at such events.[100]

What, then, of *Coney* in the courts? As limited information is available concerning the magistrates' hearings, trial and CCCR discussions, the focus here is upon the pronouncements of the CCCR judges, where a sense of unease about prize-fights and the unmanly violence and disorder they were said to involve and encourage was very much in evidence: indeed, it permeated the words of both the minority and majority. Thus, although the judges chose to argue different points or focus upon particular aspects of the case, all seemed united in their condemnation of prize-fighting and the pugilists who engaged in such competitions as well as in their desire to bring such contests to an end, thereby legally binding men to better behaviour.

For example, for Coleridge what took place in makeshift rings was a breach of the peace,[101] its effects were 'brutalizing'[102] and involved the commission of assaults – so his concerns related, at least in part, to the character of the fighting, although the coarsening and dehumanizing effects he mentioned may, of course, have been applied to both the fighters themselves and those who watched.[103] For Mathew, the combatants were 'wretched' men who suffered 'dreadful injuries' and whose lives were 'endangered' or 'sacrificed' – so he was concerned about the men who boxed, kicked, threw and wrestled each other.[104] Stephen saw broader dangers in the harm caused to the fighters and in the rowdiness of contests: 'the injuries given and received in prize-fights are injurious to the public, both because it is against the public interest that the lives and health of the combatants should be endangered by blows, and because prize-fights are disorderly exhibitions, mischievous on many obvious grounds.'[105] Hawkins condemned prize-fights and some other forms of fighting, stating that:

> ... every fight in which the object and intent of each of the combatants is to subdue the other by violent blows, is, or has a direct tendency to, a breach of the peace, and it matters not, in my opinion, whether such fight be a hostile fight begun and continued in anger, or a prize-fight for money or other advantage ... [106]

He added that although a prize-fight might begin as sport 'it is unquestionably calculated to rouse the angry feelings of both [combatants] before its conclusion'.[107] Thus, for Hawkins it was the violence, disorder and enmity which fighting occasioned in the contestants that made such contests dangerous and illegal – and the fact that a breach of the peace might be caused. Indeed, the judicial view in *Coney*, along with that in earlier cases, was that prize-fighting amounted to a display of primitive and savage urges and emotions – and these were, of course, not qualities to be recommended even in the lowest classes of Englishmen.

In contrast to prize-fighting, the status of legitimate sporting combat tended to be distinguished and received a protective approach from the judges. For Cave and Hawkins the difference in legal status related to keeping the peace and both contrasted 'fighting' with 'sport' and 'friendly encounters'. Accordingly, Cave stated that:

> ... a blow struck in anger, or which is likely or is intended to do corporal hurt, is an assault, but that a blow struck in sport, and not likely, nor intended to cause bodily harm, is not an assault, and that, an assault being a breach of the peace and unlawful, the consent of the person struck is immaterial ... a blow struck in a prize-fight is clearly an assault; but playing with single-sticks or wrestling do not involve an assault; nor does boxing with gloves in the ordinary way.[108]

So, by implication, whilst male violence in sport was civilized, legitimate and legal, conforming to Victorian ideas about manliness and appropriate exercise, the same could by no means be said to be the case in relation to bare-knuckle bouts.

Similarly, Hawkins differentiated illegal contests from lawful activities, explaining that sparring or playing a game were 'neither breaches of the peace nor are they calculated to be productive thereof'.[109] Moreover, prize-fights were different from genuinely 'friendly encounters' (such as 'amicable spar[ring] with gloves' or 'a mere friendly game') because they were 'not calculated to produce real injury'.[110] Consequently, for these judges there were clear distinctions to be drawn between unruly and illegal violence, on the one hand, and controlled and legitimate manly (if not gentlemanly) activities, on the other.

Stephen took a slightly different tack, focusing upon the relevance of the potential defence of consent to an assault charge in different contexts, but also emphasizing the distinction between fighting contests and orderly sport. In doing so, he opined:

> In cases where life and limb are exposed to no serious danger in the common course of things, I think that consent is a defence to a charge of assault, even when considerable force is used, as, for instance, in cases of wrestling, single-stick, sparring with gloves, football, and the like ... [111]

So here, it seemed to be the degree of risk of serious injury or death which fighters were assumed to face in a prize-fight that made these contests unacceptable. In comparison, the levels of danger were not adjudged by Stephen to be so extreme in sports, exhibitions, or more civilized and regulated forms of combat.

However, whilst there was clear censure of 'prize-fighting' in the unanimous confirmation of its unlawfulness in *Coney* and all of the 11 were keen to eradicate it, they disagreed as to whether it would be justifiable to extend accessorial liability for assault to all who watched such events in order to achieve this. For the three minority judges (Coleridge, Mathew and Pollock), the need to rein in this type of male behaviour justified the criminalization of all who were present at such events – excepting those with good reason for being there. They adopted this course because they thought that it would have the effect of sending out a clear message that such combat would not be tolerated and would also remove the audience, without which it was felt these contests would not survive. But, as the charges pursued in *Coney* were assaults rather than public order offences (such as those of riot, rout, affray and unlawful assembly, which had figured in earlier cases), there was no direct discussion of the danger and volatility of such gatherings of men in the minority judgments – rather the focus was upon the impact of their presence upon the fighters. Nevertheless, they were particularly vocal as to the character of those who attended prize-fighting – and, in so-saying, they echoed the words of the prosecution in *Coney*, with its depiction of the crowds as 'idle' and 'disorderly'.

Mathew, for instance, characterized the spectators at a prize-fight as the most disreputable and savage of men, referring disparagingly to 'a class of persons to whom prize-fights are attractive', blaming them for the continuance of such contests as 'pugilists fight in public for the gratification of those persons' and noting also that this was all about the money wagered by combatants and audience members. For him, 'the chief incentive to the wretched combatants to fight on until (as happens too often) dreadful injuries have been inflicted and life endangered or sacrificed, is the presence of spectators watching with keen interest every incident of the fight.'[112] Indeed, Mathew felt that the onlookers were of crucial significance as 'without spectators, I believe there would be no prize-fights'. He continued by arguing that, if juries were not directed that mere presence (without a legitimate explanation) at a prize-fight amounted to aiding and abetting assault, 'the Courts would thus have surrendered the principal means of discouraging the disgraceful exhibitions in question, which there was some reason to hope, under the pressure of the law, were gradually being discontinued.' In his view the urgent need to end prize-fights required that all those who were present, aside from those with a lawful justification (such as a police constable attempting to stop the proceedings), should be criminalized.

Similarly, Coleridge argued that 'the spectators really make the fight; without them, and in the absence of any one to look on and encourage, no two men, having no cause of personal quarrel, would meet together in solitude to knock one another about for an hour or two.' Consequently, he maintained that the 'brutalizing effects of prize-fights are chiefly due to the crowd who resort to them' – and, of course, the latter were overwhelmingly male.[113] Pollock was less vehement on this point but expressed a similar view, stating that in the case of a prize-fight 'it is usually the bystanders collected around who create and who are responsible for the fight as a matter of interest and amusement to themselves.'[114] Moreover, he argued that 'almost … the very essence of … [prize-fighting]' was that 'a large number should be present as mere spectators', but it was likely that they would 'not remain mere passive spectators, but will in some measure take an active part.'[115]

So for the minority, the need to bind men by convicting Coney, Gilliam and Tully, thereby confirming the criminality not only of prize-fighting and of supporting or deliberately watching a prize-fight, but also of mere unexplained presence at such a contest, trumped any concern about extending the reach of English criminal law (in terms of accessorial liability) too far. In contrast, the majority felt that expanding the frontiers of criminality in order to include those who merely watched a fight would have amounted to too great an encroachment on Englishmen's liberties. For example, Manisty maintained that the current law, which meant that 'every person who by his presence or otherwise encourages a fight, be it a prize or an ordinary fight, is guilty of a criminal offence', was sufficient – and that it should be 'for the jury in each particular case to say as a matter of fact whether the accused did by his presence or otherwise encourage the combatants to fight.' Moreover, he did not believe the court's decision would, as had been suggested by the prosecution, give a 'great impetus' to prize-fighting.[116] In a similar vein, Stephen felt that Littledale's pronouncement that members of the audience should be liable for what took place between the combatants, so long as they were not just 'casually passing by', 'went too far, being no doubt desirous of providing an easy and summary mode of suppressing prize-fights', although, he did not entirely rule out changing the law in this direction by statute, rather than judge-made law.[117] However, all the judges seemed united in their desire to bring about the speedy demise of prize-fighting – the minority and majority merely differed as to how far they should limit the freedom of Englishmen in order to do so (not least as this would apply to aiding and abetting in other contexts and in relation to other offences) and there was some disagreement as to the effects of not imposing liability in *Coney*.

Post *Coney*

The reaction to the CCCR decision in *Coney* was generally positive. So, whilst there was a tendency to maintain that prize-fighting should be brought to an end both because of the barbaric nature of the fights and the dangerous character of the spectators, the means of doing so suggested by the three minority judges was rejected. Thus, *The Times*'s editorial on their decision concluded that '[p]rize-fights must be put down by other methods than the indiscriminate punishment of everyone found in their vicinity.'[118] The *Law Journal* also took the side of the majority, maintaining that the correct decision had been reached as there 'was no active fact proved against' Coney.[119] Similarly, the *Daily News* was broadly in favour of the case's outcome.[120] Occupying the middle ground, the *Pall Mall Gazette* was cautious, having little to say about the case apart from the fact that it left the position of spectators somewhat uncertain because there was a danger that they might be thought to be encouraging the combatants.[121] In contrast, the view in some sporting periodicals was, unsurprisingly, of a rather different hue, with some publications reflecting a sense of nostalgia for the 'high national importance' which prize-fighting had once held as a '"noble" sport' for men.[122] Such articles and editorials recalled Egan's conception of the manly art but seemed to be very much in the minority.

Prize-fighting, of course, did not cease following *Coney* and attempts to prevent contests and to prosecute those involved continued. Indeed, there were still frequent reports of fights, interventions by law enforcers and court cases in the press in the 1880s and 1890s. For example, Figure 4 depicts police efforts to interrupt a prize-fight which took place at Southwell in Nottinghamshire on Saturday 23 February 1884. This ended in the arrests of the two combatants and one of their seconds. According to the papers, the fighters were charged with 'having been engaged … in a prize-fight' and the second with 'aiding and abetting in the fight'. There had been about 100 in the audience and the contest was described as being of 'a very severe nature'. When the defendants appeared before magistrates, their lawyer asked for clemency as, whilst there was no denial that there had been a fight, there had been no serious breach of the peace on the part of the observers. All of the men were bound over to keep the peace for 12 months.[123] Nearly a decade later in 1892 a prize-fight at Duston, Northamptonshire resulted in

Figure 4 'Prize Fight in the Midlands – Nottingham'.
Illustrated Police News, 1 March 1884, p. 1.

the death of one of the participants, William Langley. A number of those involved in bringing the fight off and some who seem to have been merely present were charged with manslaughter. At the trial on the Midland circuit *Coney* was cited. Both the surviving pugilist along with the man who organized the competition were convicted.[124] They were duly sentenced (to 12 months and seven months with hard labour respectively).[125]

Alongside such accounts, worries about bare-knuckle contests continued. In 1884 *The Times*, reported on an Old Bailey case presided over by Hawkins (who had been in the majority in *Coney*), which concerned the conviction of a number of men for their involvement in a prize-fight near Barnet. The article stated that '[t]he taste for pugilism has swiftly descended to the lower social strata.' Moreover, according to the paper, '[t]he "noble art" is in bad odour', being 'too much associated with pothouses to have much chance of regaining its old place.'[126] Such negative portrayals of prize-fighting and the men who associated themselves with it remained fairly common – as did the tendency to make unfavourable comparisons between such contests and supposedly more manly and civilized activities. Thus, in drawing attention to what he perceived to be a 'certain amount of increased interest … in pugilism' in 1888 Home Secretary Henry Matthews was careful to distinguish between illegal fighting and 'boxing or sparring with gloves'.[127]

As the above suggests, the Home Office maintained its efforts to end the contests. During the late 1880s, in particular, worries about how to police illegal fights were still a concern, with the Law Officer's opinion being sought on the matter.[128] Also, in the wake of *Coney*, the evidence needed in order to prosecute those involved in a fight was a matter which received some Home Office attention in the hope that more convictions might deter pugilists, those who organized events and potential spectators in the future.[129]

Conclusion

This chapter has revisited the well-known (to criminal lawyers) case of *Coney*, first recounting a story of the case and then recasting it in the context of nineteenth-century concerns about men. Here the case was depicted as forming a part of efforts to rein men in – and men of the supposedly lower orders, in particular. Along with other legal attempts to stop prize-fighting, the case reflected contemporary ideas about Englishmen and, what were by the 1880s, relatively well-developed anxieties about such contests. Moreover, in *Coney* unacceptable and unmanly diversions were juxtaposed with legitimate masculine pastimes, with the CCCR judges conceptualizing prize-fights (along with ordinary fights and duelling) as brutal, dangerous and criminal, whilst sparring and boxing (as well as wrestling and organized football – as opposed to street football) were portrayed as acceptable and legal ways of engaging in very English forms of sport. Inter-male 'violence' was, thus, by no means conceived of in the case as something to be universally disapproved of. Instead, only some violences were deemed to be problematic and unruly, whilst others were thought to be potentially beneficial and manly.[130]

However, this dichotomy between criminal violence masquerading as sport and manly games was hard to maintain, meaning that the legality of fighting was extremely unclear.[131] Indeed, the problem of distinguishing between sport and crime was a recurrent theme in criminal cases that resulted from fights both before and after *Coney*. For example, in 1878, the CCCR case of *Orton*[132] provided just one of many examples of this difficulty.

Orton involved a lawful boxing match, held indoors, with the spectators paying an entry fee and the fighters wearing gloves. However, the level of brutality involved meant that it was found to have crossed the line into illegality. The problem arose again in the assize case of *R v Moore* (1898)[133] when a death resulted from what was again apparently a lawful contest. Here, given the circumstances of the case, it was found to be an unlawful killing. So, what cases like *Orton* and *Moore* demonstrated was that, just because 'violence' took place in what was generally conceived of as a legitimate sporting context, this did not guarantee the legality of the activity.[134] As a consequence, the law relating to different forms of inter-male violence, was left (and still remains) relatively imprecise.[135]

It is with this thought that we leave the world of male combat and *Coney* and move on to consider *R v Dudley and Stephens* (1884). In doing so, the next chapter also focuses upon a very masculine world and a case that involved violence between men. This time though, the charge was murder.

Notes

1 (1882) LR 8 QBD 534; 46 JP 404; 51 LJMC 66; 15 Cox CC 46; 30 WR 678; 46 LT 307. These references refer to the different law reports in which the decision of the Court for Crown Cases Reserved in this case was reported. Unless otherwise stated, references to this judgment in this chapter are taken from (1882) LR 8 QBD, although the other reports of the case were consulted in constructing this chapter. As the name suggests, a law report is a published account of courtroom proceedings in a case. It is produced for lawyers and generally includes a summary of the facts which led the parties to come to court and the legal decision as well as the text of the judge's or judges' legal pronouncements.

2 Justice Stephen in *Coney* at 549.

3 Justice Mathew, ibid., at 544.

4 Whilst the decision on aiding and abetting specifically related to such contests, the impact of this ruling had a more general application to the whole area of accessorial liability.

5 Notable texts not directly cited below include: D. Ormerod and M. Gunn, 'The Legality of Boxing', *Legal Studies* 15(2), 1995, 181–203; A. Sithamparanathan, 'Noble Art of Self Defence or Unlawful Barbarism?', *Entertainment Law Review*, 13(8) 2002, 183–7; W.R. Gray, 'For Whom the Bell Tolled: The Decline of British Prize Fighting in the Victorian Era', *Journal of Popular Culture*, 21(2), 1987, 53–64; D. McArdle, 'A Few Hard Cases? Sport, Sadomasochism and Public Policy in the English Courts', *Canadian Journal of Law and Society*, 10, 1995, 109–17.

6 See: *Standard*, 14 September, 1881, p.6; *Pall Mall Gazette*, 14 September 1881, p.6; *Penny Illustrated Paper and Illustrated Times*, 17 September 1881, p.183; *Reynold's Newspaper*, 2 October 1881, p.1; *Daily News*, 20 October 1881, p.3; *The Times*, 12 December 1881, p.4; 22 December 1881, p.9, 20 March 1882, p.4; *Bell's Life in London and Sporting Chronicle*, 17 December 1881, p.4, 24 December 1881, p.11, 25 March 1882, p.5.

7 For the CCCR record of the case see TNA: PRO KB 30/4 (CCCR Pleadings).

8 Mr Benyon, who presided over the trial, included this information in his statement of the case. See *Coney* (1881–82) LR 8 QBD 534 at 535.

9 See further below.

10 The possibility that they were merely curious by-passers was, for example, mentioned by Justice Cave in *Coney* at 538.
11 See, for example, ibid., at 535.
12 See, for example: *Standard*, 14 September, 1881, p. 6; *Penny Illustrated Paper and Illustrated Times*, 17 September, 1881, p. 183; *Pall Mall Gazette*, 14 September 1881, p. 6. The bribe was reported to be £5 10s in the latter paper.
13 See, for example, the report of this Magistrates' Court hearing in *Reynolds's Newspaper*, 2 October 1881, p. 1.
14 Common assault involves putting someone in fear of immediate force and carried a maximum term of two months' imprisonment, with or without hard labour (Section 42, Offences Against the Person Act 1861). On the decision to prosecute see further the discussion of the Home Secretary's role below.
15 For a report of the trial see, in particular, *Daily News*, 20 October 1881, p. 3. The criminal work of the quarter sessions and the assizes was virtually the same (although the latter tended to deal with the most serious cases) – for present purposes, both were essentially forerunners of the Crown Court. See further, J.H. Baker, *An Introduction to English Legal History*, 4th edn, London: Butterworths, 2002, pp. 20–2, 25.
16 Ibid.
17 *Coney* at 534–5.
18 The names of these witnesses are given in some but by no means all accounts of the case. For example, see: *Reynolds's Newspaper*, 2 October 1881, p. 1; *Daily News*, 20 October 1881, p. 3.
19 See, for example, *Daily News*, 20 October 1881, p. 3.
20 Ibid.
21 Mr Benyon, who presided over the trial, quoted in *Coney* at 535.
22 For example, Justice Manisty referred to this in *Coney* at 562 and it is mentioned in *The Times*, 22 December 1881, p. 9.
23 *Coney* at 535–6.
24 6 C & P 103; 2 Nev & MMC 149; 172 Eng. Rep. 1164. See also *Old Bailey Proceedings Online* (*OBP*) (http://www.oldbaileyonline.org, version 7.0, accessed 30 March 2013), November 1833, trial of Edward Murphy (t18331128-45).
25 *Coney* at 535–6. Here Benyon gave the source of his quotation as '*Russell on Crimes*, 5th ed. vol. I, p. 818.
26 *Coney* at 536, 9.
27 Or, as one of the CCCR judges, Justice Stephen, subsequently commented, the finding seemed 'equivalent to an acquittal'. See Stephen at 552 and *The Times*, 12 December 1881, p. 4.
28 See, for example, *Daily News*, 20 October 1881, p. 3.
29 See, for example, ibid. and *Coney* at 536.
30 See Mathew in *Coney* at 546.
31 This was, for example, recorded in 15 Cox CC 46 at 48.
32 The assizes heard the most serious of criminal cases and were essentially a forerunner of the Crown Court. See further, Baker, *An Introduction to English Legal History*, pp. 20–2.
33 On the CCCR see further: J.F. Stephen, *A History of the Criminal Law of England*, London: Macmillan, 1883, vol. I, pp. 311–13; P. Handler, 'The Court for Crown Cases Reserved, 1848–1908', *Law and History Review*, 29(1), 2011, 259–88, pp. 263–4.
34 See the report of the first CCCR hearing of the case in *The Times*, 12 December 1881, p. 4.

35 The account of this stage of the proceeding presented here is drawn from *The Times*, 12 December 1881, p. 4. For other reports see, for example: *Daily News*, 12 December 1881, p. 2; *Morning Post*, 12 December 1881, p. 3; *Standard*, 12 December 1881, p. 2; *Reynolds's Newspaper*, 11 December 1881, p. 8; *Lloyd's Weekly Newspaper*, 18 December 1881, p. 3.
36 In doing so he cited authority, including *R v Young* (1838) 8 C & P 644.
37 See *The Times*, 12 December 1881, p. 4.
38 20 March 1882, p. 4. Cave's opening words were recorded in *The Times* the day after the first hearing, see 12 December 1881, p. 4.
39 *The Times* 12 December 1881, p. 4. It is possible the five disagreed, see *The Times*, 22 December 1881, p. 9.
40 The account of this stage of the proceeding reconstructed here is drawn from *The Times*, 22 December 1881, p. 9.
41 Ibid.
42 The account here is drawn from the account in *The Times*, 20 March 1882, p. 4 and the law reports.
43 See *Coney* at 552.
44 On prize-fighting and its history see: D. Brailsford, *Bareknuckles: A Social History of Prize-Fighting*, Cambridge: Lutterworth Press, 1988; B. Mee, *Bare Fists: The History of Bare-Knuckle Prize-Fighting*, New York: Overlook Press, 2001.
45 See further, Anderson, *The Legality of Boxing: A Punch Drunk Love*, London: Birkbeck Law Press, 2007, pp. 14–15, 22–5.
46 For example, in the case of James Hargrave in 1831 the fight concerned resulted in the deaths of both of the combatants. See further below.
47 For example, the illustration of the prize-fight in Figure 4 shows an all male crowd.
48 For example, *The Times* reported that 'several ladies were present' at a fight which took place near Andover in 1823 – but these were 'probably … of that itinerant class who attend like pick-pockets at large meetings, to gull the simple and unwary.' (22 May 1823, p. 4.)
49 The *Illustrated Police News*, in particular, seemed to revel in such tales, often illustrating their accounts. For example, see 21 March 1868, p. 2, 14 June 1884, pp. 1, 2, 15 July 1882, pp. 1, 2.
50 For example, the report of one fight which took place on the Birmingham Road, not far from Warwick in 1825 noted that 'an immense number of persons of all characters and quality' attended (*The Times*, 20 July 1825, p. 2). As Prince of Wales and Prince Regent, George IV was a great enthusiast for such events which he regularly attended (see, for example, Brailsford, *Bareknuckles*, pp. 25–6 and J. Anderson, *The Legality of Boxing*, pp. 18, 19). On the mixed character of those who patronized and attended fights see also, G.C. Collard *Up to Scratch: The Story of Bristol's Bareknuckle Champions*, Bristol: Packer, 1992, pp. 17–18.
51 On the golden age or years see further, for example, Mee, *Bare Fists*, ch. 3, who has it ending in 1860. Collard has it as starting in 1785 when the Championship of England was won by Tom Jackling (or Johnson), and peaking in 1795 with the racially charged contest between John Jackson and Daniel Mendoza (a London-born Spanish Jew) and ending in 1822 with the retirement of renowned fighter Tom Cribb (*Up to Scratch*, pp. 11, 16–17, 51).
52 In 1824 the *Leeds Mercury* told of a fight at Warwick at which 30,000 were in attendance (27 November, p. 2).
53 For example, see: *The Times*, 20 July 1825, p. 2; *Illustrated Police News*, 12 October 1867, pp. 1, 2. For a colourful description of the journey to a fight on two packed

special trains and police efforts to stop the contest, see Brailsford, *Bareknuckles*, p. 129.

54 For example, see Brailsford, *Bareknuckles*, p. 32 and 'The Bristolians', in Collard, *Up to Scratch*, pp. 25–51.

55 See Pierce Egan's explanation of the term in *Boxiana: Or Sketches of Ancient and Modern Pugilism, From the Days of the Renowned Boughton and Slack to the Championship of Cribb*, London: George Virtue, 1830, v. 1, p. 1. (This volume was first published in 1812 in London by G. Smeeton.)

56 See, for example, *Boxiana*, vol. 1, p. 1.

57 Ibid., pp. 2–4.

58 These quotes are taken from a poem quoted by Egan (*Boxiana*, vol. 1, p. 1).

59 See 'Male Honour and the Decline of Public Violence in Eighteenth Century London', *Social History*, 26(2), 2001, 190–208, pp. 204–5.

60 Both were published in London by John Murray.

61 Similar worries were expressed in connection with duelling. See for example, R. Shoemaker, 'Male honour', pp. 204–5.

62 *Character* included repeated references to figures such as Lord Nelson and the Duke of Wellington as embodying inspirational qualities.

63 An example of such work is provided by E.B. Tylor, *Primitive Culture: Researches into the Development of Mythology, Philosophy, Religion, Art, and Custom*, London: John Murray, 1871, vol. 2.

64 For example, see D. Pick, *Faces of Degeneration: A European Disorder c.1848–c.1918*, Cambridge: Cambridge University Press, 1989, pp. 203–16, especially pp. 203 and 213. On the prominence of such ideas in England post *Coney*, see pp. 222–4.

65 See, for example, Brailsford, *Bareknuckles*, p.135. Fears about the unruliness of spectators at prize-fights were being expressed in some quarters even in the eighteenth century (see, for example, *World and Fashionable Advertiser*, 16 October 1787, p. 3) and general worries about civil unrest led to a change in the law in order to limit public gatherings to 50 (Seditious Meetings Act 1795). Anxieties about fight spectators were a recurrent concern. In this context, in 'Pugilistic Prosecutions: Prize Fighting and the Courts in Nineteenth Century Britain' J. Anderson argued that initially the efforts to rein in and criminalize prize-fights were largely a result of concerns about keeping 'the lower classes, and their disruptive activities, in their place' (*Sports Historian*, 21(2), 2001, 37–57, p. 37). What is more, prize-fights came to have a particular association with crime and involvement in such contests was sometimes portrayed as a possible path to ruin even in the early decades of the nineteenth century. For example, in reporting upon the hanging of John Thurtell for a highly publicized murder associated with organized illegal activity in early 1820s London, *The Times* described how his 'first plunge into crime was occasioned by his predilection for prize-fighting and similar savage amusements' (10 January 1824, p. 2).

66 See further, R.F. Wheeler, 'Organised Sport and Organised Labour: The Workers Sports Movement', *Journal of Contemporary History*, 13(2), 1978, 191–210.

67 See, for example ibid., p. 194.

68 Sparring features in *Tom Brown at Oxford*, London: Macmillan, 1883 (first published 1861). See, for example, p. 80.

69 For example, see Anderson, *Legality of Boxing*, pp. 28–9.

70 See further, Brailsford's discussion of the Rules in *Bareknuckles*, pp. 158–9.

71 The case is cited in *R v Deacon and Others* (1824) Ryan & Moody 27; 171 ER 931 at 28.

72 3rd edn, London: Brooke, 1792, p. 260.

73 E.H. East, *A Treatise of the Pleas of the Crown*, London: Butterworth, 1803, v. 1, ch. V, p. 270.

74 *Coney* at 569.
75 See further: Stephen, *A History of the Criminal Law of England*, vol. I, p. 311.
76 5 C & P 170; 172 E.R. 925. Hawkins refers to it in *Coney* at 556 – although he describes it as 'a very imperfectly reported case'. Flaws include the fact that the location given is dubious; also, it is not clear from the case report what exactly Hargrave did to make him liable for aiding and abetting the manslaughter of one of the combatants. Helpfully, press reports give additional details of the evidence – and may be more reliable.
77 This account of the facts is constructed from the law reports as well as *The Times* report of the trial (10 December 1831, p. 3) and other newspaper accounts of the fight, the inquests into the fighters' deaths, and the case. See: *Examiner*, 28 August 1831, p. 558; *Standard*, 25 August 1831, p. 3, 1 September 1831, p. 3; *Hampshire Advertiser*, 27 August 1831, p. 2; *The Times*, 29 August 1831, p. 5; *The Times*, 1 September 1831, p. 4; *Jackson's Oxford Journal*, 10 September 1831, p. 4.
78 The different accounts had the contest starting in Islington or Battersea Fields. Whichever was correct, they were in agreement as to where the competition ended.
79 4 State Tr NS App A 1369; (1841) Car & M 314; 174 ER 522.
80 (1841) Car & M 314 at 318.
81 (1825) 2 C & P 234; 172 ER 106.
82 (1831) 4 C & P 537; 172 ER 814.
83 *Murphy* (1833) 6 C & P 103 at 104.
84 (1825) 2 C & P 234 at 235–5.
85 Ibid., at 234.
86 (1831) 4 C & P 537 at 537–8.
87 For example, see: 'A Day's Pleasure with the Criminal Classes', *Cornhill*, May 1864, 627–40; Brailsford, *Bareknuckles*, pp. 49–50.
88 *Billingham* provided one such illustration of what could happen when the police raided a fight.
89 This draft measure was based upon the work of James Fitzjames Stephen – the same man who was amongst those sitting in the CCCR in *Coney*. The aim of the Bill was to codify the criminal law and reduce the power of judges to make law.
90 See, for example, the explanation of this clause in *The Times*, 18 April 1879, p. 3.
91 See further: K.J.M. Smith, *James Fitzjames Stephen: Portrait of a Victorian Rationalist*, Cambridge: Cambridge University Press, 1988, pp. 78–84.
92 TNA: PRO HO 45/9590/91737. Although this seems to have been a contest at which the pugilists wore gloves, it is clear that it was still viewed by some as a prize-fight.
93 Just a very tiny selection of stories about different fights from the summer of 1881 are provided in the following newspapers: *Hull Packet and East Riding Times*, 12 August 1881, p. 2; *Pall Mall Gazette*, 20 August 1881, p. 6; *Penny Illustrated Paper and Illustrated Times*, 20 August 1881, p. 119; *Bristol Mercury and Daily Post*, 8 September, 1881, p. 2; *Leicester Chronicle and the Leicestershire Mercury*, 10 September 1881, p. 5.
94 14 September 1881, p. 6.
95 See TNA: PRO HO 34/37, pp. 138–9 (A6245/3).
96 This was widely reported in the press. See, for example: *Freeman's Journal and Daily Commercial Advertiser*, 17 October 1881, p. 7; *Huddersfield Chronicle and West Yorkshire Advertiser*, 8 October 1881, p. 3.
97 See TNA: PRO HO 158/5 (the volume covers 10 December 1879 to 20 May 1886).

98 In this context, the Midlands was a particular focus of concern in the press. This was not only resented but also disputed by some (see, for example, *Birmingham Daily News*, 10 October 1881, p. 4).
99 17 September 1861, p. 183.
100 See, for example: *Sporting Times*, 6 August 1881, p. 4; *County Gentleman, Sporting Gazette and Agricultural Journal*, 27 August 1881, p. 915.
101 *Coney* at 567.
102 Ibid., at 569.
103 Ibid., at 570.
104 Ibid., at 544.
105 Ibid., at 549.
106 Ibid., at 553.
107 Ibid., at 553–4.
108 Ibid., at 539.
109 Ibid., at 554.
110 Ibid., at 554.
111 Ibid., at 549.
112 Ibid., at 554.
113 Ibid., at 569.
114 Ibid., at 564.
115 Ibid., at 564–5.
116 Ibid., at 562.
117 Ibid., at 550. In doing so, he was reflecting his desire for a criminal code. See further notes 89 and 91 above.
118 20 March 1882, p. 9.
119 25 March 1882, p. 160.
120 20 March 1882, pp. 1–2.
121 20 March 1882, p. 3.
122 For example, the quotations here were drawn from the *County Gentleman, Sporting Gazette and Agricultural Journal*, 25 March 1882, p. 317.
123 See, for example, the report in the *Illustrated Police News*, 1 March 1884, p. 2.
124 *The Times*, 21 November 1892, p. 12.
125 *The Times*, 22 November 1892, p. 10.
126 12 January 1884, p. 9. Hawkins was criticized by the paper for being overly sympathetic towards the men. For the case see *OBP* (http://www.oldbaileyonline.org, version 7.0, accessed 30 March 2013), January 1884, trial of Edward Ryan, William Williams, Walter Head, William Ryan, John Baker, James Styles, Nicholas Thompson, Albert Woodstock, Richard Wilson, William Driscoll, Charles Thomas (t18840107-215).
127 3 HC 322, col 864, 20 February 1888.
128 See TNA: PRO HO 45/9682/A48143 (Prize fighting. Law Officer's Opinion 312(1864) as to power of arrest), 1 January 1887 – 31 December 1899.
129 See TNA: PRO HO 45/9709/A50982 (Prosecutions: Boxing contests and prize fights – evidence insufficient to support prosecutions, L.O.O.893), 1 January 1889 – 31 December 1900.
130 These kinds of distinctions between unacceptable and acceptable male violence arguably continue. I explore this in: 'Boys Will Be Boys: Masculinity and Offences Against the Person', in D. Nicolson and L. Bibbings (eds), *Feminist Perspectives on Criminal Law*, London: Cavendish, 2000, pp. 231–53; 'Men Refusing to be Violent: Conscientious Objectors to Military Service Then and Now (1916–present day)', in A. Carden-Coyne (ed.), *Gender and Conflict*

Since 1914: Historical and Interdisciplinary Perspectives, Basingstoke: Palgrave, pp. 41–54.

131 In *Coney* Stephen had described the difference as being 'a question of degree depending upon circumstances' (at 549) and for Hawkins it was a question to be left to the triers of fact on a case by case basis (at 544).

132 (1878) 43 JP 72; 14 Cox CC 226; 39 LT 293.

133 (1898) 14 TLR 229.

134 For reports of other similar cases see, for example: *Morning Post*, 5 April 1882, p. 3; *The Times*, 9 June 1886, p. 10, 24 September 1890, p. 5, 11 October 1890, p. 12. In 1892 the *Ipswich Journal* reported on a gloved fight, arguing that what had transpired was a prize-fight because of the level of brutality involved. The publication felt there was 'something excessively revolting' in watching such a contest. In contrast, '"scientific" displays' held 'under the auspices of a legitimate institution' and with law enforcement officers present were considered to be an entirely different matter (3 December 1892, p. 2).

135 The legality of 'cage fighting' for example, arguably, remains unclear. On these types of contests see further J.J. Brent and P.B. Kraska, 'Fighting is the Most Real and Honest Thing', *British Journal of Criminology*, 53(3) 357–77. (The title of this piece seems to echo some of Egan's early nineteenth-century ideas about prize-fighting, as do some of the sentiments of the fighters which are quoted within it.) On criminal law responses to male violence see, for example, Bibbings, 'Boys Will be Boys'.

Chapter 3

R v Dudley and Stephens 1884[1]

Subduing the savage

> To preserve one's life is generally speaking a duty, but it may be the plainest and the highest duty to sacrifice it. War is full of instances in which it is a man's duty not to live, but to die. The duty, in case of shipwreck, of a captain to his crew, of the crew to the passengers, of soldiers to women and children ... these duties impose on men the moral necessity, not of the preservation, but of the sacrifice of their lives for others, from which in no country, least of all, it is to be hoped, in England, will men ever shrink, as indeed, they have not shrunk.[2]

This chapter examines the infamous case of *R v Dudley and Stephens* and the extraordinary incident of inter-male violence which led to it. The defendants, Tom Dudley and Edwin Stephens, were two of four sailors who, following the sinking of the yacht they were sailing, found themselves shipwrecked and adrift at sea in a small boat, without any fresh water and with precious little food. Eventually, fearing that death was a certainty without some form of sustenance and with no prospect of rescue apparent, Dudley, with the agreement of Stephens, killed one of their number in order that they might survive. They were subsequently rescued and, following their return to England, found themselves charged with the murder of Richard Parker, on whom they had feasted.[3]

Dudley and Stephens faced a trial at the assizes[4] in Exeter, where their counsel tried to argue that they should be acquitted on the basis that they had acted from necessity. Unusually, at the close of the trial the jury returned a 'special verdict', whereby they agreed a version of the facts but left the legal questions regarding murder and necessity to the court above to decide – so there was no finding of either guilty or not guilty at this stage. The case was then transferred, complete with Dudley and Stephens, to the Queen's Bench Division of the High Court of Justice in London. The result was that the defendants were convicted and sentenced to death, as was legally required at this time. However, this sentence was subsequently commuted to a period of six months' imprisonment.

Dudley and Stephens was in several respects an extraordinary case. Of course, the happenings that formed the subject matter of the proceedings were fantastical and macabre – but there were other things that made the case distinctive. In particular, the legal procedure by which it was decided was at points confused, if not flawed. Its transfer from Exeter to London was at least clumsily handled, with some shifting of opinion as to whether the judges in London would be sitting as a reincarnation of the assizes and/or as the Queen's Bench Division.[5] There was also the fact that it was assumed, even before the case entered the courts, that if (or, perhaps, when) convicted, although the sailors would be sentenced to death, this would not be carried out – indeed, Dudley had apparently been assured by his lawyer before the trial had commenced that he would be pardoned.[6]

Beyond this, the decision in *Dudley and Stephens* was hugely significant in legal terms because it ruled on the controversial defence of necessity (at least in the context of murder). It also pronounced upon important jurisdictional questions as to the reach of English (criminal) law: Dudley and Stephens might have been English sailors who had been on an English vessel, but when the conduct in question happened they were adrift on the high seas in a small boat and very far from their country.

These aspects of the case have been written about before, most notably by A.W. Brian Simpson in the brilliant and extremely readable *Cannibalism and the Common Law* – and the present chapter owes much to this book.[7] Whilst the text below draws and builds upon this work, it adopts a different approach. In doing so, it conceives of *Dudley and Stephens* as being concerned with ideas about Englishmen, English manliness and violence.

Dudley and Stephens was very much a case concerned with men. Even on a superficial level this was immediately evident: the case focused upon what had passed between four males whilst they were adrift in the boat – and the fact that they were sailors meant that its subject matter took place in a hyper-masculine realm from which women were often absent.[8] Ideas about men also figured extremely prominently in relation to the 1884 case, not least in the courtroom discussions about law and the text of the final decision. Indeed, the very idea of a defence of necessity seemed to be conceived of in the case as something which, if accepted, would apply mainly or possibly solely to men – certainly, as the quotation which opens this chapter suggests, the examples of conduct which were cited within the courtrooms focused upon the male of the species.

More specifically, the case can be narrated as an illustration of contemporary thinking about men and of the 'binding men' narrative of this book. In *Dudley and Stephens*, worries about men translated into an urgency to prosecute and convict the sailors, whilst ensuring that an authoritative legal precedent was created in order that the parameters of acceptable English male behaviour were plainly set down. At the same time, the decision in the case itself included pronouncements as to how the English male should carry himself, whatever his rank and whether he be in his native land or roaming further afield (at least if he was part of the crew of an English vessel).

The text below begins by giving an account of the events that led to the legal proceedings, the case's progress through the courts and the decision. Following this, *Dudley and Stephens* is re-examined in the context of contemporary concerns about men and is conceived of as being a part of efforts to rein in and legally bind the male of the species. By way of conclusion, the chapter briefly considers the sailors' conception of their behaviour and reflects upon the ideas about men previously considered.

Dudley and Stephens

Numerous sources can be drawn upon in order to construct a version of the events surrounding the killing of Parker and to recount the story of the legal proceedings which ensued (although there is some variation in the different descriptions as to what actually transpired following the shipwreck). Along with the law reports of the case, the fact that a range of other contemporary documents survive means that the material is particularly rich. For example, amongst the files preserved in The National Archives are various accounts of what happened penned by Dudley, the legal depositions of Dudley and Stephens, transcripts of the trial at the Exeter assizes and the proceedings in London as well as some Home Office documents relating to the case.[9] The jury's special verdict, which provided the legally accepted version of events, has also been preserved.[10]

Local as well as national newspapers also represent a valuable source of information here, not least as they often included different material, additional commentary and more colour than official documents. The wreck and the sailors' story were widely reported and the men were interviewed about their experiences.[11] Similarly, the various legal happenings were closely followed by the papers, although the level of detail varied vastly between different publications.[12] Beyond this, illustrated newspapers often included drawings to accompany their accounts of all the happenings (see, for example, Figures 5 and 6 below). Other contemporary nineteenth-century publications included reports of the case, not least legal journals.[13] All these primary sources inform the narrative of the case and its background presented here. In addition, I am especially indebted in constructing this part of the chapter to Simpson's storytelling about *Dudley and Stephens* in *Cannibalism*. However, Simpson's tale had a very different focus and purpose from the present text and reflected his own interest in things maritime.

The shipwreck and killing[14]

The crew of the English yacht, the *Mignonette*, consisted of Captain Tom Riley Dudley, Edwin Stephens, the mate, and able seaman Edmund (Ned) Brooks, along with Richard Parker, the cabin boy (who was said to be aged between 17 and 18), all of whom seem to have been of good character, with the Captain, in particular, an experienced and respected sailor, reputed for his bravery.[15] They had been employed to sail the craft from Southampton to Sydney via the Cape of Good Hope.[16] All went well on the voyage until on Saturday 5 July 1884 the vessel sank in stormy seas 1,600 miles from the Cape. The men survived but found themselves adrift in a dinghy with no fresh water to drink and, in terms of food, only two tins of turnips. The four lived on the latter for three days, then, on the fifth day they caught a turtle, which they proceeded slowly to consume. Its remains were finished on or about the eleventh day. In terms of hydration, they managed to catch some rain in their oilskin capes, all the men drank their own urine and Parker as well as Stephens imbibed some seawater.[17]

From around the eighteenth day, Dudley, Stephens and Brooks began discussing what should be done and the idea that one of their number should be killed to provide the rest with sustenance came to be considered, this often being thought of as a customary approach within the maritime world. On at least one occasion the sailors seem to have discussed drawing lots to decide who should be killed. Parker was not included in any of these conversations and Brooks did not agree with the suggested course. At some stage Dudley proposed that, if there was no sign of rescue by the following day, then Parker, who seemed the weakest, should be killed.[18]

On Friday 25 July or thereabouts,[19] Dudley, with the agreement of Stephens but not Brooks (who seems to have either gone to or been at the other end of the boat at this point), slit Parker's throat. Dudley, Stephens and Brooks then drank Parker's blood and ate his flesh, living off his body for the next few days.[20] On Tuesday 29 July they were rescued by a German vessel, the *Moctezuma*. At this stage the contents of their boat included some scraps of flesh and bone as well as items of clothing, this apparently being all that remained of Parker.[21] They told their rescuers what had transpired and were taken to Falmouth, where they arrived on Saturday 6 September 1884.[22] Their openness as to what had happened continued and, as a consequence, the news of their shipwreck along with the story of how they survived spread quickly around the town.[23]

That same day they went to make official statements as to what had occurred at sea to the local authorities.[24] Sergeant James Laverty of the Falmouth Harbour Police was present during this process and, as a consequence of what he heard, sought warrants for their arrest. Dudley, Stephens and Brooks were duly taken into custody just hours after they had landed.[25]

The preliminary legal proceedings

On the Monday morning (8 September) the three sailors were brought before Falmouth Police Court.[26] At this hearing they were all charged with

Figure 5 'The story of the wreck of the *Mignonette.*'

Illustrated Police News, 20 September 1884, p. 1.

murder; more specifically, Dudley was technically charged as the principal, as he had wielded the knife, with the other two as accessories. The local police requested that they all be remanded until direction could be given from the Treasury as to how the prosecution should be handled. This seems to have been because the matters at hand were both important and, to say the least, unusual, suggesting that Treasury Counsel might be appointed to conduct the case.[27] The remand request was granted, so bail was at this stage refused.

The decision to go ahead with the prosecution was supported at the highest level, with the then Home Secretary, Sir William Harcourt, having a say. In doing so, he noted that this was a 'dreadful case' and highlighted the urgent need for a legal ruling on the 'terrible act'.[28] This decision, according to Simpson, had a great deal to do with the fact that a similar situation had arisen ten years before in relation to survivors of the *Euxine*, a sailing vessel owned by the then Member of Parliament for Plymouth, which was transporting coal.[29] As Simpson told it, this was the 'Leading Case that Never was' because attempts to mount a prosecution both in England and in Singapore (which was then under British control) failed due to, amongst other things, differences of opinion, evidential difficulties and the problems occasioned by communication across the vast territories of the Empire.

In August 1873 the cargo of the *Euxine* had ignited spontaneously and the vessel was abandoned by its crew. The men took to three boats. One contained eight men, four of whom were eventually picked up. Amongst their number was the second mate, British seaman James Archer, who was in charge – all the others hailed from other parts of the world. Upon rescue, they freely admitted to having killed and eaten one of their number (Francis Shufus) in order to survive.

The reaction to these happenings from legal circles included a strong feeling that Shufus's killers, having been sailors on an English vessel, should be convicted and that an authoritative legal statement should be made in the case. For example, the Solicitor-General, who presented the evidence to the Police Court in Singapore in the ultimately barren hope of getting the men committed for jury trial, felt that a prosecution was needed in order 'to show that in no case was human life to be taken without the act undergoing the most searching judicial enquiry into the causes and motives which led to its being committed.'[30] Similarly, the Attorney General in Singapore was keen for a prosecution but by an English court, as '[t]he law laid down in an English Court would have more weight in all parts of the world and would probably be considered binding in all parts of the British Dominions … it is important that the principle to govern cases of this sort in future should be authoritatively upheld.'[31] However, this was not to be. As Simpson constructed the story of this nearly case, back in England this left the officials of the Home Office and the Treasury Solicitor frustrated. Moreover, he suggested that, as a consequence, they might well 'have taken particular pains over the prosecution' of Dudley and Stephens.[32] Whether or not this was the case, once the decision to prosecute Dudley and Stephens was taken, a junior Treasury Counsel was appointed to argue the matter before the magistrates.

At the subsequent hearing of what was then the case of *Dudley, Stephens and Brooks* on Thursday 11 September, as in each stage of the legal proceedings in Cornwall and Devon, the public galleries were crowded, with people also gathering outside the building in which the legal action was taking place in the hope of getting a view of the survivors of the *Mignonette*.[33] The matter, however, was again delayed but this time the men were bailed – a remarkable occurrence in a capital case but one which, as Simpson noted, demonstrated the 'legal establishment's curious approach' to the case from start to finish; this, he wrote, was characterized by 'a determination to secure a conviction for murder, combined with a humane and slightly inconsistent desire to see that [the sailors] did not suffer unduly in consequence.'[34] Significantly, this approach was by no means generally disapproved of or seen as controversial. For instance, according to *The Times* bail was granted because the men were 'only technically charged with the highest offence a man could commit against the laws of England.'[35] Moreover, the courtroom in Falmouth greeted the decision to release the sailors with applause, demonstrating the celebrity of the men and the degree of popular sympathy towards them.[36]

By this time, local interest in the case along with support for the sailors was reflected nationally. The men's story had quickly become a matter of press attention, with regional papers around the country as well as the nationals running accounts of the happenings and opinion pieces. Indeed, thanks to the use of telegrams, some of the newspapers had been able to carry a brief version of the story on the very day of the sailors' arrival, statement giving, and arrest at Falmouth.[37]

Thursday 18 September was the date of the next hearing and it was here that the decision to drop the charge against Brooks was announced by the prosecution, having presumably been taken during the week-long break in proceedings.[38] This reflected the fact that all three of the sailors' accounts of the killing agreed that Brooks had dissented – it also, of course, provided the prosecution with their key witness, as Brooks could not perform this role if he too was on trial. Evidence was then heard and, there being deemed to be enough to support a prosecution, Dudley and Stephens were committed for trial and released on bail, charged to appear to face the 23-strong grand jury in Exeter, which would again consider whether there was enough evidence upon which to proceed with the trial proper.[39]

The proceedings and trial in Exeter

On Monday 3 November their case reached the assizes, Baron Huddleston presiding.[40] Unusually, in introducing the matter to the grand jury, the judge made a powerful argument that what the men had done legally was murder and that there was no defence of necessity in English law, citing authority for his argument.[41] In doing so, he seemed to demonstrate how keen he was for the prosecution to continue and, perhaps, how fearful he was that the case might be defeated before it had begun as a result of popular feeling in favour of the sailors. At this early point, however, he also made a point of expressing some sympathy for the defendants, stating that '[n]o person who has read the details of this painful case but must be filled with the deepest compassion for the unhappy men who were placed in this frightful position.'[42] The grand jury, unsurprisingly in the light of what the Baron had said about the legal position, delivered a 'true bill', meaning that there was considered to be a sufficient case to proceed to trial.

Thus it was that on Thursday 6 November Dudley and Stephens were tried before a 12-strong trial jury.[43] Unsurprisingly, people were keen to watch the proceedings, with *The Times* reporting that '[t]he court was densely crowded, even ladies being present throughout.'[44] Opening the case, Mr Charles for the prosecution highlighted his sympathy for the plight of the sailors but emphasized that compassion should not have any bearing upon the performance of the jurymen's 'duty'; should they find that Dudley and Stephens had committed acts which constituted the crime of murder, then they must convict. Instead, any such sympathy should properly be directed towards calls for clemency in relation to the mandatory death sentence. He went on to recount the facts, which were not disputed by the men involved, and then moved to the law. Murder, he explained, was a killing committed with malice aforethought by a person of sound mind. Malice aforethought meant that an act was done with thought and intention, rather than something committed under provocation or in hot blood. In the case of Parker's killing, the act was the result of some deliberation, rather than an act of anger and the men, he argued, were patently of sound mind. As to the contention that the men's actions constituted a justifiable and excusable homicide, this was misconceived because self-defence could not be established, there having been no threat from Parker and, according to notable jurist Sir William Blackstone, a person had no right to kill an innocent in order to assure his own survival.[45]

Then something very unusual took place which was to change the course that the legal proceedings took. Huddleston interjected, declaring his intentions as to how he meant to deal with the case. He was of a mind, he said, to ensure that it was considered by the highest legal authorities. There were two means by which this could be achieved. If the men were convicted he would reserve the case to the Court for Crown Cases Reserved (CCCR); as is explained in Chapters 1, 2 and 4 of this volume, a reservation to this court was only possible following conviction. Reservation meant that one or more of the legal questions in the case would be referred to the CCCR to rule authoritatively on – and on the basis of this its judges would either confirm or quash the conviction. However, Huddleston also highlighted a well-established (but by that time rarely used) alternative procedure. This, he said, would release the jury from the burden of delivering a guilty verdict. Instead, they could deliver a special verdict which would be limited to a finding of the facts; the questions of law being left for the court above to decide. The final stage would be to apply their legal finding to the jury's version of the facts resulting in either a conviction or an acquittal.[46]

Here then, the Baron was deliberately directing the trial in a way that attempted to shape the jury's choices; rather than a finding of guilty or not guilty, they could either convict the men or they could merely decide upon the facts. In either case the same common law judges who presided over the assizes around the country would have the final say as to the law, in whichever court they were sitting – and Huddleston indicated in no uncertain terms that *their* decision was not expected to be in doubt as legally the men were unquestionably guilty. All this served to demonstrate that acquittal was not an option that he was prepared to entertain (something that the defence commented upon at the time)[47] – and that he seemed determined to have an authoritative legal statement made by a panel of the most senior judges, in order that a clear precedent would be created.

Following this remarkable intervention, Charles continued with the case for the prosecution, with Brooks giving evidence as to what had taken place on the high seas.[48] Others were called to confirm what had happened following the sailors' rescue.[49] The depositions authored by the sailors were also placed before the court, as were other versions of the story written by Dudley, including a lengthy account produced for the Board of Trade.[50]

Mr Collins for the defence then had the opportunity to put the case for Dudley and Stephens. However, he did so in the knowledge that Huddleston had already made it clear that to his mind the defendants were guilty as 'there was no justification' for the sailors to kill Parker.[51] Collins's task was, consequently, an especially difficult one, the Baron already having taken a view as to the law, as well as having said how he intended things would proceed both within and beyond the trial. Nevertheless, Collins made a brave attempt at defending the men. In cross-examination of prosecution witnesses he had already managed to get Brooks to testify as to the sailors' sufferings and their extreme predicament – with no reasonable prospect of relief.[52] In presenting the case for the defence Collins challenged the court's jurisdiction to try the matter, maintaining that although under the Merchant Shipping Act 1854 it could try offences committed on British ships on the high seas, a 'ship' was defined as a vessel 'not propelled by oars' – and the alleged offence here had been committed in just such a boat. Huddleston, seemingly in a great deal of haste and not expecting this line of argument, promptly reserved the question.[53] Presumably he did so on the basis that he was anticipating a special verdict, as for the matter to be reserved to the CCCR he would have needed to have ruled on this (and there would need to be a conviction of at least one of the men for the case to reach that court).

Collins then addressed the jury, reminding them that men in the direst of situations had been known to resort to the desperate remedy adopted by the defendants but 'no Government in any civilized country had … prosecuted the unhappy survivors on a charge of murder.'[54] The facts, he said, were not disputed, but the men were of good character and had acted in a way that was abhorrent to them only because of their perilous situation. Given this, necessity should provide them with a defence. Moreover, it made no difference that the sailors had opted not to draw lots to make their selection but rather had chosen the weakest. His parting shot was to tell the jurymen that none of the three sailors had thought that they had acted wrongly in the grave and unusual circumstances in which they had found themselves, let alone that they had committed a criminal offence.[55]

However, the Baron cut matters short, directing the jury that they had no choice but to accept his statement as to the law, whatever might have been argued by the defence. He then proceeded to manoeuvre the 12 men towards delivering a special verdict, justifying his prescriptive approach in a rather repetitive and somewhat circular manner. In doing so, he largely reiterated what he had previously said about his view of the legal position and his plans for the case to be referred whether there was a conviction or a special verdict – acquittal again being ruled out.[56] No objections to the special verdict procedure having been raised, Huddleston produced his ready-made draft special

The Pictorial World

AN ILLUSTRATED WEEKLY NEWSPAPER

No. 116, New Series.—(Vol. V.) NOVEMBER 13th, 1884. Price Sixpence, Post Free, 6½d.

REGISTERED AT THE GENERAL POST OFFICE FOR TRANSMISSION ABROAD.

1. The Castle Gate. 2. Captain Dudley. 3. The Mate. 4. Master Wiese, of the *Montezuma*, who rescued the crew. 5. His Lordship informs the Jury of *his* intentions. 6. Edwin Brooks as witness. 7. Mr. Collins, Q.C., for the Defence. 8. The Trial: The case for the Prosecution.

THE LOSS OF THE YACHT "MIGNONETTE": TRIAL OF THE SURVIVORS AT EXETER.

Figure 6 'The Loss of the Yacht *Mignonette*: Trial of the Survivors at Exeter.'

Pictorial World, 13 November 1884, p. 1.

verdict for the jurymen to comment on and approve[57] ('like a conjurer with a rabbit', according to Simpson[58]).

By this deft stroke, as *The Times* explained, he avoided what he seemed to fear most and what others involved in the administration of criminal justice might well also have been concerned about; namely the possibility of an acquittal because of 'the popular prejudice in favour of the prisoner [*sic*]', which would have meant that the case would be closed with no possibility of a review or of more authoritative pronouncements as to the legal position.[59] Accordingly, the special verdict stated the basic facts as to the shipwreck and killing as purportedly decided by the jury – although it had, of course, essentially been written by the judge. It specified that if the three had not had the sustenance provided by Parker's body, they would 'probably' not have survived long enough to be rescued, that the boy was likely to have died first and that at the time of the killing there was no prospect of rescue. So the finding of the facts reflected the view that the only way for any lives to be saved was through the murder of one of the crew in order that the others could eat. However, it also stated that, if it was indeed necessary to kill someone, there was no particular justification for killing Parker, rather than one of the others. The decision as to the law and the full verdict were thereby deferred. In addition, a plea for mercy to be exercised towards the sailors, were they to be convicted, was included within the special verdict.

At the close of the case in Exeter the proceedings along with the sailors were left in a somewhat uncertain position. Dudley and Stephens were bailed to appear before the next assizes, which were to be held at Bodmin.[60] However, they also seem to have been directed or advised to follow the Baron and their case to London.

The proceedings in London

In the first instance, *Dudley and Stephens* was adjourned to Huddleston's rooms at the Royal Court of Justice, London, pending consideration by a panel of judges. At this stage there was disagreement as to the correct procedure and there followed some debate and manoeuvring. The Baron had suggested that the Cornwall assizes would reconvene in London, with a panel of his fellow judges, who presided over the assizes around the country, making a decision as to the law. If this had happened, he seems to have assumed that the case would then have moved back to Cornwall for the confirmation of what was expected to be a conviction and sentencing. This was not, however, what transpired.[61]

On Thursday 4 December *Dudley and Stephens* was, indeed, argued and decided before five of the assize judges. However, they decided that they were sitting as the Queen's Bench Division of the High Court – of which the assizes were a part. The panel consisted of Huddleston, Lord Chief Justice Coleridge, Justices Grove and Denman and Baron Pollock.[62]

Dudley and Stephens were allowed to be present in the court and sat on the solicitors' bench.[63] At the outset, Collins, again speaking for Dudley and Stephens, challenged the wording of the special verdict and, in this context, suggested that the proceedings in Exeter might not have been valid. His protestations, however, were not accepted.[64] Then the arguments proper began, with the Attorney General, Sir Henry James appearing for the prosecution, thereby demonstrating the importance which the matter was accorded. He maintained that no form of defence could apply to the case, as only deliberate killing by way of execution following conviction or during a war was justified and self-defence could not be extended to include circumstances where the victim posed no risk to the killer or a third party he was seeking to protect.[65] Collins then put his case, arguing, for example, that necessity not only existed but should provide a defence in the current case. In doing so, he referred to authorities, including the esteemed writings of one of the five judges' brethren (Justice Stephen), as well as the words of other legal texts and cases. He also stressed the unusually extreme circumstances in which Dudley and Stephens found themselves and tried to defeat the notion that they had intended to kill by asserting that the men's goal had been 'to preserve their lives'. At every point, however, he was met with a fierce rejection of the arguments he presented – with all the judges intervening, although Coleridge was the most dominant.[66] Indeed, the press reports of the exchanges, in particular, gave the sense that the five's minds were well and truly made up and that Collins's task was a hopeless one.[67]

At the conclusion of the defence case 'the court retired for luncheon',[68] with a brief but significant parting comment from the Lord Chief Justice. He indicated that the judges probably would not hear the Attorney General's response to the defence arguments.[69] One can only assume that this was because their decision, if it had not been clear from the outset, had been made by this point.

The decision

Upon their return, Coleridge announced that they would convict the two sailors but was somewhat at a loss as how properly to proceed. Indeed, the author of the Queen's Bench report of the decision also seems a little confused as he has Coleridge as stating that '[t]he court are of opinion that the conviction must be affirmed' – but there was, of course, no conviction to confirm.[70] As to what else needed to be done, following some discussion it was decided that the reasons for the judgment along with the passing of sentence would be delayed for four days but that both would be tasks for the Queen's Bench judges. This still left some issues unresolved, however. Dudley and Stephens, who were present in court, were still bailed to appear at the assizes in Bodmin should the present court decide that the law was such that they were guilty, Huddleston having assumed that matters would be concluded in the South West. His view did not carry the day though, as it was decided that everything would be finalized in London.[71] Following some discussion, the sailors, were returned to custody to await the Court's formal decision and pronouncement of their sentence. With a display of compassion in keeping with their treatment thus far, it was decided that they would spend the next few days in Holloway Prison, this being judged by Coleridge to be 'so far as it can be, the most comfortable' place to be held.[72]

On Tuesday 9 December Coleridge delivered the reasons for the judgment and passed sentence on Dudley and Stephens. He rejected the arguments regarding the questions of jurisdiction and procedure, focusing upon establishing that necessity was no defence to murder. In the absence of statutory guidance and domestic case law, the judgment considered legal writers, the relationship between law and morality, notions of acceptable and expected behaviour (both on land and at sea) and stories of seafarers in crisis. The conclusion, in terms of the law, was that necessity was no defence to murder, at least in the present circumstances.

Dudley and Stephens were, as the law required, sentenced to death, although Coleridge did not don the black cap as was the convention in the assizes when passing the capital sentence.[73] However, as has been suggested, it was generally thought that this would not be carried out. Indeed, the papers reported that things were immediately set in motion to address this matter and it was widely assumed that the solution would take the form of a complete pardon. In fact, the 'pardon' which was granted was described as being only partial and the sentence was in fact commuted to six months' imprisonment.[74] Now ordinary prisoners, the men served their time at Holloway under normal prison conditions[75] and seem subsequently, as Simpson noted, to have very much disappeared from the public gaze.[76]

Binding men and denying degeneracy

Dudley and Stephens was crucially important from a legal perspective as it authoritatively set the boundaries of criminal liability in relation to murder and the defence of necessity.[77] However, as suggested above, it was also very much a case concerned with men and ideas about manliness – or rather Englishmen and English manliness – and attempts to delimit what was expected of the nation's menfolk. Before this particular version of the binding men narrative is explored in relation to the case, however, the contemporary context needs to be sketched in order to provide a backdrop to what unfolded in 1884.

The pre-*Dudley and Stephens* context

As we shall see, key concerns about men which surfaced within *Dudley and Stephens*, as well as in discussions about the case and its subject matter, included worries about degeneration, parasitism, atavism, selfishness and heathenism. Connected to these notions, there were anxieties about Englishmen who behaved as savages or monsters. From the middle of the nineteenth century onwards fears that sections of the population, in particular the English male population, were in moral and/or physical decline were being expressed in various circles. These worries tended to focus upon the lower classes, not least the urban poor, although this is not to say that unease was solely directed towards one section of society. Degeneration theory was a key facet of this thinking. Whilst it might not have reached its height until the final decade of the nineteenth century, these ideas had been influential for some decades previously.[78] For example, Edwin Ray Lankester's *Degeneration: A Chapter in Darwinism* (1880),[79] an important text in this genre, was published not long before *Dudley and Stephens*. Whilst the author spent much time talking about non-human species and of the downward path of reverse evolution which might lead them to parasitism, he also related his ideas to humankind.[80] Thus, he maintained that any race might degenerate, just as it could evolve. Moreover, his writings suggested that no nationality, including the English, was immune to decline. Indeed, Lankester argued that the signs of this were already evident in 'civilised Europe'. The feared downward progression could, however, to his mind be prevented – and this was something that was needed even in England.[81]

Other writers who embraced evolutionary ideas also had thoughts about humanity. For example, Edward Burnett Tylor theorized that the human races could be arranged hierarchically, from the most savage and underdeveloped to the most civilized. His schema placed northern Europeans at the pinnacle of the breed – but also identified the savage types who had survived even in superior cultures, pointing to the lower classes within contemporary England and in an 1871 publication he gave the example of the superstitious ploughman with his basic tools and simple life.[82] To some, such ideas provided a justification for efforts to civilize the inferior types of the Empire. However, as Tylor's comments illustrate, this thinking suggested that Englishmen too had primitive and perhaps even savage tendencies, which might require taming.

The very idea that Englishmen could display the characteristics of such under-evolved or lesser peoples – or that they might perhaps be degenerating to their level – was an alarming prospect. This was a particular concern in the context of thinking about the nation's place in the world. After all, England and its people ruled the Empire, which was supposedly inhabited by inferior races – and the English male's presumed superiority was a crucial facet of imperial discourse. In this context, if Englishmen did not live up to the standards that were expected of them, something needed to be done to change them – or their unbecoming behaviour needed to be in some way rejected and punished in the hope that this might go some way towards reasserting the pre-eminence of the English.[83]

These kinds of theories, along with other concerns about the nation's men, were hugely influential and were oft repeated across a range of different spheres in the years before *Dudley and Stephens*. For example, writings from early English criminology and psychiatry drew upon thinking about reverse evolution or underdevelopment within western races. In this context, commentators often focused upon male behaviour, hypothesizing as to criminality and its causes. Here two dominant views prevailed (although these were sometimes confusingly conflated): either some individuals had an inherent predisposition to crime (so their inferiority was innate) or criminals were ordinary folk who had taken the decision to breach the law (their degeneration being a conscious choice). In both cases, the failure was troubling – and arguments were presented as to how such men and their behaviour should be addressed.[84]

In sharp juxtaposition with but not unconnected to such concerns, the image of an idealized, intensely patriotic version of the English male was also identifiable in the period before *Dudley and Stephens* and such thinking was also to play a role in the case itself. Here men were required to be worlds away from the primitive peoples of the Empire – they had to be civilized, law-abiding, self-sacrificing, exercise restraint and embody Christian morality – and, as if that was not enough, men were also expected to be heroic. In the context of such thinking, the idea that in the direst of circumstances an Englishman could abandon his national identity and give way to his animal urges with impunity had to be rejected at all costs.

In this vein, the Muscular Christianity movement preached the need for men to be disciplined, stoical and learn the value of altruism – and advocates sought to rectify deficiencies in the English male, whether because of under-development or as a result of decline. Notably, Charles Kingsley argued that men, in particular, should adopt healthy lifestyles in order to avoid the temptation and barbarism to which their biology could otherwise lead them. His proposed solution focused upon such things as 'healthy habitations', 'personal cleanliness', 'physical exercise' and 'development of brain-power', which he argued would 'regenerate the human system'. Additionally, he stressed that men should 'obey those laws of nature which are the voice of God.'[85]

Samuel Smiles's extremely popular and influential self-improvement writings were also especially significant in relation to ideas about men and male behaviour. In a series of books, most notably *Self-Help: With Illustrations of Conduct and Perseverance* (1859),[86] Smiles advocated a model of masculinity which he argued all should strive towards, thereby benefiting not only themselves but their country by preventing degeneration and allowing each man to be the best he could be. Like Kingsley, Smiles's ideas represented a Christian vision of how men should behave and amongst the characteristics he advocated to his male readership were self-reliance, self-control, steadfastness, bravery, chivalry, duty, virtue, morality and self-denial.

For example, he devoted a chapter of *Character*, first published in 1871,[87] to 'Self Control', arguing that: 'there can be no true manhood without it … To be morally free–to be more than an animal–man must be able to resist instinctive impulse'.[88] Thus, Smiles emphasized the importance of an individual holding himself in restraint in order to distinguish himself from the beasts. Indeed, he saw adversity as the 'touchstone of character', suffering as 'divinely appointed' and pain as 'remedial'.[89]

Smiles's was very much a middle-class, gentlemanly vision of how men should be, however, at points his work suggested that all classes of the nation's menfolk could demonstrate the manly qualities he espoused. For example, he explained that 'roughs picked up in the streets, or raw unkempt country lads taken from the plough' could 'exhibit the unmistakable characteristics of true bravery and heroism!' Most significantly for present purposes, however, he cited the circumstances of the wreck of the *Birkenhead* as just such an instance.[90]

HMS *Birkenhead* was a Navy troopship which struck a rock and sank in 1852. There were not enough lifeboats to carry all aboard so Lieutenant-Colonel Seton ordered that the men should remain on the ship in order that the women and children could have a chance of survival. Most of the men obeyed and many perished as a consequence.[91] The story was often recalled as an indicator of what England expected of its men and it was also said to be the source of the notion that women and children should be prioritized in a disaster.

Dudley and Stephens

If the story of the *Birkenhead* demonstrated what was expected of Englishmen when in danger on the seas, according to these contemporary ideas about men, the tales of the *Euxine* and the *Mignonette* provided extreme examples of what they should *not* do. Indeed, from even the most fleeting of glances at the facts of the case as depicted in the trial transcripts, in the law reports and the statements of the men involved, let alone the contemporary newspapers, it is clear that *Dudley and Stephens* resonated with a good deal of the anxieties about men depicted above. For instance, the sailors' actions seemed to have more in common with the cannibal savages of imperial lands than with contemporary notions of English manliness. Moreover, in the context of Simpson's story of *Dudley and Stephens*, they had followed the more primal (and hyper-masculine) 'custom of the sea' (which entailed that they select one of their number to be sacrificed so that the rest might have a better chance at survival), rather than abide by the more modern and civilized law of England.[92] Such ideas were frequently reflected in press coverage of the case from the start. For example, the view of the *Daily News* on the Falmouth proceedings included the warning that 'it can never be held among civilised people that men placed in mortal peril by hunger are justified in living on each other', as '[t]hat would be to go back to animalism and savagery'.[93]

In terms of evolutionary thinking in the fledgling field of criminology, Dudley, Stephens and, to some extent, Brooks's behaviour seemed to indicate that they had, when in the direst of circumstances and suffering perhaps from a form of 'famine-madness',[94] degenerated into more primitive beings, with barbarism, selfishness and survival at all costs coming to the fore and what was considered the right, legal and Godly course thereby perverted. Indeed, it seemed that these men, who had apparently previously been of good character, had somehow descended into criminality – whether by giving way to their natural savage urges or by rational choice.

Certainly, the statements made by Dudley and Stephens, along with the evidence of Brooks, seemed to emphasize their fall by highlighting the gruesome nature of their actions. By their own words, all three seemed to be suggesting that animalistic urges had been released by their plight. This was most graphically illustrated in comments like Stephens's 'we ate a good deal – I should think quite half of the body before we were picked up, and I can say that we partook of it with quite as much relish as ordinary food'.[95] Brooks made similar observations, including the following, which gives a sense of the feeling that there was something transformative, perhaps supernaturally so, about their actions: 'after drinking the blood I felt quite strong – in fact we all made use of the expression that we were quite different men'.[96]

Alternatively, in terms of Smiles's writings, the men had failed to show the self-restraint, self-sacrifice, stoicism and the sense of duty that was expected of Englishmen when facing death. Moreover, they had also not demonstrated the physical and moral fortitude which Muscular Christianity sought to imbue in men. Instead, they had chosen to take another's life in order to secure their own survival.

It is with all this in mind that we return to the legal proceedings in *Dudley and Stephens*, from the decision to prosecute, the hearings in Falmouth, the grand jury decision and trial in Exeter to the decision of the Queen's Bench Division in London. In this context, ideas about men and concerns about the behaviour of the sailors figured in discussions as to how the case should be handled as well as in the courtrooms in which it was heard. Indeed, the case might be seen as representing a restatement and a defence of an idealized form of English masculinity which echoed contemporary ideas about men.

With graphic evidence as to the gruesome happenings in the *Mignonette*'s boat appearing in the men's official accounts of their experiences and in the press in England and around the world,[97] the urgency to prosecute and convict Dudley and Stephens can, amongst other things, be depicted as an attempt to convey a strong message about how Englishmen should behave when in danger. In addition, the knowledge that at home some sections of the public and the press tended to view the sailors not merely with sympathy but as celebrities and heroes (Simpson described Dudley and Stephens as being seen as 'folk heroes' in some quarters[98]) heightened the need to state unequivocally and authoritatively what was to be expected of the nation's menfolk. Indeed, in *Cannibalism* Simpson observed that the Home Secretary, in particular, seemed to have been especially exercised by the fact that Dudley was in some quarters seen as an heroic adventurer, not least as this view reflected what was to Victorian minds a very pagan conception of 'what a man must do'.[99]

However, for a prosecution to succeed (and with the story of the *Euxine* in mind) there was a need to establish that the English courts had jurisdiction over the matter – and, more particularly, over English sailors adrift in foreign waters. As Simpson argued, the failure to bring a case against the survivors of the coal-bearing vessel a decade earlier had been a matter of frustration and unease as there was a strong desire for a clear ruling as to the illegality of such conduct. Part of this disquiet might arguably be recast in terms of concerns about the likely perceptions of both the men in the case and the law of England, with worries centring upon what this incident of killing and cannibalism said about those who sailed under the country's flag. Indeed, the reaction of the Treasury and Home Office to the case of the *Mignonette* can be portrayed in similar terms; here too there was a sense of urgency not merely that the law on murder and necessity should be clear and technical questions of jurisdiction resolved, but that Dudley and Stephens should be convicted and that Englishmen aboard English vessels would thereby be legally bound to behave as civilized men.

Both at the assizes and at the Queen's Bench Division there were discussions as to whether the English courts had authority over English sailors on English (or British) vessels. In Exeter, Huddleston had deflected Collins's arguments about this by reserving the issue. However, in London Coleridge addressed the jurisdictional question. In order to do so he focused upon section 267 of the Merchant Shipping Act 1854, explaining that Dudley and Stephens were subject to English law because they were crew upon a British vessel at the time of the killing and the Act extended to offences committed 'either ashore or afloat'. The Act imposed English standards upon such men, as under it they were brought 'within the jurisdiction of the Admiralty of England'.[100] Indeed, several of the judges seemed to go beyond this on 4 December, when the Queen's Bench Division heard the case and decided to convict. Thus, in the courtroom discussions, Denman declared that a British subject was under the jurisdiction of English criminal law wherever he was in the world and *The Times* described Coleridge's view as being that the national registration of the boat 'has nothing to do with it' as '[t]he men were Englishmen on the high seas; they do not lose their subjugation to our law by being in a foreign vessel.'[101] These were, of course, less (or perhaps more) than legalistic views, with Denman, in particular, feeling that the English should always adhere to the law of their land.

Aside from the crucial matter of the English courts' jurisdiction over English sailors on English vessels, other aspects of the courtroom proceedings in *Dudley and Stephens* arose from worries about the male of the species and invoked ideas about men. In particular, Huddleston's determination that there should be a prosecution and a conviction could be seen as an attempt to demonstrate that the sailors' behaviour was not something that was acceptable for Englishmen, whatever their class, and, in so doing, to bind not only the two sailors but other males as well. His procedural manoeuvring, together with the pressure he brought to bear on both the grand and trial jurymen in Exeter, ensured that the trial went ahead, that there was an authoritative and very public legal ruling by the judges of the Queen's Bench Division and meant that the men were found guilty. Moreover, the Baron made a number of statements as to morality, law and necessity focusing upon the defendants' selection of the weakest of their number as a victim – to him this indicated that their conduct had fallen far short of that which he expected of men even in the most perilous of circumstances. For example, in seeking to convince the jury to return a special verdict he was critical of the defendants, calling their manliness into question. Thus, he opined that 'on all the grounds of law and morality' a group of men could not kill one to save the rest and that in such circumstances it would certainly not be justifiable to sacrifice the weakest amongst them.[102]

However, in terms of what transpired in the various courtrooms in which the case was considered, it was in Coleridge's judgment that ideas about men were most powerfully conveyed. The Lord Chief Justice juxtaposed qualities which were portrayed as unEnglish, immoral, primitive, monstrous (ideas associated with degeneration, the lower races of Empire and criminality) and unmanly, against ways of being that were truly masculine, stoical, civilized and quintessentially English. In fact, much of his judgment was concerned with how Englishmen should behave; but let us turn first to his conception of what took place following the loss of the *Mignonette*, which, of course, helped to provide a justification for the defendants' conviction.

Coleridge depicted what transpired on board the boat in terms that emphasized the gruesome and barbaric nature of the sailors' actions. Thus, whilst not choosing to rehearse the full story, he referred to '[o]ther details yet more harrowing, facts still more loathsome and appalling', which were put before the jury and were recorded in Huddleston's notes of the trial.[103] This is not to say that he made no further mention of the happenings. For example, he recounted that 'the prisoners put to death a weak and unoffending boy upon the chance of preserving their own lives by feeding upon his flesh and blood after he was killed, and with the certainty of depriving *him* of any possible chance of survival.'[104] Here, Dudley and Stephens were presented as rational, cold and inhuman parasites who had made a calculated decision to extinguish the life of a boy whose strength was failing and who had done nothing wrong.

These were themes which were repeated at various points in the judgment. For instance, the vulnerability of Parker was highlighted again when Coleridge stated that 'the boy was incapable of resistance, and, in fact, made none' and that he posed no threat to the defendants as 'it is not even suggested that his death was due to any violence on his part attempted against, or even so much as feared by, those who killed him.'[105] Later in the text there was again a reference to 'the deliberate killing of this unoffending and unresisting boy'[106] and to the fact that '[i]n this case the weakest, the youngest, the most unresisting, was chosen'[107] rather than 'one of the grown men'.[108] This was not, then, a case of justifiable self-defence but rather of deliberate and premeditated murder – what is more, it was selfishness at its worst.

At the same time as castigating the way in which Dudley and Stephens had behaved, Coleridge spent some time in his judgment dwelling upon how men in their position should conduct themselves. Indeed, the Lord Chief Justice's text provided a model for an idealized form of very English and most definitely Christian manliness. These comments too reflected contemporary ideas about the male of the species, including those espoused by the Muscular Christianity movement and in the work of Smiles. For example, as is demonstrated by the epigraph to this chapter, Coleridge emphasized the importance of duty, courage and selflessness by stating that whilst '[t]o preserve one's life is generally speaking a duty, but it may be the plainest and the highest duty to sacrifice it'. Moreover, 'duties impose on men the moral necessity, not of the preservation, but of the sacrifice of their lives for others' – and these were duties 'from which in no country, least of all, it is to be hoped, in England, will men ever shrink, as indeed, they have not shrunk.'[109] Additionally, this was a Christly model of altruism as 'the duty of dying for others' was one entirely in keeping with 'the Great Example whom we profess to follow' and this emphasis on Christian moral standards was also evident in Coleridge's reference to England as a 'Christian country'.[110]

Significantly, like Smiles before him, Coleridge made mention of a well-known cultural reference point in order to demonstrate what was expected of shipwrecked Englishmen. For the judge 'the noble case of the Birkenhead' demonstrated '[t]he duty, in case of shipwreck, of a captain to his crew, of the crew to the passengers, of soldiers to women and children'.[111] According to this conception of manliness, far from being killed and consumed, Parker, as the youngest, the least experienced and most vulnerable of the shipwrecked sailors should have been protected, with his interests placed above those of his fellows. So, the Captain should have looked to his welfare, rather than planned his demise.

In the light of all these observations about what men should and should not do and what qualities they should embody, there was clearly no place for a defence of necessity within the English criminal law, especially when it came to murder. Thus, Coleridge felt that 'it is quite plain that such a principle once accepted might be made the legal cloak for unbridled passion and atrocious crime.'[112] There was, therefore, an 'awful danger of admitting the principle which has been contended for.'[113] Coleridge was assisted in his rejection of necessity by the great legal authority, Lord Hale, who he quoted. In commenting upon the idea of such a defence, Hale had stated that 'I take it that here in England, that rule, at least by the laws of England, is false'. He had reinforced the point, by adding that 'if a person, being under necessity for want of victuals or clothes, shall upon that account clandestinely … steal another man's goods, it is felony, and a crime by the laws of England'.[114] Here then, the emphasis was on the need for law to require people (and, in the current context, men) to endure hardship and resist the 'temptation' to commit crime.[115] Moreover, to Coleridge the idea of necessity, along with the selfishness and self-preservation with which it was associated, was not supportable in 'a Christian country'[116] and he rejected the idea that men could respond to life-threatening circumstances by turning their back upon the law of the land as 'a proposition which appeared to us to be at once dangerous, immoral, and opposed to all legal principle and analogy.'[117] Such lawlessness, along with the lack of control that it involved, was not, therefore, something that could be borne.

So, the defence of necessity was rejected by Coleridge and the other Queen's Bench judges and the conduct of Dudley in killing Parker and of Stephens in being a party to it was castigated as unmanly and unEnglish and found to be murder. However, as we have seen, in the Exeter and London courtrooms a good deal of sympathy was expressed for the defendants and the situation in which they found themselves. Indeed, this approach was even evident in terms of the presentation of the prosecution case. It probably reflected an awareness of, along with a sensitivity to, the level of public feeling for the sailors – but it may also have demonstrated genuine compassion for the sailors. Let us pause and consider the Queen's Bench judgment in the light of this observation.

Coleridge undoubtedly showed a good deal of understanding for the men he passed judgment upon. For example, demonstrating his appreciation for the seriousness and difficulty of the sailors' plight, he stated that '[i]t must not be supposed that in refusing to admit temptation to be an excuse for crime it is forgotten how terrible the temptation was; how awful the suffering; how hard in such trials to keep the judgment straight and the conduct pure.'[118] In addition, whilst he castigated the killing of an innocent in order that others might survive and drew attention to the calculated and animalistic actions which had brought this about, he also made a point of recognizing the extreme nature of the position in which the sailors had found themselves.

Indeed, towards the end of his judgment he emphasized that '[i]t is not suggested that in this particular case the deeds were "devilish"'.[119]

So, there was contradiction within Coleridge's judgment, with him both condeming the defendants' actions and demonstrating compassion for them. More significantly, he expressed doubts as to whether the standards to which he and his fellows were holding men were in fact ones which were achievable. Thus, he noted that 'the prisoners were subject to terrible temptation and to sufferings which might breakdown the bodily power of the strongest man and would try the conscience of the best'.[120] In fact, he even seemed to express doubts as to whether the judges themselves might be able to live up to the legal requirements they were effectively imposing upon Dudley and Stephens and Englishmen in general:

> We are often compelled to set up standards we cannot reach ourselves, and to lay down rules we could not ourselves satisfy ... But a man has no right to declare temptation to be an excuse, though he might himself have yielded to it, nor allow compassion for the criminal to change or weaken in any manner the legal definition of the crime.[121]

So, here, the idealized manly qualities described by Coleridge were acknowledged to perhaps be aspirational rather than achievable – at least in circumstances such as those in which Dudley and Stephens found themselves. In keeping with this sensitivity, in the Queen's Bench judgment there was also mention of the possibility of clemency, with Coleridge stating that the court had no choice but to 'ascertain' and 'declare' the law and 'if in any case the law appears to be too severe on individuals, to leave it to the Sovereign to exercise that prerogative of mercy'.[122]

Post *Dudley and Stephens*

Despite this evidence of judicial sympathy for the plight of Dudley and Stephens whilst they were adrift and the recognition that few men might be expected to behave as the law was in effect requiring them to do, the defendants had nonetheless been convicted of murder and sentenced to death. The question now was what exactly should happen to them. It fell to the Home Secretary to make this decision. In this he had before him the jury's pleas for clemency, letters and petitions requesting that the sailors be pardoned,[123] along with the knowledge that there had been reference to leniency by the Queen's Bench judges – and, of course, there was the popular sympathy for the men as well as the notion of Dudley as a hero – and this, as we have seen, was something that particularly troubled him.

However, Harcourt rejected the possibility of an unconditional pardon, feeling that the adoption of this course would have the untenable effect of 'pronounc[ing] it an innocent act and deserving no punishment.' Moreover, this would 'condemn the law' as it would amount to stating that 'it has arrived at an unjust conclusion.'[124] The answer, it was resolved, was a commutation of sentence but not to a punishment which might be taken to be either unduly harsh or overly lenient. This decision was accordingly announced in mid-December 1884.[125] So, even at this stage of the proceedings, it seems that conveying the right message not only about the law but also about how Englishmen should behave remained a concern for those charged with the administration of the criminal justice system. Thus, as Simpson noted, the 'determination to secure a conviction for murder, combined with a humane and slightly inconsistent desire to see that [the sailors] did not suffer unduly in consequence' continued to the last.[126]

Beyond the Home Office and the various courtrooms where the case was considered and, aside from the popular feeling in favour of Dudley and Stephens, reaction to the case and the commutation of the sailors' sentences often reflected the views of Huddleston and Coleridge as to how males should and should not behave. Moreover, there was also a sense that conviction followed by clemency was the correct outcome.

For example, in the days following the Queen's Bench decision but before the Home Secretary had commuted the sentence, the periodical *John Bull* expressed approval of the case's outcome, was concerned about the level of support for the sailors and expressed a view as to the appropriate punishment. In doing so, its coverage highlighted fears of degeneration. In terms of what the sailors had done, the publication felt that it would be 'difficult to conceive of a more revolting and cowardly crime' than to 'foully [*sic*] slaughter a helpless lad' in order to save their 'loathsome lives'. Moreover, the paper argued that 'to admit that the pangs of hunger can excuse a similar atrocity is to degrade man to the level of the brutes' and expressed 'horror' that 'a portion of the public held that this revolting crime might be regarded as justifiable homicide', seeing this as 'strange evidence of depraved sentiment' on the part of the populous. Instead, the magazine felt that 'the natural instincts even of the most savage and degraded of barbarous peoples would have revolted against cowardly murder and cannibalism.' It was, therefore, hoped that 'a sentence of salutary severity' would 'effectively assert the elementary principles of justice and morality.'[127]

The *Standard* also seemed to draw upon concerns about atavistic behaviour in men, noting in its commentary on the judgment that if necessity were accepted, the result would be a backwards drift to brutality.[128] *The Times*'s approving editorial on the Queen's Bench decision felt it necessary to 'protest against the notion that in the extremity of hunger or thirst men are considered as released from all duties towards each other'. Echoing the concerns expressed by the judges, the paper's editorial addressed the dangers of allowing that strong men can sacrifice the weak, including women and children, in order to survive. Instead, men in dire circumstances should 'die heroically', like miners 'who are walled up in a subterranean gallery, with no food or water', or soldiers who refuse to opt for horrors such as those of which the crew of the *Mignonette* were guilty.[129] However, in keeping with the seemingly inconsistent approach to the case by legal authorities, the editorial emphasized that '[t]here was no wish to deal hardly with Dudley and Stephens', but also noted that the sailors had 'been the subjects of somewhat mawkish, ill-directed sympathy.'[130]

In broader legal circles too, there was support both for the decision in *Dudley and Stephens* and for its vision of how men should conduct themselves. For example, the *Law Journal* stated that:

> A man is not entitled to take the life of another in order to save his own, however great the necessity may be, unless that other is trying to take his life. He must accept his own lot, and die like a man. He has no right to consider his own life as more important than another's. The man who acts on the consideration that the life of others is of more importance than his own is a hero, and the man who acts on the converse estimate of himself in regard to an innocent person is a criminal.[131]

Here then, was a very clear perspective not only on what a man should not do but how he should behave when placed in danger – and this again reflected the kinds of ideas about manliness advocated by the likes of Smiles. Patently, an Englishman should at all costs demonstrate stoicism and selflessness even to the last; what is more, he should aim to act the hero.

Conclusion

This chapter has both constructed a detailed history of *Dudley and Stephens* and told a story about the case in which it was portrayed as being an attempt to bind men to a particularly idealized vision of Englishness when faced with the most desperate of plights. The defence of necessity was thereby rejected and the sailors were convicted. Despite the finding of guilt, however, a good deal of compassion for Dudley and Stephens was in evidence both within and beyond the courtrooms in which their case was decided – and in delivering the final judgment Coleridge was particularly keen not to castigate the defendants for their actions, not least as he felt that many men might struggle to live up to the standards of behaviour which he and his fellow judges were effectively imposing. *Dudley and Stephens* was then, to some extent, a case where abstract ideas about law and Englishmen were on trial and this was perhaps reflected in the fact that it was widely presumed that the men would not face execution for what they had done. However, the judgment was by no means merely symbolic; Dudley and Stephens did not escape punishment entirely and (with the procedure by which it was decided unchallenged) their case created a precedent which would bind future courts and, therefore, men (and women, although in cases involving females it might be presumed that judicial pronouncements would reflect distinct ideas as to sex and gender) who might try to claim that their criminality was negated by the extreme necessity of the situation in which they found themselves. Moreover, as *The Times*'s editorial on the Queen's Bench decision was at pains to point out, such understanding and clemency as was generally thought to be due to Dudley and Stephens would not be accorded to anyone who in the future was found to have conducted themselves in a manner similar to the sailors.[132]

This is not the whole story, however (as if it were ever possible to produce such a creature), not least because more can be said about the case in regard to men and manliness. Consequently, in moving towards its close, this chapter briefly turns to consider one more twist in the tale of the loss of the *Mignonette* by focusing upon the two sailors' perspectives on their actions. The defendants had their own particular view of what had passed in the boat – and there appeared to be considerable sympathy for their standpoint amongst the general public. In addition, the sailors' ideas seemed, according to Simpson, to be shared by other seafaring men and those who were familiar with their ways.[133] Indeed, it was fairly evident that there were those who felt the defendants' conduct had been justified because the custom of the sea should protect them from the legal niceties which applied on dry land. Thus, for example, in the early days of the legal proceedings the *Daily News* noted that 'public feeling at Falmouth, and, indeed, throughout the west of England' was not only 'one of deep sympathy for the unhappy men', but also that 'scarcely a word of condemnation of their desperate action is heard from any quarter'[134] – and a number of papers (including *The Times*) had made reference to the general mood towards Dudley and Stephens, which seemed to see them as 'only technically' guilty of murder. With this in mind, it is to Dudley and Stephen's versions of events that we now turn.

In stark contrast to conceptions of their behaviour as unmanly, unEnglish and barbaric, the defendants' accounts of their adventure embodied very different ideas about what a man should do in such circumstances as they had found themselves. As Dudley, in particular, but also Stephens saw it, they were honest men who did what they had to; what is more, their openness revealed that they believed they had done nothing wrong, let alone anything criminal. Thus, both the defendants appeared to have agreed that they had a duty to try to survive in order to provide for their families and protect them from the destitution which might well follow the loss of a male provider. In their view, they had decided that the boy was the obvious one to be sacrificed as he was closest to death and had no wife or children to support – and he was suffering, so killing him would be an act of kindness rather than of brutality. For example, Dudley recorded that he had asked Stephens: 'What is to be done? I believe the boy is dying. You have a wife and five children, and I have a wife and three children.'[135] In another of his accounts of their discussions he wrote that 'I said then it must be done it may save three lives so we put an end to his suffering'.[136]

For Dudley, there was also the sense that, as the captain, it was for him to look to the best for his crew – and that this, in the circumstances, might mean killing one of their number in order that the others might have a chance of survival. He, therefore, sought to take charge of the situation, as he had throughout (by being the last to leave the sinking yacht in an effort to try to get food and water, by making a sea anchor, plugging a hole in the boat, rationing the tins and by being the first to suggest killing and consuming someone for food in order that the rest might live). Thus, to his mind his actions were to be conceived of as manly and rational, if not heroic, rather than cowardly or in any way atavistic or savage.[137]

Consequently, re-examining Dudley and Stephens from the perspective of the sailors, it becomes evident that they were putting forward their own version of manliness which was both classed and specific to their livelihoods and, as Simpson highlighted, accorded with their knowledge of and adherence to the customs of the sea rather than the law of the land.[138] Here what the present analysis adds to Simpson's brilliant story of the case is the sense that these customs were very much concerned with the way in which men should behave in the most dire of situations; they provided a context-specific recipe for manliness.

Moreover, the sailors' ideas about male behaviour were by no means totally distinct from those espoused by Coleridge, Smiles and Kingsley. Indeed, the characteristics embraced here included a sense of duty and courage as well as a need to protect women – and theirs was very much a Christian model of behaviour. Thus, Dudley portrayed himself as a man of God even at the very moment of the murder, telling how 'I then offered a prayer for the poor boy's soul if were [sic] to commit such a rash act asked for forgiveness from our Maker'.[139]

It is at this point that we leave the masculine maritime world and head for dry land. The next two chapters consider men's violence towards women, looking first at sexual violence in the context of *R v Clarence* (1888)[140] and then marital non-sexual abuse focusing upon *R v Jackson* (1891).[141] And so it is to the East End of London that we now turn our attention.

Notes

1 (1884) 14 QBD 273; 49 JP 69; 54 LJMC 32; 15 Cox CC 624; 33 WR 347; [1881–5] All ER Rep 61; 52 LT 107; 1 TLR 118. These references refer to the different law reports in which the Court for Crown Cases Reserved decision was reported. Unless otherwise stated, references to this judgment in this chapter are taken from (1884) 14 QBD 273, although the other reports of the case were consulted in constructing this chapter. As the name suggests, a law report is a published account of

courtroom proceedings in a case. It is produced for lawyers and generally includes a summary of the facts which led the parties to come to court and the legal decision as well as the text of the judge's or judges' legal pronouncements.

2 Lord Chief Justice Coleridge in *Dudley and Stephens* at 287.

3 No charges were brought as to their use of Parker's body as cannibalism was not a criminal offence.

4 The assizes heard the most serious of criminal cases and were essentially a forerunner of the Crown Court. Circuit judges travelled the country, presiding over cases. On the assizes see further, J.H. Baker, *An Introduction to English Legal History*, 4th edn, London: Butterworths, 2002, pp. 20–2.

5 The *Law Journal* was of the view that there was scope for an appeal by way of a writ of error specifically because the procedure used to try and convict Dudley and Stephens was incorrect. See 'Obiter Dicta', 6 December 1884, p. 725 and 'The Case of the Mignonette', 13 December 1884, pp. 742–4. See also A.W.B. Simpson, *Cannibalism and the Common Law: The Story of the Tragic Last Voyage of the Mignonette and the Strange Legal Proceedings to Which It Gave Rise*, Chicago: University of Chicago Press, 1984, p. 223.

6 See Simpson, *Cannibalism*, p. 204 and HO 144/141/A36934 (petition regarding sentence from Dudley to Home Secretary, 7 January 1885). The assumption was widely reported in the press. For example, see: *Daily News*, 10 December 1884, p. 2; *The Times*, 10 December 1884, p. 9.

7 See also, for example: H. Stephen, 'Murder by Necessity', *Law Quarterly Review*, 1, 1885, 51–61; M.G. Mallin, 'In Warm Blood: Some Historical and Procedural Aspects of Regina v Dudley and Stephens', *University of Chicago Law Review*, 34, 1967, 377–407; G. Williams, 'A Commentary on *R v Dudley and Stephens*', *Cambrian Law Review*, 8, 1977, 94–9; D. McCormick, *Blood on the Sea: The Terrible Story of the Yawl 'Mignonette'*, London: Muller, 1962.

8 The focus upon men was also evident in Simpson's tale-telling in *Cannibalism*. Indeed, despite the fact that he was not consciously writing about gender, this text was very much concerned with the male of the species, with its accounts of the maritime world and the sailors.

9 See TNA: PRO KB 6/6(2), DPP 4/17, HO 144/141/A36934, HO 34/52. Simpson gives a more complete list of the available archive material, *Cannibalism*, p. 326.

10 The initial text of the verdict was reproduced in *The Times*, 7 November 1884, p. 11. Its amended form, following some of the defence objections being accepted, is given at the beginning of the Queen's Bench law report (*Dudley and Stephens* at 273–5). For the amendments, the objections and the judicial response, see, for example: TNA: PRO DPP 4/17, pp. 240–3. See also Simpson, *Cannibalism*, pp. 226–9.

11 For example, early reports of the wreck include: *Birmingham Daily Post*, 8 September 1884, p. 8; *North-Eastern Daily Gazette*, 6 September 1884, p. 4 (2nd edn); *Belfast News-Letter*, 8 September 1884, p. 5; *Aberdeen Weekly Journal*, 9 September 1884, p. 3. Interviews with Stephens were published in a number of papers: *Daily News*, 13 September 1884, p. 6; *Lloyd's Weekly Newspaper*, 14 September 1884, p. 7; *Reynolds's Newspaper*, 14 September 1884, p. 5.

12 *The Times* gave a particularly good account of the proceedings in London, complete with some helpful supplementary commentary (5 December 1884, p. 3 and 10 December 1884, pp. 3, 6, 9).

13 For example, see: 'Homicide by Necessity', *Criminal Law Magazine and Reporter*, 6, 1885, 95–102 and 361–78.

14 The story told in this section is constructed from the special verdict, the sailor's different accounts, newspaper reports and Simpson's *Cannibalism*.

15 This was reflected, for example, by Brooks's statements about Dudley within the legal proceedings, see TNA: PRO DPP 4/17, pp. 36, 109. On Dudley's career and standing see further Simpson, *Cannibalism*, pp. 22–4 – as regards the other sailors see pp. 30–8.
16 See Simpson, *Cannibalism*, pp. 42–3.
17 For example, see TNA: PRO DPP 4/17, pp. 9, 12, 17–18, 32–3 and KB 6/6 (2).
18 For example, see TNA: PRO DPP 4/17, pp. 18–19, 31, 33 and KB 6/6 (2).
19 There was a lack of clarity as to days in the sailors' various accounts but the 20th was taken by the court as the agreed day. See Simpson, *Cannibalism*, pp. 61–2.
20 For example, see TNA: PRO DPP 4/17, pp. 18, 34–5 and KB 6/6 (2).
21 For example, see TNA: PRO DPP 4/17, p. 28 and KB 6/6 (2).
22 For example, see TNA: PRO DPP 4/17, p. 19 and KB 6/6 (2).
23 For example, see the account of Dudley's conversation with the man who piloted the *Moctezuma* into Falmouth harbour in Simpson, *Cannibalism*, pp. 2–3.
24 Brooks's original account no longer survives, so it is not clear what he said. See Simpson's *Cannibalism*, pp. 7, 10. Dudley made six or seven different written accounts of the events, which included some factual variations, some of which are cited here.
25 My very brief summary of the events upon their arrival in Falmouth relies largely upon Simpson, *Cannibalism*, pp. 2–11.
26 The information about the police court hearings depicted here is drawn from press reports of the case, cross-referenced with Simpson, *Cannibalism*, ch. 4. For press reports see, for example: *Morning Post*, 9 September 1884, p. 2; *Standard*, 9 September 1884, p. 3; *Bristol Mercury and Daily Post*, 9 September 1884, p. 8.
27 See, for example, *Standard*, 9 September 1884, p. 3.
28 See: TNA: PRO HO 144/141/A36934, communications between the Board of Trade and Home Office dated the week of the 8 September 1884; TNA: PRO HO 34/52, pp. 239–40; Simpson, *Cannibalism*, p. 77.
29 See 'Regina v Archer and Miller: The Leading Case that Never Was', *Oxford Journal of Legal Studies*, 2(2), 1982, 181–96 and *Cannibalism*, ch. 7.
30 Quoted by Simpson, 'Regina v Archer and Miller', p. 189.
31 Quoted by Simpson, ibid., p. 192.
32 See *Cannibalism*, p. 195.
33 For example, see the reports of this hearing in *The Times*, 12 September 1884, p. 4; *Daily News*, 11 September 1884, p. 5; *Royal Cornwall Gazette*, 12 September 1884, p. 4. For reports of subsequent Falmouth proceedings see, for example: *Birmingham Daily* Post, 19 September 1884, p. 5; *North-Eastern Daily Gazette*, 19 September 1884, p. 2; *York Herald*, 19 September 1884, p. 5.
34 *Cannibalism*, p. 79.
35 12 September 1884, p. 4.
36 Ibid.
37 See, for example, *North-Eastern Daily Gazette*, 6 September 1884 (2nd edn), p. 4.
38 On this hearing see, for example: *Bristol Mercury and Daily Post*, 19 September 1884, p. 8; *Daily News*, 19 September 1884, p. 2; *Royal Cornwall Gazette Falmouth Packet*, 19 September 1884, pp. 6, 8.
39 On the role and composition of the grand jury in relation to Dudley and Stephens see Simpson *Cannibalism*, pp. 198–9.
40 The story of the happenings on this day is drawn from press reports of the proceedings, supplemented by Simpson's description and analysis, *Cannibalism*, ch. 8. See, for example: *Daily News*, 4 November 1884, p. 3; *Morning Post*, 4 November 1884, p. 3; *The Times*, 4 November 1884, p. 3; *Royal Cornwall Gazette*, 7 November, 1884, p. 5.

41 For example, see: *Daily News*, 4 November 1884, p. 3; *Morning Post*, 4 November 1884, p. 3; *The Times*, 4 November 1884, p. 3. Simpson commented on how 'exceptional and indeed irregular' this was; see *Cannibalism*, p. 202.
42 For example, see *Daily News*, 4 November 1884, p. 3.
43 This being an entirely different panel from the 23 who had just decided that the matter could proceed. The story of the trial told here is drawn from the transcript of the proceedings (TNA: PRO DPP 4/17, pp. 47–219) and newspaper reports. For press reports of the court proceedings that day see, for example: *The Times*, 7 November 1884, p. 11; *Daily News*, 7 November 1884, p. 3; *Morning Post*, 7 November 1884, p. 6; *Standard*, 7 November 1884, p. 3; *Lloyd's Weekly Newspaper*, 9 November 1884, p. 5; *Royal Cornwall Gazette*, 14 November 1884, p. 4.
44 7 November 1884, p. 11.
45 TNA: PRO DPP 4/17, pp. 47–75. In terms of press reports see, for example, *The Times*, 7 November 1884, p. 11.
46 See TNA: PRO DPP 4/17, pp. 76–81.
47 Ibid., p. 79 and see, for example, *Daily News*, 7 November 1884, p. 3. Contemporary commentators differed as to whether an acquittal was a real possibility – and whether a judge should attempt to pre-empt any such concern. See, in particular, 'The Case of the Mignonette', *Law Journal*, 13 December 1884, p. 742.
48 See TNA: PRO DPP 4/17, pp. 82–110. See also his Falmouth deposition at pp. 32–7.
49 See TNA: PRO DPP 4/17, pp. 111–18.
50 See ibid., pp. 119–39.
51 See Huddleston's comment, ibid., p. 81.
52 This was achieved with the help of Huddleston, see *The Times*, 7 November 1884, p. 11 and TNA: PRO DPP 4/17, pp. 99–102, 104–8, 110.
53 TNA: PRO DPP 4/17, pp. 144–52, see especially pp. 149–50. See also, for example, *The Times*, 7 November 1884, p. 11.
54 See, for example, *The Times*, 7 November 1884, p. 11 and TNA: PRO DPP 4/17, p. 165.
55 See, for example, *The Times*, 7 November 1884, p. 11 and TNA: PRO DPP 4/17, p. 181.
56 TNA: PRO DPP 4/17, pp.186–206.
57 See TNA: PRO DPP 4/17, pp. 206–219. In fact, he had offered this text for the lawyers' perusal earlier in the proceedings, see pp. 79–80.
58 *Cannibalism*, p. 213.
59 10 December 1884, p. 3. Such concerns were being expressed elsewhere as well. For example, see 'The Case of the Mignonette', *Law Journal*, 13 December 1884, p. 742.
60 See, for example, *The Times*, 5 December 1884, p. 3.
61 For the procedural discussions as to where the case should be heard see, in particular, TNA: PRO DPP 4/17, pp. 221–38. The *Law Journal* felt that the procedure adopted was incorrect and could have resulted in a successful appeal by way of writ of error. See: 'Obiter Dicta', 8 November 1884, p. 666; 'Case of the Mignonette', 29 November 1884, p. 711; 'Obiter Dicta', 6 December 1884, p. 725; 'Obiter Dicta', 13 December 1884, p. 742; 'The Case of the Mignonette', 13 December 1884, pp. 742–3. Simpson also provided a helpful discussion of these procedural issues; see *Cannibalism*, pp. 208–23, 236–7.
62 The story of the London proceedings on 4 December given here is drawn from a number of sources, as each record details slightly different things. Aside from the law reports, these include the official transcript (TNA: PRO DPP 4/17, pp. 239–390), different press accounts and other contemporary publications.
63 *The Times*, 5 December 1884, p. 3.

64 See: *Dudley and Stephens* at 275–8; TNA: PRO DPP 4/17, pp. 241–66; *The Times*, 5 December 1884, p. 3.
65 See TNA: PRO DPP 4/17, pp. 267–80.
66 For Collins's arguments see ibid., pp. 281–366.
67 See, for example: *The Times*, 5 December 1884, p. 3; *Morning Post*, 5 December 1884, p. 6.
68 Something that was made much of, given the fact that they were in the middle of judging a case about 'extreme hunger', in a humorous sketch in *Funny Folks*, 20 December 1884, p. 404.
69 See, for example, the report carried in the *Morning Post*, 5 December 1884, p. 6 and TNA: PRO DPP 4/17, p. 366.
70 *Dudley and Stephens* at 278.
71 See, in particular, the discussions in TNA: PRO DPP 4/17, pp. 366–90.
72 See, for example, the report in the *Morning Post*, 5 December 1884, p. 6 and TNA: PRO DPP 4/17, p. 390.
73 *Dudley and Stephens* at 288.
74 See TNA: PRO KB 33/46 Thomas Dudley and Edwin Stephens; Conditional Pardons, 15 December 1884.
75 On their first days in prison and the wait for news as to the capital sentence see, for example: *Daily News*, 10 December 1884, p. 2.
76 See *Cannibalism*, pp. 282–305.
77 For a discussion of more recent consideration of developments in relation to necessity see, for example, R. Huxtable, 'Logical Separation? Conjoined Twins, Slippery Slopes and Resource Allocation', *Journal of Social Welfare and Family Law*, 23(4), 2001, 459–71.
78 On degeneracy see, for example: W. Greenslade, *Degeneration, Culture and the Novel 1880–1940*, Cambridge: Cambridge University Press, 1994, especially ch. 1; D. Pick, *Faces of Degeneration: A European Disorder c.1848–c.1918*, Cambridge: Cambridge University Press, 1989.
79 London: Macmillan.
80 Ibid., p. 33.
81 Ibid., pp. 58–62.
82 See 'The Science of Culture' in *Primitive Culture: Researches into the Development of Mythology, Philosophy, Religion, Art, and Custom*, London: John Murray, 1871, vol. 2, pp. 115–17.
83 On the idea of 'degeneration within' civilized European nations as well as in the savage of empire, see, for example, Pick, *Faces of Degeneration*, pp. 37–44 (although, here his focus is upon France).
84 In terms of early criminology in England and its links with psychiatry, including these kinds of discussions, see further, D. Garland, 'British Criminology Before 1935', *British Journal of Criminology*, 28(2), 1988, 1–17, pp. 3–5. On the links made between crime and degeneration in England, see, for example, Pick, *Faces of Degeneration*, ch. 7.
85 *Health and Education*, London: Isbister, 1874, pp. 11, 22, 67.
86 London: John Murray.
87 London: John Murray. The references here are from the 1874 edition (London: John Murray).
88 P.158. Andrew Smith's *Victorian Demons: Medicine, Masculinity and the Gothic at the Fin-de-Siècle* gives an excellent introduction to the thinking of Lankaster, Kingsley and Smiles, along with other contemporary theorists and writings about men – and his take on the topic seems to fit very well with the subject matter of *Dudley and Stephens* (Manchester: Manchester University Press, 2004, pp. 17–21, ch. 1).

89 *Character*, pp. 364–6.
90 See *Character*, p. 159.
91 On the *Birkenhead* see, for example, A.C. Addison, *The Story of the Birkenhead: A Record of British Heroism*, London: Unwin, 1902.
92 On the custom see *Cannibalism*, ch. 5.
93 11 September 1884, p. 5.
94 This phrase is used in 'The Case of the Mignonette', *Law Journal*, 13 December 1884, p. 743.
95 TNA: PRO KB 6/6(2).
96 Ibid.
97 See, for example, the *New York Times*, 7, 28 September, 7 November, 8, 10 December 1884. These articles are available at http://www.nytimes.com (accessed 30 March 2013).
98 *Cannibalism*, p. 83.
99 Ibid., p. 89.
100 See, TNA: PRO DPP 4/17, pp. 359–65 and *Dudley and Stephens* at 280–1.
101 See TNA: PRO DPP 4/17, pp. 364–5 and *The Times*, 5 December 1884, p. 3.
102 This is the form of words recorded in *The Times* report, 7 November 1884, p. 11.
103 *Dudley and Stephens* at 279.
104 Ibid.
105 Ibid.
106 Ibid., at 286.
107 Ibid., at 287.
108 Ibid., at 288.
109 Ibid., at 287.
110 Ibid.
111 Ibid.
112 Ibid., at 288.
113 Ibid., at 287.
114 Ibid., at 283.
115 Ibid., at 288.
116 Ibid., at 287.
117 Ibid., at 281.
118 Ibid., at 288.
119 Ibid.
120 Ibid., at 279.
121 Ibid., at 288.
122 Ibid.
123 A number of such pleas from the public are included in TNA: PRO HO 144/141/A36934.
124 Ibid. These passages are quoted and discussed by Simpson in *Cannibalism*, p. 247.
125 See ibid. and Simpson's discussion of the decision in *Cannibalism*, pp. 242–8. The communication of the news to the prisoners was reported in *The Times*, 15 December 1884, p. 6.
126 *Cannibalism*, p. 79.
127 6 December 1884, p. 798.
128 15 December 1884, p. 4.
129 10 December 1884, p. 9.
130 10 December 1884, p. 9.
131 'The Case of the Mignonette', 13 December 1884, p. 744.
132 10 December 1884, p. 9.

133 On the well-known tradition of killing and cannibalism at sea see, for example, *Cannibalism*, p. 140.
134 11 September 1884, p. 5.
135 TNA: PRO KB 6/6(2).
136 TNA: PRO KB 6/6(2). See also TNA: PRO DPP 4/17, p. 18.
137 For example, his account in the depositions put before the trial court had him deciding to kill Parker when his fellows shrank from so acting, see TNA: PRO DPP 4/17, p. 18 and see generally pp. 13–20.
138 See, in particular, *Cannibalism*, ch. 5.
139 TNA: PRO KB 6/6(2). See also Dudley's description of this prayer in the deposition laid before the court in Exeter; TNA: PRO DPP 4/17, p. 18.
140 (1888) 22 QBD 23; 53 JP 149; 58 LJMC 10; 16 Cox CC 511; 37 WR 166; [1886–90] All ER Rep 133; 59 LT 780; 5 TLR 61.
141 [1891–4] All ER Rep 61; [1891] 1 QB 671; 60 LJQB 346; 64 LT 679; 55 JP 246; 7 TLR 382.

Chapter 4

R v Clarence 1888[1]

Supervising sex

> I cannot … be a party to a judgment which in effect would proclaim to the world that by the law of England in this year 1888 a man may deliberately, knowingly, and maliciously perpetrate upon the body of his wife the abominable outrage charged against the prisoner, and yet not be punishable criminally for such atrocious barbarity.[2]

The *Clarence* case concerned a wife, Selina Clarence, who contracted a sexually transmitted infection or (as such ailments were then known) venereal disease from her husband, Charles Clarence, through vaginal intercourse. Charles[3] was charged, prosecuted and convicted of two *non-sexual* offences against the person in relation to the disease transmission. This being a difficult and controversial case, it was then sent by the judge to the Court for Crown Cases Reserved (CCCR) so that the legal questions concerned could be authoritatively ruled upon, thereby creating a precedent which would be applied by future courts. In the CCCR a majority of nine proceeded to find that Charles had committed no offence, whether *non-sexual* or *sexual*, the other four judges being minded to confirm the jury's decision. As a consequence, the husband's convictions were quashed.[4] In so deciding, the court considered a number of legal questions. These included: the 'marital rape exemption', by which a wife was deemed to have consented to 'natural' sexual relations with her husband for the duration of the contract (meaning that, although a husband could be convicted of non-sexual abuse in relation to his wife,[5] he could not be convicted of raping or indecently assaulting his spouse – but would find himself in a very different position if anal intercourse was alleged[6]); the effect of fraudulently obtained consent to sexual intercourse; and the legal implications of disease transmission.

So, *Clarence* involved an ultimately unsuccessful attempt to legally categorize what Charles had done as a form of *non-sexual* violence perpetrated against Selina. However, as the brief account of the case given above suggests, *Clarence* was actually very much about *sex*, the legal supervision of sexual relations between men and women and, more specifically, between husbands and wives. Indeed, this is how it is cast here. Thus, the stories told in this chapter focus upon male sexual behaviour towards women and consider closely related ideas regarding male sexual immorality, including: attitudes towards extra-marital and marital sexual relations; thinking about the rights, privileges and duties of a husband towards his wife in relation to sexual matters; and worries concerning the spread of venereal diseases by men.

Clarence has been written about before in the context of historical work on sex, wives and women working as prostitutes and has been considered by legal academics looking at offences against the person, marital rape and disease transmission.[7] Also, there is scholarship on gender, law and marriage in the period that considers the case and provides useful information about the milieu in which it took place.[8] Such work is drawn upon here and forms a backdrop to the story-telling and argument. However, this chapter differs from previous writings about *Clarence* in a number of respects. First, it offers a little more factual detail about the Clarences and the court case than has previously been provided. Secondly, its focus is on both cases heard in the trial courts around the country and those reserved for review by a panel of judges in London. Thirdly and most importantly, it considers the case in terms of contemporary ideas about men.

The text below begins by recounting the events which led to *Clarence*, what happened in the courts and the decision. It then moves to the construction of a tale about the case which develops this book's 'binding men' narrative by setting the litigation in the context of late Victorian concerns about men's sexual conduct in relation to adult women[9] and efforts to rein in and legally bind the male of the species to better sexual behaviour – with the focus on criminal law. In terms of the case itself, as there is little information about the trial and the attempt to restrain men within *Clarence* was ultimately unsuccessful, it is the views of the minority of the CCCR that form the focus of attention. However, the majority judgments briefly figure, not least as they too featured a variety of strong but sometimes very different views about men, women and sex. To set these in context, there is some discussion of wider resistance to imposing legal limits upon male sexual freedom and the related notion that females rather than males were largely to blame for the spread of sexual diseases is also considered. So, whilst this chapter focuses upon efforts to set boundaries, including legal restrictions, upon male sexual behaviour, it also includes consideration of opposition to this – opposition which, of course carried the day in *Clarence*; although, as we shall see, things were not always this straightforward as, for instance, in the case of at least one of the majority judges the decision not to hold Charles criminally liable for his actions seemed to have been taken somewhat reluctantly.

Clarence

The account provided in this section is reconstructed from a number of different sources. The fullest version of the facts which led to *Clarence*, along with the courtroom proceedings and eventual decision, was provided by the law reports of the CCCR's decision. In terms of the trial, the Central Criminal Court censored its record, with the Old Bailey Proceedings merely stating that its subject matter was 'unfit for publication' and other surviving documents give little by way of additional information.[10] Newspapers seemed to follow this lead, meaning that little can be said about what transpired at trial. When *Clarence* reached the CCCR it was reported in the press, although the details tended to be obscured.[11] For example, *The Times* covered the proceedings in the CCCR[12] and, along with the *British Medical Journal*, it published a good report of the court's decision, although neither actually stated what the disease was or how it was transmitted.[13] A few professional journals included commentaries on the case, as did some other contemporary commentators, providing additional information.[14] Surviving documents relating to the CCCR case do not add much to the story provided in other sources.[15] However, searching census data and registers of marriages and births has in this case aided the provision of a little more background as to the wife and husband at the centre of *Clarence*.

The infection of Selina

From the facts found by the jury it appeared that on Tuesday 20 December 1887[16] Charles James Clarence (aged 28)[17] and Selina Clarence had consensual sexual relations (or as the statement of the facts had it, he 'had connection with her'),[18] which we can surmise involved penile-vaginal sex. At the time, Charles apparently knew that he had gonorrhoea and that he was likely to transmit this to his wife. He did not, however, tell Selina about the state of his health and she contracted the infection. Whilst she had consented to the sexual activity, she maintained that she would not have done so had she known about her husband's condition.

Beyond this, reports and records of the case give precious little information. However, a little foraging means that a few further details can be provided. Censuses and records of births, deaths and marriages[19] reveal that Selina, whose maiden name was Foster, was born in 1862 or 1863 and the couple were married on 12 August 1880 at St Mary Magdalene Church, Woolwich, London. They apparently had two children: Charles James Foster Clarence's baptism was recorded as taking place on 27 September 1885 (born 5 September), whilst Ethel A. Clarence was recorded as having been born in 1882 or 4, depending on the record. On the 1885 baptism record of their son, the father's occupation was given as Clerk and the family were living at 9 Oliffe (or Olliffe) Terrace, Manchester Road on the Isle of

Dogs in the East End of London,[20] a relatively respectable, wholly working-class area.[21] Moving forward to the years after the case, by the 1891 census Selina's occupation was given as 'Certificated Teacher of Elementary School' and she was living with the children in Canal Street, Mile End; there was no mention of Charles in the entry.[22]

All this seems to indicate that Charles and Selina were not without learning, were by no means amongst the poorest of the East End's inhabitants and might well have been viewed as being relatively respectable for their class. Whatever Selina and Charles's precise circumstances, it appears that Selina chose to seek justice for her husband's transmission of venereal disease to her (and perhaps also indirectly for the adultery which had presumably led to his infection) through the criminal law.

The trial

Charles Clarence was tried at the Central Criminal Court (the Old Bailey) during the Sessions which commenced on Monday 23 April 1888. There he faced two counts under the Offences Against the Person Act 1861. The charges were that, by infecting her with gonorrhoea, he unlawfully and maliciously inflicted grievous bodily harm upon his wife (section 20) and that, in so doing, he had also assaulted her occasioning actual bodily harm (section 47). Charles was not legally represented at this stage in the proceedings.

Whatever the contentions that were put before and discussed in the Old Bailey in relation to these issues, at the close of arguments, the Recorder of London, who presided over the case, told the jury that, if they found the facts to be proved, they could convict Charles on either count, despite the fact that he was married to Selina.[23] On the basis of this judicial direction the panel of 12 men decided to find Charles guilty on both counts but also made a recommendation of mercy, which seemed to suggest that they were not totally unsympathetic towards the defendant.[24] This was not the end of the matter, though, as the Recorder felt it to be of sufficient importance and uncertainty to reserve judgment, respite sentence and refer the legal issues for an authoritative statement. Thus, the arguments were to be considered by the CCCR. Charles seemed at this point to have been remanded in custody[25] but, according to the Old Bailey records, was subsequently released on bail on 13 June, following the first CCCR hearing of the case (see further below), with his mother acting as surety.[26]

The review

The CCCR had been created in 1848 by the Crown Cases Act. It was a court of review rather than a court of appeal – in fact, there was no court of criminal appeal until one was created by the 1907 Criminal Appeal Act, which in turn brought the older court to an end. The CCCR consisted of all the common law judges who went on circuit, presiding over the assizes[27] around the country (the exact number of judges increased during its lifespan). In the normal course, cases were heard by a panel of five of the judges; however, where the five were divided and felt the matter to be of sufficient importance or controversy, it could be considered by all the available judges (as happened in the present case).

The CCCR could only hear cases which had resulted in a conviction and was empowered to consider only matters referred to it by a judge. Neither the defence nor the prosecution had any say in whether a case should be referred, although lawyers could ask for this to be considered. Generally, if the decision was taken to reserve a case to the CCCR, sentencing would either be respited or, once sentence was passed, a convicted person would be released on bail, whilst the legal questions and their consequences were resolved.

On the day the case came before the CCCR for consideration, the judge who had presided over the trial would state or present the basic facts (on paper and sometimes also appearing in person), as well as the legal questions to be resolved, to the judges.[28] Matters would then be argued by prosecution counsel (assuming there was one) and, if a defendant was represented, their lawyer, with the judges often interjecting repeatedly. Occasionally there would be no one representing either side of the matter, so the judges would merely discuss it amongst themselves.[29] The CCCR could only rule upon the matters of law reserved for its consideration – and they were left to accept the findings of the jury as to the facts of the case. The effect of such a decision would be either to quash or to affirm a conviction; if the latter course was decided upon, the 'prisoner' or 'defendant' would be recalled to the trial court, so that the sentence could be either confirmed or pronounced ('appellant' was not the correct term as this was no appeal – and 'prisoner' was often used regardless of whether the person was in custody). Where the result was an acquittal this would be noted at the next sitting of the trial court and the defendants would be formally discharged.[30]

Clarence was scheduled to be heard by the CCCR on Saturday 9 June 1888, with Lord Chief Justice Coleridge, along with Justices Manisty, Hawkins, Wills and Grantham forming the judicial panel.[31] However, Coleridge put the proceedings off for a week. According to the report in *The Times*, upon entering the courtroom he first set down that the prisoner should be provided with counsel by the Treasury as 'it was a case of greatest importance, involving questions of serious difficulty'. He then stated that the case should be heard before all the judges because initial discussions had made it clear that differences of opinion already existed.[32] Thus, the case was postponed to allow for counsel to be arranged and to permit all 15 of the panel to be present.

The case came before the CCCR on Saturday 16 June 1888. Of the 15 judges, two were not available, so the case was heard by Lord Chief Justice

Coleridge, Barons Pollock and Huddleston, Justices Stephen, Manisty, Mathew, A.L. Smith, Wills, Grantham, Field, Hawkins, Day and Charles.[33] The Recorder's statement of the case called upon the 13 to consider whether his legal direction was right and, in doing so, whether Charles could be convicted on both or either of the counts.

As a result of Coleridge's intervention on 9 June, at this hearing Charles was represented by one Forrest Fulton, instructed by the Solicitor to the Treasury. The prosecution case was put by Mr Poland. From the limited information available, it seemed that a great deal, if not most, of the two-hour long courtroom argument and discussion which ensued[34] concerned the laws relating to sex and marriage, along with some consideration of previous cases concerning disease transmission, including the communication of venereal diseases.[35] Thus, on behalf of the defence, Fulton's arguments regarding the section 20 charge of unlawfully and maliciously inflicting grievous bodily harm included discussion of what he portrayed as the long-established rule that a husband could not be convicted of raping his wife, as by marriage she had consented to sexual relations with him for as long as the union should endure.[36] This was based upon the words of Chief Justice Hale, who in 1736 had written that 'by their mutual matrimonial consent and contract the wife hath given up herself in this kind to her husband, which she cannot retract'.[37] As a result of this, Fulton argued that what Charles had done (having sexual connection with his wife) could not be described as 'unlawful' and this was an element of the offence which had to be proved if a guilty verdict was to be reached.[38] Moreover, he opined that the section required the infliction of grievous bodily harm to be 'malicious', meaning that it be intentional – and there was nothing to show that Charles had intended to infect his wife.[39]

In terms of the section 47 charge of assault occasioning actual bodily harm, Fulton maintained that '[i]f coition, as between husband and wife, cannot constitute rape, it follows that coition cannot as between them constitute an assault by the husband',[40] so Charles had not committed the offence. What is more, he emphasized that not only was consent to 'coition' on the part of a wife a matrimonial obligation, but the wife in the present case had actually consented to the specific sexual encounter which had caused her to be infected with gonorrhoea – so according to him all this meant that there could be no conviction under section 47.[41]

In addition, in order to sustain his arguments Fulton dismissed and distinguished recent cases where it had been found that the transmission of venereal disease could, at least in some instances, constitute offences against the person. He also distinguished those authorities which suggested that some kinds of fraud might vitiate consent in the context of sexual offences (some of these cases are considered below).[42]

Poland for the prosecution argued that Charles was guilty on both counts, rejecting the proposition that a husband could not be convicted of raping his wife.[43] Controversially, he did so by maintaining that Hale's pronouncements regarding marriage were 'not supported by any other authority'. So, if 'the prisoner had effected his purpose by force, the prosecutrix [Selina] knowing his condition and resisting', this would have constituted rape.

In addition, Poland contended that Selina should not be viewed as having consented to the specific occurrence of sexual intercourse which caused her to be infected because her agreement was given when she was unaware of her husband's condition (that is, her consent was fraudulently obtained) and would not have been forthcoming had she known of the true state of affairs. So, for Poland, the marital exemption not being valid and consent being absent, Charles had been rightly convicted under sections 20 and 47 as his conduct was both 'unlawful' and an 'assault'.

Unsurprisingly, in so arguing Poland relied upon the very past cases (on venereal disease transmission and fraud) that Fulton had rejected. Indeed, having dismissed the marital rape exemption, he in effect maintained that they should be extended so as to apply to offences committed within marriage.[44]

Following the lawyers' representations, the judges retired to consider their decision. After half an hour they re-emerged.[45] The matter had continued to be controversial and the men were, as Coleridge's previous comments had suggested might be the case, divided, so judgment was reserved. Indeed, Coleridge stated that 'they may take some time' and Charles was to remain on bail.[46]

The decision

The judgments were finally handed down on Saturday 10 November 1888.[47] The majority – Wills, Stephen, Grantham, Mathew, Smith, Huddleston, Manisty, Pollock and Coleridge – took the husband's side, deciding that no offence could have been committed. Field, Hawkins, Day and Charles dissented, finding for the prosecution.[48]

In general terms, most of the judges came to the conclusion that no offences were committed in *Clarence* as through the contract of marriage a wife consented to sexual relations with her husband, although the multiple majority judgments explored the issues in slightly different ways and rehearsed other arguments as well. For the minority, amongst other things, the consent of a wife in marriage was not absolute and Charles's behaviour constituted the offences against the person of which he had been convicted by the jury at trial.

Binding men and criminalizing male sexual violence

That *Clarence* was a controversial and legally important case was clear from the way in which it was handled in the courts. Not only was it reserved to the CCCR, but it was also argued before the full court and there was a delay in the delivery of judgment because the judges could not agree upon its proper outcome. However, tightly entwined with the legal issues in the case were ideas about men. More specifically, despite the fact that the case concerned non-sexual offences against the person, it was very much about men's sexual relations with women. Consequently, it is possible to re-narrate *Clarence* in terms of contemporary ideas about men, sex, violence and (im)morality, with the views of the minority in the CCCR depicted as forming a part of efforts to rein in and legally bind men in the latter half of the nineteenth century.

The pre-*Clarence* context

Worries about male sexual conduct towards women to whom they were not married were frequently expressed in the nineteenth century, with such concerns often linked to thinking about men's immorality. Here the focus often fell upon the working classes and, in particular, the lowliest members of society, who were frequently presumed to be disreputable, lawless and Godless, although the behaviour of other classes of men could also be a source of unease – and, of course, this concentration on the bad behaviour of the poorest did not necessarily have much to do with how debauched and criminal their behaviour actually was in comparison to that of other sections of society.

Various sources both encouraged and fed these classed anxieties. In particular, there was the work of social reformers and researchers, with their investigations into the lives of the poor and stories of crime. The writings of Henry Mayhew on London, for example, suggested that sexual depravity and criminality was rife amongst the nethermost orders of society, at least in the capital. His findings were first circulated in the *Morning Chronicle*, but were subsequently collected together in book form and, consequently, reached a wide audience. The fourth and final volume of his *London Labour and London Poor* was published in 1861 and dealt, amongst other things, with prostitution.[49] Whilst the focus was upon categorizing the girls and women involved and describing their lives, his stories also purportedly revealed the conduct of the men who inhabited this world, highlighting sexual dissolution in the lower levels of society, with occasional glimpses of unprincipled conduct in all classes of men.[50]

Newspapers also served to highlight concerns about men and sex by their reporting of alleged attacks against women and any resultant trials in the criminal courts – and they too tended to centre upon the lives of the poor. The more populist and sensationalist publications, including the illustrated press, along with local papers, devoted large amounts of space to crime stories and some of this related to offences of a sexual nature, including the rape and indecent assault of women. However, as reports of *Clarence* demonstrated, the press at this time sometimes (but not always) censored the details and were, as Kim Stevenson has observed, 'ambiguous and cryptic'.[51] Nevertheless, even in such expurgated accounts the implications of sexual impropriety were usually still clear, not least because any charges which were brought against a man were generally cited and some papers revelled in signifying the sexual nature of the incident, either by the use of sensationalist descriptions in their article headings, or by emphasizing the fact that the specifics of the allegations were not judged to be appropriate for publication.

For instance, in February 1878 the *Bristol Mercury and Daily Post* included a story headed 'Alleged Outrage at Weston-Super-Mare' concerning Ellen Courtney, who was harassed, chased and indecently assaulted by Thomas Harris, 'a respectably-attired young man'.[52] The following year the same paper reported 'The Gross Outrage on a Bristol Woman Near Glastonbury.' Thomas Pike was accused of raping and robbing Mary Brooks as she walked from Glastonbury to Butleigh with her nine-year-old son, Richard.[53] Both these stories gave some information about what was alleged to have taken place – and they hinted at more. In contrast, the details of an attack by a police constable on 19-year-old Jessie Henderson at Birkenhead, which appeared to have included rape, was deemed to be 'not fit for publication' by the *Cheshire Observer* in 1872; the headline disguised the nature of the crime, merely announcing that there was a 'Double Charge of Felony Against a Policeman'.[54]

It was not unusual for such press stories of alleged sex crimes and of trials for sexual offences to include the expression of anxieties as to the behaviour of the man or men involved – or more general concerns about male sexual conduct towards women. For example, in January 1870 the *Essex Standard* reported the conviction of William Cousens, who worked for a grocer and draper, for assaulting two domestic servants, Esther Young and Rhoda Kettle, during a religious service. The facts given indicate that the non-consensual touching was sexual. Reference was made in evidence presented by the vicar and by their employer, who supported the young women, to the fact that there had been a number of complaints that women had been 'insulted and interfered with … by idle youths' and they felt that such behaviour needed to be stopped. Consequently, the case was 'put forward on public grounds.'[55]

In the context of such accounts of male immorality and sexual violence, it was not surprising that a range of commentators and campaigners bemoaned men's conduct towards women.[56] Again, such thinking often focused upon the lower classes, who tended to be thought of as being either especially wanting in decency and ethics or most prone to temptation, although this is by no means to say that that men of other classes were never considered in relation to these anxieties. In particular, as a result of what Judith Walkowitz has referred to as the traditional 'casual acceptance of male sexual licence' by some within the upper classes, the attitudes and behaviour of males from this section of society were also a matter of concern[57] – but here unease often centred upon their conduct towards girls rather than women.[58]

Worries about the male of the species tended to rehearse familiar contemporary themes, including, for example, fears that some men might either be under-evolved or were degenerating into more primitive or animalistic states both physically and morally. Indeed, in the work of writers who inclined towards evolutionary theory, concerns were expressed that some people and, in particular, men, seemed to be behaving in ways which fell below the standards to be expected of a great, if not the greatest, nation.[59] Here, incontinent sexual behaviour was a matter of concern, with men sometimes being described as falling prey to their base biological needs, rather than rising above the bodily and exercising self-control. This kind of thinking was often echoed in writings about men, sex and immorality, not least in the contexts of venereal disease transmission and prostitution.[60]

Unsurprisingly, anxieties about men and sex outside of wedlock were expressed by those aiming to ensure adherence to Christian ethics. Indeed, innumerable religious tracts and public lectures of the period warned of high levels of male immorality and sought to rectify the situation. These efforts were often directed at young working-class men in urban areas, who were perceived to be at greatest risk of being led into sin. In 1884, a talk by Alfred S. Dyer, a Quaker and campaigner for social purity, offered 'Safeguards Against Immorality; and Facts that Men Ought to Know'.[61] Dyer preached about the extent of depravity and the dangers of failing to be chaste and pure, with extra-marital sex his main concern. His arguments indicated just how alarmed he was about the conduct of young men, as did the urgency with which he advocated 'a well-occupied mind, plenty of out-door exercise, and a resolute avoidance of vicious companions.'[62]

In a similar vein, in *A Young Man's Questions Answered* (1880) by H. Butter, which seems to have been in existence both as an instructional talk and in printed form since the 1860s, the author warned of the dangers of fornication and adultery, maintaining that 'it is according to God's law that a man should attach himself to one woman in that most intimate relation, Marriage ...'.[63] Moreover, Butter stressed that 'all vices carry their punishment', warning that:

> a young man may, perchance, practice it for some time with apparent impunity; or he may, on the other hand – unhappily, as he will doubtless consider it – at once contract a disease so loathsome that he dares not avow it, but strives to conceal it, that it may either carry him to an early grave, or, after the doctors have done their best for him, leave him debilitated for life, a burden to himself and others.[64]

As this quotation demonstrated, in the context of concerns about male sexual immorality, not only was extra-marital sex considered sinful but those who engaged in such intemperance were considered likely to bring suffering upon themselves in this world, let alone the next.

Another focus of concerns about men, morality and sex was provided by those who campaigned for women's rights. In this context, attention during the 1860s to 1880s centred upon two issues often linked together: what was often referred to as 'the social evil' (prostitution) and the spread of 'the scourge' (venereal disease) – and here the focus tended to fall upon the male of the species as being the (primary) problem. So, in terms of prostitution, the women (and children) who were lured or forced into selling sex were viewed as being victimized by men and the transmission of venereal disease was attributed to the licence accorded to (or practised by) men when it came to sex. Such arguments came together in the resistance to and campaigns to abolish the Contagious Diseases Acts (CDAs) of the 1860s (and, given the facts in *Clarence*, they are of particular interest here).[65]

These measures were conceived of as a means to address a very particular problem: to reduce the incidence of venereal disease in the military. The Acts were essentially framed in a way that constructed female prostitutes as being responsible for the spread of infection. Significantly, they seemed also to be founded upon the assumption that *some* men at least could not (be expected to) resist their biological impulses, so prostitution was conceived of as an inevitable evil. Indeed, the wider idea of the unavoidability of prostitution because of *all* men's supposedly natural needs also had cultural currency in this period, with this sometimes seemingly being taken to mean that males had rights to sexual liberty which needed to be protected and defended (as will become evident, this was a view from which the judiciary was by no means entirely immune in the wider context of sexual offences as well as in *Clarence*).

The CDAs applied only to particular geographical areas. The focus was on localities where there was a military presence and the legislation provided that women who were found, on the basis of the word of a policeman, to be a 'common prostitute' were required to be regularly examined. If they were discovered to be infected with venereal disease, they could be detained for a period of up to nine months.[66]

In contrast, opponents of this legislation blamed male ethics and societal double standards about men's and women's sexuality (whereby men were accorded a degree of licence, whereas women were not) for the very existence of prostitution, let alone the spread of sexually transmitted infections. Their emphasis tended to be on the urgent need for men to repair their ways and often echoed contemporary concerns about degeneration and reverse evolution. For example, in 1873 in a letter published by an anti-CDAs journal, W. Littleton rejected the argument that men were 'mere animals', tied to their biology, which required them to satisfy their sexual needs. In his view this was 'a doctrine most dangerous to the moral welfare of the nation'. Rather, men had souls and were 'responsible to the higher law of morals and religion'; therefore, both women *and* men should be held to the same high moral standards when it came to matters of sex.[67] In other words, males' sexual liberty needed to be restrained and their morals improved.

The following year Josephine E. Butler, perhaps the most well-known campaigner against the Acts, called for the 'casting off of national evils … and the revival of a higher morality.'[68] Indeed, she viewed the CDAs as protecting men's vices[69] and targeting only women's immorality, arguing instead that '[u]ntil war be waged against impure men, as well as against impure women', it would be impossible to address the problem of prostitution.[70] Thus, English 'spiritual leaders ought directly to deal with the false and guilty theory, deeply rooted in the minds of men – religious as well as worldly – that impurity is necessary for men', so that female prostitution might no longer be 'in the heart of Christendom'.[71] So it was not just the CDAs and prostitution that Butler challenged, it was also ideas about men's supposed need for sex, which she saw as spurious. Moreover, she viewed the female of the species as being morally superior in matters of sexual ethics and, therefore, most able to bring about radical change in men. Indeed, to her mind there were 'comparatively few men who have the strength of motive which women have to assail this particular form of evil'.[72]

In their opposition to the CDAs, both Littleton and Butler directed attention towards conceptions of maleness, men's behaviour and, in particular, the fallacy of male sexual necessity. They also stressed the importance of English Christian morality – and the dangers for the country of allowing the continuance of double standards of morality underpinned their arguments. Consequently, men's behaviour when it came to matters of sex was not only to their minds a cause of great concern, but was something that needed to be addressed and remedied, so that they behaved as civilized humans rather than as beasts.

In 1886 the anti-CDA campaigners were successful and the Acts were repealed.[73] However, discussions about prostitution, along with the spread of venereal disease, continued. Indeed, as we shall see, some of these ideas were to be rehearsed again in *Clarence* two years later.

In the context of worries about men and sex, husbands' sexual behaviour towards their wives was also a source of unease. Here reports of legal cases often drew attention to the problem of abuse. In the field of civil and, more specifically, matrimonial law sexual conduct often figured in separation and divorce proceedings – and this was something which was to be drawn upon by the minority judgments in *Clarence.* Moreover, such cases tended to involve spouses from all but the very poorest sections of society, meaning that men's sexual misdeeds (at least within wedlock) were shown to be evident across all classes of men.[74]

In matrimonial law a man's behaviour could be argued to constitute 'legal cruelty' and this, if established, was enough to obtain a separation, although evidence of adultery was also needed in order to obtain a divorce. However, as a result of the marital rape exemption, evidence of sexual abuse could most often only be drawn upon indirectly. Thus, as A. James Hammerton's work has demonstrated, allegations of non-sexual cruelty could often seem to relate to sexual attacks, with claims of assaults which took place in bed 'with no explanation of precipitating arguments', suggesting that what had transpired related to some form of unwanted sexual conduct.[75]

From records and press reports of criminal cases it seems that a similar approach might also sometimes have been used within the criminal courts at this time, with husbands facing charges of non-sexual violence in connection with sexual attacks (it being well established that non-sexual wife abuse was a crime). Consequently, husbands might have found themselves convicted in relation to their 'natural' as well as their 'unnatural' sexual behaviour towards their wives. For example, an account of a husband's attack on his wife in Kingsdown, Bristol in 1881 tells how it began in the bedroom but ended up on the street as she had run away from him, eventually throwing herself from a window in order to escape. At this stage the police intervened and he was subsequently convicted of assaulting his wife. As he had previously been sentenced to two months imprisonment for the same crime, this time he was given three.[76]

Returning to the civil law, sometimes sexual behaviour figured more directly in matrimonial cases as cruelty could be established if 'unnatural' anal intercourse was proved to the satisfaction of the court – and some cases proceeded on this basis.[77] Of more relevance to Clarence, however, was the fact that the marital rape exemption had effectively been tempered in matrimonial law, meaning that the idea of disease transmission as a civil wrong was well-established by the time of *Clarence* – as was to be noted by the prosecution and the CCCR (minority) judges Hawkins and Field.[78] Thus, as Gail Savage and Hammerton have demonstrated, the 'wilful communication of venereal disease' was frequently used by wives in order to establish legal cruelty in separation and divorce cases.[79]

This issue was to attract some considerable attention in the years just prior to *Clarence* when the infamous Campbell separation and divorce cases came before the courts. This continuing saga included allegations that Lord Colin Campbell had infected his wife, Lady Gertrude Elizabeth Campbell, with syphilis. This, along with other aspects of the case, was widely reported in the press and the litigation along with the parties gathered some notoriety. (Figure 7 depicts the couple in court in 1886.)[80]

In the light of such civil cases and their often quite open (as compared to criminal cases) coverage in the newspapers and with knowledge of the effect of Hale's pronouncement, it was not surprising that men's sexual behaviour in marriage was a matter of concern amongst those who fought for the rights of women. One such writer and campaigner was John Stuart Mill, who

Figure 7 'Scenes and Incidents in the Colin Campbell Divorce Case.'

Illustrated Police News, 25 December 1886, p. 1.

worked alongside Harriet Taylor. In *The Subjection of Women* (1869), a work credited to Mill, he drew attention to the plight of those wives who found themselves 'chained' to a 'tyrant' who was legally able to 'claim from her and enforce the lowest degradation of a human being'.[81]

Sexual excess and violence within marriage was also a particular worry for commentators whose interests lay in contemporary thinking about evolution. Thus, as Joanna Bourke has argued, for those influenced by theories of degeneration, a husband who forced his wife to engage in sexual relations was regressing and showing himself to be little more than an animal, rather than holding himself to the high standards required of a modern Victorian man.[82]

As some of the above suggests, a good deal of the unease about male sexual incontinence was accompanied by efforts to suggest how all Englishmen, whatever their class, should behave. Here, particularly middle-class ideals of masculine sexual morality tended to be advanced, with preachers, writers, lecturers and campaigners seeking to explain what was to be expected of all men in the supposedly advanced and civilized world of late nineteenth-century England, as well as offering advice as to how best to avoid the temptations of the flesh. Along with the likes of Dyer, who sought to educate the young and preach religion, and those, like Butler, who fought for women's rights and thought that women, with their higher sense of morality, should guide men to better behaviour, one of the most prominent and influential of writers who sought to improve men was Samuel Smiles. In works such as *Self Help: With Illustrations of Conduct and Perseverance* (1859)[83] and *Character* (1871),[84] Smiles advised people, but particularly men, on how they should behave. In relation to matters of sex, for example, he seemed to be addressing only the male of the species, who he assumed (unlike women) had strong sexual desires, when he wrote of the need to 'resist instinctive impulse' and avoid vice.[85] Instead, he directed men to focus upon 'valiant self-discipline, self-respect, and self control' and aim for 'chastity, virtue, and temperance.'[86] Indeed, as Smiles explained, self-control in all things, not least as regards chastity, was crucial, as it was 'the chief distinction between man and animal; and, indeed, there can be no true manhood without it.' For '[l]et a man give the reins to his impulses and passions, and from that moment he yields up his moral freedom.'[87] In addition, in relation to married men's infidelity he stressed that both women and men should 'maintain a high standard of purity', emphasizing that '[t]he same moral law applies alike to both' as 'the notion that because of a difference in sex, man [*sic*] were at liberty to set morality at defiance, and to do that with impunity, which, if done by a woman, would stain her character for life' could not be countenanced.[88]

It was not only in relation to extra-marital relations that such advice was offered; self-control along with self-denial was also often advocated for husbands *within* marriage. Thus, Mill and Taylor's work argued for legal equality in marriage, which would entail that husbands be respectful of their wives, treating them as friends rather than as servants or slaves of their sexual appetites.[89] Although his outlook and purpose was distinct from Mill and Taylor, Dyer too pressed the need for men to exercise 'proper self-restraint *within* the marriage relationship' [emphasis added] when it came to sex.[90] Likewise, Smiles focused upon wedlock, portraying an idealized companionate model, in which domesticity, friendship, respect, restraint and purity were key elements.[91]

The views of those who advocated rights for wives and argued for sexual moderation in marriage were, however, by no means shared by all. In particular, it was often assumed that the marital rape exemption was both the legal approach and the right approach. For instance, in 1870 James Schouler maintained that 'wilfully declining matrimonial intimacy and companionship' was nothing short of a 'breach of duty, tending to subvert the true ends of marriage' and, consequently, a spouse's 'sallies of passion' were expected to be passively borne by wives.[92] In addition, as Butter's tract for young men suggested, marriage was sometimes seen as God-given and so the only truly moral context in which to engage in sexual relations. Moreover, the purpose of wedlock was often said to be to provide a legitimate outlet for men's supposed bodily needs.

As will become apparent in the discussion of the majority's judicial pronouncements in the CCCR in *Clarence*, in consequence of these conceptions of matrimony, it seemed to be assumed by some, apparently as a result of the application of (some sort of twisted) logic, that nothing sexual that took place within marriage could be wrong in the relation to morality or law (or at least nothing that conformed to ideas about 'natural' sex). But, leaving such views aside for the moment, let us return to the theme of binding men and, more specifically, worries about the sexual intemperance of the less fair sex.

At the same time that concerns about men and sex were circulating, there were parallel efforts within legal spheres to address the problem of male behaviour towards women. Here expanding the boundaries of the criminal law and, in particular, of sexual offences was the focus, with the CCCR playing a key role. Some of these attempts at change had had a degree of success by the time *Clarence* came before the courts in 1888 – and many of them were cited in the case. But, unlike *Clarence*, they did not involve husbands and wives because of the contemporary legal acceptance of Hale's words as to the overriding legality of sexual activity between married couples.

A number of cases in the years prior to *Clarence* suggested that judges were seeking to rein in male sexual behaviour towards women. In particular, a series of decisions had developed the notion that, in an expanding number of circumstances, a woman's apparent consent to sexual activity could be found to be legally invalid where there had been some prior fraud on the part of the defendant. This meant that even where there had apparently been consent at the time of a sexual encounter there could still be a conviction for a sexual offence. For example, in the CCCR case of *R v Flattery* (1877)[93] it was found that a man's fraud as to the nature of the activity vitiated a woman's consent to intercourse. John Flattery offered medical advice for a fee (*The Times* described him as a 'herbalist').[94] He was consulted by 19-year-old Lavinia Thompson and her mother about the former's ill-health. Flattery claimed that he could cure Lavinia by performing a surgical procedure. Both Lavinia and her mother agreed to this and the man took the daughter into a room, put her on the floor 'and then and there had carnal sexual connection with her'. She offered only 'feeble resistance', believing that she was being treated. Flattery was convicted of rape at the Leeds winter assizes, Justice Hawkins presiding. Hawkins then reserved the matter. The question for the CCCR was whether this form of fraudulently induced submission could amount to consent and, therefore, justify the conviction.[95] Justices Kelly,

Mellor, Denman and Field, along with Baron Huddleston decided the case – and it is worth noting at this point that Hawkins, Field and Huddleston were subsequently to sit in judgment of *Clarence*, with the former two in the minority and, therefore, in favour of affirming Charles's conviction.

The decision in *Flattery* was unanimous, with all the judges of the view that this was rape because there was no consent to sexual connection; the consent to the supposed operation being, to their mind, irrelevant as it was fraudulently obtained. The conviction was, therefore, affirmed. Flattery was subsequently sentenced to seven years penal servitude.[96]

Any apparent criticism or disgust at Flattery's conduct was not directly expressed within the judgments, apart from the description of his actions as involving 'fraud and false pretences'.[97] However, this is not to say that no inferences can be drawn from what was said – or rather, what was not said by the judges. The very few words with which the conviction was affirmed, along with the scant time given to the arguments presented by counsel for Flattery, were telling. Perhaps even more significantly, although counsel for the prosecution appeared in court, the law report stated that he 'was not called upon',[98] suggesting that, although the judges heard from the defence counsel, they had no need to hear the opposing arguments, having already decided that the jury's finding of guilty was correct.

Also significant in *Flattery* was the view expressed about the earlier case of *R v Barrow* (1868),[99] with all five judges feeling the need to comment negatively upon it, despite the fact that it could merely have been distinguished. *Barrow* was another sexual offences case involving fraud. Harriet Geldart was in bed with her husband and their baby when Barrow climbed into the bed and initiated sexual intimacy with her. She was half awake and went along with the penetrative intercourse which ensued because she thought he was her spouse. At some point she realized that all was not as she had believed it to be and, as a result, a charge of rape came to be brought against Barrow. The defendant was convicted but the matter was reserved to the CCCR.

The CCCR found that she was neither asleep nor unconscious and had consented so no crime had been committed as, although her consent was obtained by fraud, this was not sufficient to have the effect of turning the encounter into a rape. Barrow's conviction was, therefore, quashed. Significantly, in *Flattery* all the CCCR judges felt the need to say that they desired to revisit the decision in *Barrow*. The implication of this being that they were of the view that where a man fraudulently induced consent by deception as to his identity (at least where he impersonated a woman's husband), it should be found that there was no consent on the part of the woman. In such situations a conviction was, therefore, the correct outcome.

In so finding, the judges in *Flattery* were in fact following two earlier decisions – *R v Saunders* (1838)[100] and *R v Williams* (1838)[101] – in which impersonation of a husband was found to have negated a wife's apparent consent. Thus, the disapproving mentions of *Barrow* in *Flattery* seemed to mark a reversal of judicial opinion and a wish to return to the previous law.[102] What is more, their view appeared to have been shared by legislators as it was subsequently enshrined in statute in 1885. Section 4 of the Criminal Law Amendment Act 1885 helpfully stated, amongst other things, that:

> Whereas doubts have been entertained whether a man who induces a married woman to permit him to have connexion with her by personating her husband is or is not guilty of rape, it is hereby enacted and declared that every such offender shall be deemed to be guilty of rape.

So, in legislation as well as in cases, there were efforts to bind men to better behaviour in their sexual conduct towards women.

In another move towards reining in men's sexual behaviour, in 1878 the CCCR seemed to confirm the view, which had been briefly called into question by the 1866 case of *Bennett*[103] (see further below), that a sleeping or unconscious victim could not consent to sexual activity. The facts of *R v Young* (1878),[104] a rape case referred to the CCCR, were similar to those of *Barrow*; indeed, the doubt which had been cast upon *Barrow* in *Flattery* was discussed by the court (which comprised of Coleridge along with Justices Mellor, Lush, Cleasby and Lopes – with Huddleston as the trial judge). In *Young*, Johanna Hurley had been asleep in bed with her husband and two children when John Young 'proceeded to have connection with her'. She woke up and first thought he was her husband, but realized when he spoke that he was not and she immediately 'flung' him off her. The jury found that there was no consent and there was no reason for the prisoner to believe that she had consented. Huddleston directed a guilty verdict.[105] Given the nature of the jury's findings of the facts, the CCCR's decision to confirm the conviction seemed to have been taken on the basis that Hurley was asleep when the sexual activity had begun and there was, thus, no consent. So *Young* returned criminal law to its previous state as regards a sleeping victim.[106]

In the field of criminal evidence law, there had also been modest developments in the direction of criminalizing male sexual behaviour towards women before 1888. In 1871 the CCCR was called upon to make a legal ruling in *R v Holmes and Furness*.[107] Here two men had been charged and convicted of indecently assaulting Sarah Palmer. In cross-examination at the trial she had been asked about her past sexual history. Counsel for the men questioned whether she 'had had connection with' a third man by the name of Robert Sharp. She denied this and Sharp was brought as a witness by the defence and asked whether Palmer had ever had 'connection' with him, but he was stopped from answering as a result of objections from counsel for the prosecution. Following the jury's decision to convict Holmes and Furness the case was reserved. The point to be ruled upon was whether

Sharp's response should have been allowed. The five CCCR judges all found that the correct approach had been taken – once the question had been asked of her and answered, Palmer had to be taken at her word. Whilst some variation of opinion was in evidence as to how much this approach should be applied to different facts, Justice Byles took the view that a woman could not be contradicted as to her previous sexual history.[108] Moreover, he added that this had to be so because, to his mind, 'a rape may be committed upon a prostitute.'[109] This was a particularly radical statement for its time and one which, consequently, provided a significant illustration of this judge's feeling that men should be legally bound to higher standards of sexual behaviour.

There were also criminal cases demonstrating this tendency to rein in men's sexual activities that were more closely related to the facts in *Clarence* (although their outcome was not wholly positive). Two relatively recent trials had involved the successful prosecution of men for offences against the person arising from their communication of venereal disease to a female through vaginal intercourse. In both cases the victims were female children but the legal approach was one which would also be applicable to women.

In *R v Bennett* (1866)[110] a man was prosecuted for an indecent assault upon his unnamed 13-year-old niece at Taunton assizes. The girl was taken to have consented to sexual intercourse because she had agreed to sleep in the same bed with him (the age of consent effectively then being 12).[111] Indeed, consent was found despite the fact that she was asleep or unconscious when the sexual activity took place[112] (a decision which was subsequently to occasion some harsh criticism[113] because it had long been accepted that consent could not be present in such circumstances and – as we have seen – *Young* subsequently returned criminal law to its former state).[114] As a consequence of this ruling, the judge found that there could be no rape. However, he also stated that, as she did not consent to the aggravated circumstances (the risk of infection with what was probably syphilis),[115] there could be an assault and, in this case, an indecent assault (although, it is worth noting that, following this judicial reasoning, a non-sexual assault charge might have been more fitting as it was the harm caused by the infection that she was deemed not to have consented to rather than any sexual or indecent conduct). The jury having found Bennett guilty, he was sentenced to two years' imprisonment with hard labour.

The first instance case[116] of *R v Sinclair* (1867)[117] followed *Bennett* and it too involved the communication of venereal disease by a male to a girl through vaginal intercourse. However, as will become apparent, there was an important difference between this case and *Bennett*. Eighteen-year-old William Henry Sinclair faced two trials at the Central Criminal Court for his behaviour towards Emma Sinclair, who was described as being 'just above twelve years of age'[118] and was, therefore, also just over the then age of consent (whether William and Emma were related is not recorded). The Old Bailey Proceeding gives little information regarding either case. In the first it is merely stated that he was charged with '[f]eloniously ravishing and carnally knowing' (in other words, raping) the victim and was found not guilty, although this seems to have been on the ground that she was found to have consented.[119] The same source offers similarly scant facts in relation to the second trial, merely stating that he 'was *again* indicted for an assault on the same person' – but that this time he was convicted and sentenced to 12 months' imprisonment.[120] The latter trial was included within the pages of the law reports, however, so a little more information can be added to that provided by the court records.

Penetrative vaginal intercourse took place between Emma and William. As a result of the connection, she contracted gonorrhoea. Siginificantly, Sinclair appears to have been charged with two counts of *non-sexual* assault under sections 47 and 20 of the 1861 Act (the very same offences as Charles faced in *Clarence*, whereas in *Bennett* the charge was for a *sexual* offence).[121] The judge, Justice Shee, directed that if the girl had consented or had demonstrated 'such absence of resistance as would reasonably imply consent', there could be no finding of assault. However, he added that her consent might be vitiated by the prisoner's behaviour if the jury found four elements to have existed: first, that he knew of his condition; secondly, that he knew of the likely consequences of engaging in intercourse; thirdly, that he did not tell the girl; and, finally, that she would not have consented had she been in possession of all the facts. Here 'the deceit practised upon her' would entail that she had not consented in the context of non-sexual offences against the person and the disease transmission would constitute an assault.[122]

As was noted above, although both *Bennett* and *Sinclair* involved girl victims, the legal finding that the communication of venereal disease during consensual penetrative intercourse could sometimes constitute an offence against the person also applied to women (although the question remained as to whether the crime should properly be categorized as a *sexual* and/or *non-sexual* offence). Thus, the decisions were of potentially vast importance. What is more, in terms of the binding men narrative being constructed here, they arguably represented a hugely significant development, given that this was a time when women often tended to be blamed for the spread of sexually transmitted diseases (as the CDAs demonstrated). Against their having much weight in future courts, however, was the fact that they were first instance cases involving the pronouncements of single judges, rather than CCCR reviews where a panel would decide the matter. However, this was less of an issue in the nineteenth century, as Coleridge had himself previously noted, when the authoritativeness of a case might be influenced by, for example, the identity of the particular judge involved.[123]

So, the cases of *Flattery*, *Young*, *Holmes*, *Bennett* and *Sinclair* along with section 4 of the Criminal Law Amendment Act 1885, seemed to show something of a trend towards criminalizing male sexual violence against women – and, in doing so, these legal labours were, of course, in keeping with the anxieties about male brutishness, unGodliness and lack of self-restraint which we have seen were circulating at the time. This is, of course, by no means to say that the judicial efforts during this period were entirely concerned with curtailing male liberty when it came to matters of sex. Indeed, at the same time there seemed to be concern about the nature and extent of the expansion of the criminal law insofar as it penalized men for their sexual conduct towards women. For example, in the CCCR Kelly in *Holmes* made it clear that he thought that where the woman was a 'common prostitute', or there was evidence that she had previously 'had connection' with a man accused of rape, attempted rape or indecent assault, 'such evidence is undoubtedly admissible, for it has a direct bearing upon the question of consent.'[124]

There was also in criminal cases sometimes a tendency amongst the judiciary to express a seeming anxiety about the effect of shifting the law in such a way as to potentially penalize more men. An example, of this was provided by Denman in *Flattery*. Whilst affirming the defendant's conviction and agreeing that *Barrow* should be reconsidered, the judge also saw the need to emphasize that men required some protection from liability. He stated that '[t]here may be cases where a woman does not consent in fact, but in which her conduct is such that the man reasonably believes she does.'[125] Thus, Denman seems to have been worried that, if the legal approach to consent to sexual intercourse were to be altered too much, men would be in danger of being convicted for, to his mind, genuinely and understandably mistaking consent because of a woman's behaviour.

Clarence

This background of conflicting opinion as to male sexual behaviour towards women and the extent to which men should be supervised by law was the context within which *Clarence* came before the courts and, in particular, the CCCR. So the question here was which view would hold sway. This was by no means a straightforward matter, despite the fact that the leanings of some of the 13 who considered it might have been at least guessed at from their involvement in previous cases (in particular, the decisions of Hawkins and Field in *Flattery* might have suggested that they would favour affirming Charles's conviction rather than quashing it – and, indeed, this was the course they opted for). This was because *Clarence* was distinct from previous cases, making it more difficult to deduce how the judges might react. Primarily the difference lay in the fact that it involved sexual intercourse between a husband and a wife.

In the end, as we have seen, the CCCR in *Clarence* was split, with four judges finding that Charles's conviction should stand and nine quashing it. Much of what was said by those in both camps, however, focused upon matters of sex and sexual offences, although there was also talk about the parameters of the two non-sexual crimes with which Charles was charged. Moreover, although both sections 47 and 20 were not gender-specific offences, meaning that both men and women (whether or not they were married to each other) would face prosecution for sexual disease transmission if the defendant's conviction were affirmed, most of the focus was upon the behaviour of the male of the species.

Let us turn first to the pronouncements made in support of affirming Charles' conviction by the minority judges. Of the four, only Hawkins and Field gave judgments, as Day concurred with Hawkins and Charles with Field. Their words can be portrayed as embodying contemporary concerns about men and, in particular, husbands. More specifically, in the context of the 'binding men' narrative of this book, the dissenting judgments in *Clarence* can be constructed as an attempt to criminalize, not only Charles Clarence, but also other men who might behave similarly in the future, by seeking, albeit unsuccessfully, to create a clear precedent regarding the transmission of venereal disease through consensual sexual activity where the accused, but not the victim, knew the risk. At the same time, their pronouncements suggested how men should behave, at least in marriage.

In legal terms, Hawkins's judgment primarily rested upon three findings: that a wife's 'obligation' in marriage to 'submit' to sexual intercourse with her husband was not without limitations; that a husband had duties of restraint in marriage; and that venereal disease transmission could result in convictions under sections 47 and 20. For example, drawing on civil law cases, he maintained that the 'marital privilege' did not mean that a husband could endanger his spouse's health or cause her serious injury – and this would cover situations where he knew that he had venereal disease and intercourse would likely infect her. Such behaviour was, to his mind, not only dangerous but also unlawful.[126] His argument was that, whilst a woman's consent to sexual intercourse *might* bar a charge of rape in circumstances such as those in the present case, the 'infectious contact' could still constitute a non-sexual offence against the person. In this regard he cited *Bennett* (one of the venereal disease transmission cases which had resulted in a conviction) with approval and drew attention to the fact that he felt this was precisely the distinction which had been drawn in the case.[127]

Hawkins, however, went still further. Indeed, so keen was he to affirm the conviction in *Clarence* that he was prepared to do so even if this meant that a husband in such circumstances would also be guilty of rape as, although he thought that it would be very rare for a jury to convict a husband, he could 'imagine a state of circumstances under which a husband might deservedly be punished with the penalty attached to rape'.[128] This was a radical statement for the time, particularly for a judge (although not, as we have seen, for women's rights campaigners), revealing the depth of his feelings about the case.

Hawkins was also particularly vocal as to how he saw what Charles had done, describing it 'an offence as cruel and as contrary to the obligation a man owes to his wife to protect her from harm, as can well be conceived.'[129] As this quotation suggests, his judgment displayed a sense of consternation and disgust at the defendant's behaviour. For example, he made a point of commenting upon the assumed origin of Charles's affliction and, in so doing, drew attention to the husband's presumed immorality; the 'loathsome disease' was, Hawkins said, 'contracted through his own infidelity'. What is more, he emphasized the seriousness of the consequences for Selina, noting that Charles had 'endanger[ed] her health' by his actions.[130]

The strength of his feeling about the case was also demonstrated by his indication that a wife might be justified in killing a husband who sought to force intercourse upon her when he was infected with venereal disease. Thus, Hawkins argued that a wife could resist 'even to the death' a connection with her infected husband – and, significantly, he emphasized this despite conceding that there was no legal authority for his view.[131] Indeed, the judge said that he could not 'conceive it possible seriously to doubt' the latter, as to his mind any such sexual connection would be justified only with the express (fully informed) consent of a wife.[132]

Accordingly, in Hawkins's opinion a married man in such a condition as Charles should 'forego his privilege' because it could not be exercised 'without at the same time doing something ... which is unlawful and dangerous to another'.[133] Sexual abstinence was, therefore, the only moral and legal course and, if a husband failed to exercise self-control in this regard, he must face the criminal consequences of his disregard for the well-being of his spouse.[134] Indeed, to rule otherwise would, he felt, be beyond even 'the most liberal construction of [a husband's] matrimonial privilege'.[135]

In closing, Hawkins was keen to reaffirm his loathing for the conduct in *Clarence* (in fact, he attacked it in far stronger terms than he had previously). But he also chose to emphasize the great distance between his own views and those of the majority of his fellow judges and to highlight what he saw as the wider impact of the decision in terms of what it said about the English law regarding husbands' powers. Given the vehemence with which this was done, it is worth returning to the epigraph to this chapter. Having stated that 'this conviction is right and in accordance with the law', Hawkins added that he could not 'be a party to [the] judgment' because of what it would 'in effect ... proclaim to the world'. His objection lay in the fact that *Clarence* meant that:

> ... by the law of England in this year 1888 a man may deliberately, knowingly, and maliciously perpetrate upon the body of his wife the abominable outrage charged against the prisoner, and yet not be punishable criminally for such atrocious barbarity.[136]

Here, then, he condemned the majority's decision in no uncertain terms. To Hawkins's mind it sent an indefensible message: namely, that the supposedly civilized England of the latter part of the nineteenth century actually allowed a husband to perpetrate such savage treatment against his wife with legal impunity. In contrast, Hawkins maintained that all Englishmen had obligations towards their wives and it was important that the law of the land should be seen to uphold these. Consequently, his judgment echoed contemporary ideas about men, sex and marriage, as well as the ideals of sexual ethics portrayed in lectures, tracts and books which advocated how Englishmen, of whatever class, should conduct themselves, not least within wedlock. Indeed, it indicated that, rather than acting like primitives by responding to animalistic urges, having no regard for the well-being of their partners, all English husbands should be required to be chivalrous and respectful towards their lifelong companions – and they should exercise sexual restraint.

As the above suggests, for Hawkins, *Clarence* was very much a case about regulating husbands' sexual conduct towards their wives. Nevertheless, his judgment, had it been adopted by the majority, would have allowed allegations of non-sexual offences against the person committed by disease transmission through sexual intercourse which occurred outside as well as inside marriage (and these crimes could have been committed by men or women). Indeed, Hawkins specifically discussed this, feeling that prosecutions would rarely be brought in cases arising from a consensual 'illicit communion' because of the shame and ridicule which would be brought upon those involved. What is more, parties to such encounters would most likely be judged by juries to have 'entered into the immoral communion tacitly consenting to take all risks.'[137] So overall, whilst he accepted that his decision would apply to disease transmission beyond wedlock, his comments suggested that, in terms of consensual interactions he was not only little concerned about this but that he took a low view of those men (and women) who willingly engaged in extra-marital sexual relations. As to venereal disease transmission through rape, the implication of his reasoning was that this would undoubtedly be criminal.

The other minority judge to give reasons for his decision was Field. Key to his thinking was an even more radical rejection of the long-accepted position, based upon the words of Hale, that a husband could not in law rape his wife. In so saying, Field took the view that Charles and men who conducted themselves in similar ways towards their wives might be convicted of rape. Like the prosecutor, Poland, he argued that Hale's supposedly authoritative statement was based on no previous authority. As a result, he stated that 'I should hesitate before I adopted it.' Instead, Field maintained that there could 'be many cases in which a wife may lawfully refuse intercourse, and in which, if the husband imposed it by violence, he might be held guilty of a crime' and cited an eighteenth-century divorce case to support his view that the sexual rights of husbands in marriage were by no means unlimited.[138]

Despite this, it was clear from what he said that Field contemplated the offence of marital rape would be applied only in relatively extreme circumstances.[139] However, the importance of his pronouncements on Hale should not be underestimated. For a judge at this time they were at the very least remarkable – all the more so when one considers that it was not until 1991 that the then House of Lords finally did away with the marital rape exemption in its entirety.[140] Moreover, his views seemed to some degree to echo those of some of the campaigners for women's rights in the period, with their arguments about wives' sexual slavery.

Field's decision also relied on the idea that *Clarence* involved a fraud. He argued that Selina had consented to 'a natural and healthy connection', as Charles had 'wilfully left her in ignorance as to, the real nature and character of that act.'[141] In his view the husband had, consequently, deceived his wife into agreeing to something other than what had transpired and had thereby caused her harm – and in these circumstances her consent was not true consent. In doing so, Field cited with approval legal authorities on fraud vitiating consent in the context of sexual activity, focusing in terms of case law upon *Saunders* and *Williams* in relation to the impersonation of a husband, *Flattery* in the case of fraud as to the nature of the act and *Bennett* and *Sinclair* where the fraud related to the 'physical nature and conditions of the act'.[142] So, for him men's sexual behaviour towards women, whether within or beyond marriage, should be legally restrained in instances of deception.

Moreover, in both his rejection of the marital exemption and his finding of fraud there was direct criticism of Charles. Field described him as acting in the knowledge both that 'he had a foul and infectious disease' and that 'the infection of his wife would be the natural and reasonable consequence of intercourse'. Nevertheless, he 'solicited intercourse' by 'wilfully suppressing' his condition, 'wilfully [leaving Selina] in ignorance' and making a 'false representation by act and conduct' as to his physical health. In consequence, she was led to believe that she was consenting to the 'natural and healthy connection' to which she was 'bound' and to which she 'had been accustomed' to consent. Like Hawkins, Field then went on to specify how Charles should have conducted himself, stating that '[t]here was, I think, a clear duty cast upon the prisoner before he solicited the intercourse to communicate his condition to his wife'.[143]

Unlike Hawkins, however, Field did not specifically consider the implications of his decision in relation to men's immorality outside of marriage, instead focusing upon husbands' behaviour towards their wives. Consequently, the judgments of both Hawkins and Field might be said to have been aimed primarily at legally binding husbands' behaviour towards their wives, rather than at men's sexual morality more generally.

These, then, were the approaches of the judges who sided with the jury in their conviction of Charles Clarence. Amongst other things, they reflected anxieties as to the behaviour of husbands towards their spouses in relation to sex, along with a strong sense of the duties a man owed to his wife and, in particular, a desire to ensure that there were consequences as regards the criminal law if a husband failed to live up to them. Indeed, Hawkins and Field, with the agreement of Day and Charles, were primarily seeking to uphold a model of male marital morality, rather than a code for men to uphold in all their sexual relations. However, there were signs that men's sexual conduct was a broader matter of concern, particularly, for example, in Hawkins's reference to how Charles became infected and his discussion of the impact of his judgment upon disease transmission outside of wedlock.

Hawkins and Field along with Day and Charles did not win the day, however, and the majority of the judges took a different view in terms of both the law and the significance of the case for the male of the species. Here, as Kate Gleeson has noted in her consideration of *Clarence*, the chief anxieties concerned the consequences for husbands and for men in general if Charles's conviction was affirmed.[144] Floodgates arguments played a role in this context, with concerns about the allegations that women might level at men. More generally, whilst the majority judgments did not quite amount to an unqualified defence of male sexual rights within marriage and their freedoms beyond wedlock, they suggested a sense of alarm at the idea that men might be held to be legally bound in the manner proposed by the prosecution.

Indeed, the majority focused a good deal of their attention upon the dangers inherent in the possible opening up of a new field of criminal liability in relation to men – and, by implication perhaps, the resultant restriction upon male sexual liberty. Wills, in particular, feared the consequences of doing so. His excitable pronouncements were largely organized around identifying and considering the dire and unsupportable implications (to his thinking) of the various arguments for imposing liability. Moreover, they were in stark contrast to Hawkins's approach to men who bought or had extra-maritial sex. For example, according to Wills, allowing the implied or actual consent of Selina to be negated might mean that 'every man ... who knowingly gives a piece of bad money to a prostitute to procure her consent to intercourse, or who seduces a woman by representing himself to be what he is not, is guilty of assault, and, it seems to me, therefore, of rape'.[145] Whilst he described the latter situation as a case of consent obtained by fraud, he felt that 'it would be childish to say that she did not consent'.[146] The vehemence of this denial was clear – indeed, the very suggestion that fraud might vitiate consent in these circumstances was to him absurd. At the same time, Wills made no comment on such men's behaviour here – either in relation to their seeking out prostitutes or in attempting to cheat women. Nor was there anything said about the women who in his fictitious examples were variously tricked into having sexual relations with a man.

He continued at some length in this alarmist vein, rehearsing a series of scenarios in which his focus was the effects of affirming Charles's conviction upon men in the future.[147] In particular, he was vexed that men might be victims of blackmail. Thus, he warned that a 'new field of extortion may be developed, and very possibly a fresh illustration afforded of the futility of trying to teach morals by the application of the criminal law to cases occupying the doubtful ground between immorality and crime, and of the dangers which always beset such attempts.'[148] Consequently, for Wills, it was male interests that were important, not women's – and certainly not those of women working as prostitutes. Indeed, the idea of legally binding men to better behaviour could not have been further from his thoughts.

Whilst Wills provided an extreme, almost caricatured version of the majority view, his sentiments and concerns were echoed by the others. Yet this is not to say that the majority were anything but disgusted by Charles's behaviour (as a husband). For instance, even Wills cast Charles as a scoundrel, describing his behaviour as 'wicked and cruel'[149] and Stephen was similarly condemnatory of the defendant, describing what had transpired as 'abominable conduct'[150] and subsequently referring to 'the abominable nature of the prisoner's conduct'.[151]

There were also signs that some of the majority were not entirely happy with their findings as to the law and the decision reached. Most notably, Lord Chief Justice Coleridge revealed that he had actually changed his mind.[152] Moreover, there was some evidence of unease concerning the marital rape exemption, with even Wills describing the latter as 'a proposition to which I certainly am not prepared to assent, and for which there seems to me to be no sufficient authority.'[153] However, clearly not all the majority shared such thoughts: notably, Smith defended a husband's marital right, regardless of whether he was 'sound in body' or not.[154]

Post *Clarence*

The immediate reaction to *Clarence* was limited (perhaps as a result of its subject matter); the press, for example, merely reported the decision briefly. Amongst those publications that did respond to it, there was a tendency to support the approach of the majority, as it seemed to have been accepted (in accordance with Wills's thinking) that ruling Charles's actions were covered by the existing law would have had consequences that were at best untenable and at worst disastrous. The *Saturday Review*, for example, took such a view, warning that if Field, along with the 'sentimental' Hawkins, had won the day, the effect would have been to produce an 'avalanche of unsavoury cases'.[155] This having been said, the article did not rule out the specific criminalization by Parliament of venereal disease transmission and made mention of this as a possibility, although presumably with the proviso that the offence should be clearly (de)limited.[156] Indeed, there appeared to be some support for legislation, with the *British Medical Journal* positively advocating this course, at least in relation to syphilis.[157] Thus, even where there was approval of the decision in *Clarence*, there could be a feeling that something ought to be done to legally bind men to better sexual behaviour; although it was unclear whether such views related to men (and women) both within and outside of marriage.

What tended to unite responses to *Clarence*, however, were their opinions of Charles and his behaviour towards his wife. So, for example, the *British Medical Journal* felt that '[t]he language used by the judges in reference to the act as abominable, cruel, wicked, foul, and atrocious barbarity, and a most malignant injury, is not one whit too strong.'[158] Similarly, the *Saturday Review* considered 'the conduct of the husband ... [to be] abominable beyond all words of censure.'[159] Indeed, in commentary on the case Charles was often portrayed as a degenerate who had failed to exercise the self-control to be expected in such circumstances.

As for the application of *Clarence* in the courts during the closing decade of the nineteenth century, *Bennett* and *Sinclair* were taken to have been overruled by the case and *Clarence* was interpreted to mean that venereal disease transmission could not be an offence in any circumstances. So, far from binding men to better behaviour, the subsequent interpretation of *Clarence* meant that men's potential liability for their sexual conduct towards women actually shrank. This was something which was met with disquiet in some quarters. For example, within the *British Medical Journal*'s 'Public Health' section consternation was expressed at the outcome of an 1891 Old Bailey case.[160] Twenty-two-year-old Linden Howard was charged with the abduction of a girl, Alice Sarah Sargeant, under the age of 18 (she was in fact 16) and with 'assaulting the girl by communicating a disease.' The assault charge was, however, dropped during the trial on the basis of the decision in *Clarence*. Nevertheless, Howard was convicted of abduction and sentenced to nine months' imprisonment.[161] Whilst the *Journal* article briefly criticized the 'very slight punishment of nine months' imprisonment', its focus was upon the interpretation of *Clarence*. The 1888 case, it was argued, was wrongly applied here, as it had been decided on the basis that the parties were husband and wife. In *Howard* the facts were different and distinguishable and, consequently, there should have been a conviction. The piece concluded with the comment, 'the sooner the communication of venereal disease is made an indictable offence the better.'

Beyond this, *Clarence*, appeared to have marked a halt in what had seemed to be an increasing acceptance that different forms of fraud might vitiate consent in relation to sexual offences. Moreover, despite the conflicting statements on marital rape, the 1888 case also came to be seen as a confirmation of Hale's exemption. This meant that what might be narrated as the gradual expansion of criminal laws regarding sex and crime in the nineteenth century appeared to have been somewhat derailed by *Clarence*, at least as regarded the conduct of men towards women.[162] So, here too, far from binding husbands in relation to their sexual conduct towards their wives, let alone men's behaviour towards women outside of wedlock, *Clarence* could be viewed as serving as a legal protection of men's sexual freedom.

Beyond legal spheres, concerns about men, morality, sex and marriage persisted after *Clarence*, with advocates of women's rights, in particular, campaigning for changes to social attitudes and male behaviour as well as to law. These efforts included calls for the marital rape exemption to be done away with. In the years immediately following *Clarence* perhaps the most notable example of these labours was provided by the work of Elizabeth Clarke Wolstenholme Elmy. Having first publically argued against husbands' immunity from prosecution in 1880, she continued to work towards its abolition through that decade. In the 1890s, in the wake of the Court of Appeal's decision in *R v Jackson* (1891),[163] which confirmed that a husband's physical dominion over his wife was by no means absolute (see Chapter 5), she tried to get the issue re-examined and (unsuccessfully) attempted to get a Bill placed before Parliament so that the exemption would at least be publically discussed.[164]

In other contexts, concerns about sexually violent men continued to be expressed, as did the view that men who sexually abused women and, in particular, husbands who forced sexual activity upon their wives, were brutes and degenerates. For example, in 1890 Henry Havelock Ellis maintained that sexually violent men exhibited the physical signs of decline, including atavistic traits like hairiness.[165]

In relation to disease transmission too, concerns about the behaviour of men in general and husbands in particular did not end with *Clarence*. To take an example from the sphere of fiction, Sarah Grand's 1893 novel, *The Heavenly Twins*, included the story of Edith, who married a man infected with syphilis. She caught the disease, which she passed on to her child, then went insane and died of the ailment.[166] Grand's purpose here was, in part, to use the work to educate the public on sexual matters – but she also wanted to highlight the harm that she felt was caused to women by degenerate men. For example, one of her characters, commenting upon Edith's plight, stated that '[i]t's dirty men makes the misery'.[167] Grand herself was subsequently to say that 'I hope that we should soon see the marriage of certain men made a criminal offence.'[168]

Wolstenholme Elmy also addressed the issue of venereal disease transmission within marriage and wrote about *Clarence*. In an 1898 *Westminster Review* article she expressed abhorrence at the decision and went on to highlight the fact that, whilst 'the majority of men are better than the law, there are base men who abuse to the utmost the power which the law gives them'.[169] For this author, 'the decent veil of legal marriage too often covers horrors not to be expressed.' Moreover, as she saw it, the result was that through marriage a woman became her husband's 'sexual slave'.[170] In this context, she again argued that the marital rape exemption should be revoked; however, as we have seen, in this regard her endeavours, along with those of others who followed her for the next 90 or so years, were to prove unsuccessful.[171]

Moving forward to the early years of the twentieth century, efforts to penalize men who transmitted venereal diseases to their wives continued and there were attempts to ensure that the victims could gain some form of legal remedy for their situation. In 1909 Helena Swanwick, a prominent feminist and suffragist, submitted to the Royal Commission on Divorce and Matrimonial Causes that the transmission of venereal disease in marriage should be both a criminal offence and a ground for divorce. Again, it was primarily male behaviour and its effects upon women which concerned Swanwick and the other women who gave evidence in support of this view.[172] In 1913 suffragette leader Christabel Pankhurst was to champion the subject in *The Great Scourge and How to End It* – and she too placed the blame firmly upon the male of the species.[173] Thus, she highlighted the fact that innocent wives were infected by their husbands', seeing the only solution as being chastity for men – and votes for women.[174]

Conclusion

This chapter has revisited the well-known (to criminal lawyers) case of *Clarence*, first recounting a story of the case and then recasting it in the context of nineteenth-century concerns about men's sexual conduct towards women both within and outside marriage. Here legal efforts to bind the male of the species to better behaviour in matters of sex were considered alongside the minority judges' attempts to affirm Charles's conviction for non-sexual offences against the person. In this context, Hawkins and Field's judgments were portrayed as reflecting contemporary concerns about men, sexual morality and marriage, and efforts to rein in men.

However, Hawkins and Field failed to convince a sufficient number of their brother judges to side with them and, as a result, the sexual transmission of disease, which had previously been held to be (at least in some circumstances) an offence of violence, was no longer (in any circumstances) a crime. Instead, arguments about the marital rights of husbands (and perhaps male sexual liberty) seemed to have won the day, although disease transmission did remain something that could be used to establish legal cruelty in matrimonial proceedings.[175]

Following *Clarence*, attempts to restrain husbands' legal dominion over their wives were once again soon to become the focus of the courts. As was briefly mentioned above, within a little over two years the infamous 'Clitheroe abduction' litigation (or *R v Jackson* as it was known in legal circles) was to place these questions firmly before members of the judiciary, in both the criminal and civil courts. Here, though, non-sexual physical violence committed by a husband against his wife was the focus of attention and most of the legal action played out in the civil courts. It is this controversy which forms the subject matter of the next and final chapter.

Notes

1 (1888) 22 QBD 23; 53 JP 149; 58 LJMC 10; 16 Cox CC 511; 37 WR 166; [1886–90] All ER Rep 33; 59 LT 780; 5 TLR 61. Unless otherwise stated, the references to the Court for Crown Cases Reserved decision in this chapter are from (1888) 22 QBD 23, although the other reports of the case were consulted in constructing this chapter. As the name suggests, a law report is a published account of courtroom proceedings in a case. It is produced for lawyers and generally includes a summary of the facts which led the parties to come to court and the legal decision as well as the text of the judge's or judges' pronouncements on law.

2 Justice Hawkins in *Clarence* at 55.

3 I have chosen to refer to the husband and wife by their first names here in order to avoid referring to them as Mrs and Mr Clarence or using their first and second names at each mention, as this seemed to be overly cumbersome.

4 This was recorded by the Central Criminal Court. See *Old Bailey Proceedings Online* (*OBP*) (http://www.oldbaileyonline.org, version 7.0, accessed 30 March 2013), October 1888 (t18881022), index, vii.

5 See further Chapter 5.

6 Rape at that time only applied to non-consensual vaginal penetration. 'Indecent assault' was the forerunner of what is now 'sexual assault' (see sections 52 and 62, Offences Against the Person Act 1861 and section 3, Sexual Offences Act 2003). No one could validly consent to anal intercourse at this time. See section 61, Offences Against the Person Act 1861. Given the different attitudes towards anal intercourse and its illegality (along with the fact that such activity did not figure in *Clarence*), the offence of sodomy is only briefly considered in this chapter.

7 In particular, see: K. Gleeson, 'Sex, Wives, and Prostitutes: Debating *Clarence*' in J. Rowbotham and K. Stevenson (eds), *Criminal Conversations: Victorian Crimes, Social Panic, and Moral Outrage*, Columbus, OH: Ohio State University Press, 2005, ch. 13 and 'The Problem of Clarence, Brutal at His Best: James Fitzjames Stephen and the Doctrine of Sexual Inequality', *Nottingham Law Journal*, 14(1), 2005, 1–16; C. Withey, 'Biological GBH: overruling Clarence?', *New Law Journal*, 153(7104), 2003, 1698, 1707.

8 For example, see: M.L. Shanley, *Feminism, Marriage, and the Law in Victorian England, 1850–1895*, London: IB Tauris, 1989; A.J. Hammerton, *Cruelty and Companionship: Conflict in Nineteenth Century Married Life*, London: Routledge, 1992.

9 Chapter 1 considers male sexual conduct towards girls.

10 *OBP* (http://www.oldbaileyonline.org, version 7.0, accessed 30 March 2013), April 1888, trial of Charles James Clarence (28) (t18880423–429a). The National Archives (TNA) PRO CRIM 4/1030.

11 See, for example: *Morning Post*, 12 November 1888, p. 6; *Standard*, 12 November 1888, p. 2; *Reynolds's Newspaper*, 11 November 1888, p. 8; *Daily News*, 12 November 1888, p. 4; *The Pall Mall Gazette*, 12 November 1888, p. 7; *Lloyd's Weekly Newspaper* (Special Sunday Morning Edition), 11 November 1888, p. 12; *Bury and Norwich Post, and Suffolk Standard*, 13 November 1888, p. 2; *Huddersfield Daily Chronicle*, 12 November 1888, p. 4.

12 11 June 1888, p. 4, 18 June 1888, p. 4.

13 *The Times*, 12 November 1888, p. 3; 'Regina v Clarence', *British Medical Journal*, 2(1455), 17 November 1888, 1135.

14 For example, see: 'Regina v Clarence', *British Medical Journal*, 2(1455), 17 November 1888, 1121; 'Marital Cruelty', *Saturday Review of Politics, Literature,*

Science and Art, 66(1725), 17 November 1888, 577–8; 'Criminal Law', *Law Magazine and Review*, 14 (Quarterly Digest), 1888–9, 5th ser., 35–6.
15 See TNA: PRO KB 30/4 and CRIM 12/94.
16 *Clarence* at 23–4. There is no record of the circumstances which led Selina to be so specific about the date on which she was infected.
17 Charles's age is given in the *OBP*, April 1888, Charles James Clarence (t18880423–429a).
18 *Clarence* at 23.
19 These were accessed via http://www.ancestry.co.uk (accessed 30 March 2013).
20 The Terrace was actually Nos 176–202C Manchester Road, see H. Hobhouse, 'Cubitt Town: The Inland Area', in *Survey of London: Volumes 43 and 44: Poplar, Blackwall and Isle of Dogs* (1994), pp. 498–514, http://www.british-history.ac.uk/report.aspx?compid=46526 (accessed 30 March 2013).
21 See, for example, ibid., pp. 375–87.
22 Selina was listed as head of household.
23 This is taken from the brief summary of the facts in the law report (at 24).
24 *OBP*, April 1888, trial of Charles James Clarence (t18880423–429a).
25 See TNA: PRO KB 30/4.
26 TNA: PRO CRIM 4/1010.
27 The assizes heard the most serious of criminal cases and were essentially a forerunner of the Crown Court. On the assizes see further, J.H. Baker, *An Introduction to English Legal History*, 4th edn, London: Butterworths, 2002, pp. 20–2.
28 Some of these documents, signed by the judges concerned, are preserved in TNA: PRO KB 30 (CCCR, Pleadings) – the (rather grubby) statement of the case in *Clarence* is in KB 30/4.
29 For example, this was indeed the case in *R v Barrow* (1868) LR 1 CCCR 156; 38 LJMC 20; 11 Cox CC 191; 17 WR 102; 19 LT 293. *Barrow* is considered later in this chapter.
30 On the CCCR see further: J.F. Stephen, *A History of the Criminal Law of England*, London: Macmillan, 1883, vol. I, pp. 311–13; P. Handler, 'The Court for Crown Cases Reserved, 1848–1908', *Law and History Review*, 29(1), 2011, 259–88, pp. 263–4.
31 See *The Times*, 11 June 1888, p. 4.
32 Ibid.
33 One was abroad as a result of ill-health and the other was in Chambers, see *The Times*, 18 June, 1888, p. 4.
34 The length of the hearing was recorded in *The Times*, ibid.
35 The account of the arguments provided here is taken from the law reports of the case.
36 *Clarence* at 24.
37 Sir M. Hale, *The History of the Pleas of the Crown*, London: Lincoln's Inn, 1736, vol. 1, 629.
38 *Clarence* at 24.
39 Ibid., at 24.
40 Ibid., at 25.
41 Ibid.
42 Ibid.
43 Poland's arguments are summarized in *Clarence* at p. 26.
44 Ibid.
45 The length of their deliberations was given in *The Times*, 18 June, 1888, p. 4.
46 Ibid.

47 Day, Charles and Grantham were absent but conveyed their views through others on the bench; see *The Times*, 12 November 1888, p. 3.
48 Day agreed with Hawkins and Charles with Field (*Clarence* at 55, 61).
49 This volume was co-authored by B. Hemyng, J. Binny and A. Halliday. London: Griffin, Bohn.
50 See the section of the book on 'Prostitution' authored by Mayhew and Hemyng, pp. 35–272.
51 '"Crimes of Moral Outrage": Victorian Encryptions of Sexual Violence', in Rowbotham and Stevenson, *Criminal Conversations*, ch. 14, p. 233 and generally.
52 2 February 1878, p. 8.
53 14 February 1879, p. 8.
54 8 June 1872, p. 7.
55 *Essex Standard, and General Advertiser for the Eastern Counties*, 4 February 1870, p. 3.
56 Other authors have identified similar trends. For example, Leonore Davidoff described Victorian society as becoming concerned about sex and sexual behaviour (especially as regarded men). 'Class and Gender in Victorian Britain', in J.L. Newton, M.P. Ryan and J. Walkowitz (eds), *Sex and Class in Women's History*, London: Routledge, 1983, p. 20.
57 *Prostitution and Victorian Society: Women, Class, and the State*, Cambridge: Cambridge University Press, 1980, p. 3.
58 See further Chapter 1.
59 Influential writers in this genre included Edward Burnett Tylor – see, for example, *Primitive Culture: Researches into the Development of Mythology, Philosophy, Religion, Art, and Custom*, two vols, London: John Murray, 1871.
60 For example, see: *Shield*, 24 December, p. 338, 14 June 1873, p. 194, 9 August 1873, p. 262, 3 November 1877, p. 275.
61 This was also published in pamphlet form (London: Dyer Brothers).
62 Ibid., p. 8.
63 London: W.H. Guest, p. 7.
64 Ibid., pp. 9–10.
65 The Contagious Diseases Act 1864 was subsequently amended by the Contagious Diseases Acts 1866 and 1869.
66 On the Acts see further, Walkowitz, *Prostitution*.
67 Letter, *Shield*, 9 August 1873, p. 262.
68 *Some Thoughts on the Present Aspect of the Crusade: Against the State Regulation of Vice*, Liverpool: T. Brakell, 1874.
69 *The Constitution Violated. An Essay [Advocating the Repeal of the Contagious Diseases Acts 1866, 1868 and 1869]*, Edinburgh; Edmonston and Douglas, 1871, p. 43.
70 Ibid., p. 91.
71 *Some Thoughts*, p. 9.
72 Ibid., p. 14.
73 Contagious Diseases Acts Repeal Act 1886.
74 Indeed, the working class were by no means entirely excluded from this branch of law in the period. For example, see G. Savage, '"The Wilful Communication of a Loathsome Disease": Marital Conflict and Venereal Disease in Victorian England', *Victorian Studies*, 34(1), 1990, 35–54, pp. 45–6.
75 See *Cruelty and Companionship*, pp. 108 and Bourke, 'Sexual Violence', p. 421.
76 The spouses were George and Mrs Prigg (the latter's first name was not given), see *Bristol Mercury and Daily Post*, 27 January 1881, p. 6, 5 February, 1881, p. 7.
77 See, for example, Hammerton, *Cruelty and Companionship*, p. 109.

78 See *Clarence* at 26, 51, 58.
79 See Savage '"The Wilful Communication of a Loathsome Disease"' and Hammerton, *Cruelty and Companionship*, pp. 109–10.
80 For example, see: *Birmingham Daily Post*, 10 July 1884, p.5; *North-Eastern Daily Gazette*, 9 July 1884, p. 4. See further Savage, 'The Wilful Communication', p. 36, who describes the case as having 'enjoyed an exceptional notoriety'.
81 London: Longmans, Green, Reader and Dyer 1869, p. 522. See further, J. Bourke, 'Sexual Violence, Marital Guidance, and Victorian Bodies: An Aesthesiology', *Victorian Studies*, 50(3), 2008, 419–36, pp. 422–3.
82 See, in particular, 'Sexual Violence, Marital Guidance, and Victorian Bodies', pp. 423–4.
83 London: John Murray.
84 London: John Murray. The references here are to the 1874 edition (London: John Murray).
85 For example, see *Character*, p. 158.
86 Ibid., p.159.
87 Ibid., p. 158 and on self-control see generally ch. VI.
88 Ibid., p. 304.
89 See, for example, *The Subjection of Women*, pp. 172–3.
90 *Safeguards Against Immorality*, p. 8.
91 See *Character*, ch. XI.
92 *A Treatise on the Law of Domestic Relations*, Boston, MA: Little, Brown & Co., p. 37, quoted in Bourke, ibid., p. 422.
93 (1877) 2 QBD 410; 46 LJMC 130; 13 Cox CC 388; 25 WR 398; 36 LT 32.
94 12 March, 1877, p. 10.
95 Flattery (1877) 2 QBD 410 at 411–3.
96 *The Times*, 12 March 1877, p. 10.
97 Kelly, 2 QBD 410 at 413.
98 Ibid., at 413.
99 Significantly, as we shall see, this view was to result in statutory change less than a decade later in 1885.
100 (1838) 8 C & P 265.
101 (1838) 8 C & P 286.
102 Justice Kelly, who had been the trial judge in *Barrow* but did not have a part in the CCCR decision, had in fact always felt that the initial conviction was correct (see *Barrow* LR 1 CCCR 156 at 158). By 1877, as one of the judges in *Flattery*, he was referring to it and other cases which supported its approach as 'decisions which I regret', (1877) 2 QBD 410 at 413).
103 (1866) 176 ER 925; 4 F & F 1105.
104 (1878) 38 LT 540; 14 Cox CC 114.
105 In fact, he did so on the basis that in *Flattery* the CCCR had expressed a wish to reconsider *Barrow* and a conviction would allow the matter to be reserved – so the case was sent to the CCCR on the question of fraud, rather than the fact that the victim was asleep.
106 Consequently, the issue of any fraud on the part of Young did not figure in the judgments.
107 (1871) LR 1 CCCR 334; 36 JP 564; 41 LJMC 12; 12 Cox CC 137; 20 WR 123; 25 LT 669.
108 This issue remains a source of controversy and disagreement. See, for example: J. Temkin, 'Sexual History Evidence – Beware the Backlash', *Criminal Law Review*, 2003, 217–42; D. Birch, 'Untangling Sexual History', *Criminal Law Review*, June 2003, 370–83.

109 (1871) LR 1 CCR 334 at 337.
110 (1866) 176 ER 925; 4 F & F 1105.
111 See further Chapter 1.
112 The defendant had given her alcohol each evening and she had gone to sleep quickly, remembering nothing of her nights with Bennett.
113 For example, see the comments of Justice Fitzgerald in the Irish case of *Hegarty v Shine* (1878) LR 2 Ir 273; 14 Cox CC 124 at 129.
114 On the alarmingly uncertain position of the sleeping or unconscious complainant today see section 75(2)(d), Sexual Offences Act 2003.
115 The precise affliction is not specified in the brief report, which merely refers to it as a 'foul disease' and as 'venereal disease' (at 1106).
116 A court of first instance is the court where a case commences or a court of trial, as opposed to a court of review or appeal.
117 (1867) 13 Cox CC 28.
118 Ibid., at 28.
119 *OBP* (http://www.oldbaileyonline.org, version 7.0, accessed 30 March 2013), August 1867, trial of William Henry Sinclair (t18670819-756).
120 *OBP* (http://www.oldbaileyonline.org, version 7.0, accessed 30 March 2013), August 1867, trial of William Henry Sinclair (t18670819-777).
121 The report is not entirely clear as to the charges.
122 She seemed to have been taken to have consented to sexual activity as a result of a lack of evidence of resistance. Indeed, in the second trial it was accepted by the prosecution counsel that, as there was no evidence of her resistance, a conviction for rape could not be supported (*Sinclair* at 28).
123 See Coleridge in *R v Coney* (1882) LR 8 QBD 534 at 569.
124 (1871) LR 1 CCR 334 at 337.
125 Flattery (1877) 2 QBD 410 at 414.
126 *Clarence* at 51–2.
127 Ibid., at 52–3.
128 Ibid., at 52.
129 Ibid., at 54.
130 Ibid., at 51.
131 Ibid.
132 Ibid.
133 Ibid., at 51–2.
134 Ibid., at 52.
135 Ibid., at 51.
136 Ibid., at 55.
137 Ibid., at 54.
138 Ibid., at 57–8. See *Popkin v Popkin* (1794) 1 Hagg Ecc 765 at 767; 162 ER 745.
139 He gave the example of a wife who refused intercourse because of her own ill health but whose husband then, with the help of a third person, 'forcibly perpetrated the act', *Clarence* at 57–8.
140 Although the marital rape exemption was restricted by the courts from the middle of the twentieth century, it was not until 1991 that the then House of Lords finally overturned it in *R v R* [1992] 1 AC 599; [1991] 4 All ER 481; [1991] 3 WLR 767; [1992] 94 Cr App Rep 216. This was then enacted in legislation: section 142, Criminal Justice and Public Order Act 1994.
141 *Clarence* at 59.
142 Ibid., at 59–61. In doing so, he dismissed the Irish case of *Hegarty v Shine*, which was cast by the defence as calling *Bennett* and *Sinclair* into some doubt.
143 Ibid., at 58–9.

144 'Sex, Wives, and Prostitutes'.
145 *Clarence* at 28.
146 Ibid., at 27.
147 See, for example, ibid., at 28–9.
148 Ibid., at 32–3.
149 Ibid., at 34.
150 Ibid., at 40.
151 Ibid., at 46.
152 Ibid., at 65.
153 Ibid., at 33.
154 Ibid., at 37.
155 'Marital Cruelty', pp. 577–8.
156 Ibid., p. 578.
157 'Regina v. Clarence', 2(1455), 17 November 1888, 1121.
158 Ibid.
159 'Marital Cruelty', p. 578.
160 'An Action for Assault', 2(1605), 3 October 1891, 776.
161 See *The Times* reports of the case: 21 September 1891, p. 3; 22 September 1891, p. 5. There was also a brief Old Bailey record of the trial. See *OBP* (http://www.oldbaileyonline.org, version 7.0, accessed 30 March 2013), September 1891, trial of Linden Howard (22) (t18910914-712). As to abduction, see further Chapter 1.
162 What is more, this change post-*Clarence* might also be said to have been further evidenced by the revision of the majority's view in *Holmes* that a female complainant's statements as to her past sexual history could not be contradicted (in the CCCR case of *R v Riley* (1887) 18 QBD 481; 56 LJMC 52; 16 Cox CC 191; 35 WR 382; 56 LT 371 it was decided that evidence that a woman had in the past consented to sexual intercourse with a man accused of indecently assaulting her was admissible). Past sexual history evidence remains an area of controversy. See, for example: L. Kelly, J. Temkin and S. Griffiths, *Section 41: An Evaluation of New Legislation Limiting Sexual History Evidence in Rape Trials*, London: Home Office, 2006. http://webarchive.nationalarchives.gov.uk/20110218135832/http://rds.homeoffice.gov.uk/rds/pdfs06/rdsolr2006.pdf (accessed 30 March 2013).
163 [1891–94] All ER Rep 61; [1891] 1 QB 671; 60 LJQB 346; 64 LT 679; 55 JP 246; 7 TLR 382. See Chapter 5.
164 See Shanley, *Feminism Marriage and the Law*, p. 185.
165 See further Bourke, 'Sexual Violence', pp. 423–5.
166 London: Heinemann.
167 Ibid., p. 178.
168 Interview in *The Humanitarian*, March 1896, quoted in L. Bland, *Banishing the Beast: English Feminism and Sexual Morality 1885–1914*, London: Penguin, 1995, p. 149. See further the discussion of Grand in *Banishing the Beast*, pp. 146–9.
169 Ignota, 'Judicial Sexual Bias' *Westminster Review*, 149(3), March 1898, 279–88. Ignota was one of Elizabeth Clarke Wolstenholme Elmy's pseudonyms.
170 Ibid., p. 285.
171 On Wolstenholme Elmy's efforts regarding the legal exemption, see further, for example, Shanley, *Feminism, Marriage, and the Law*, pp. 184–7.
172 See Savage, 'The Wilful Communication', pp. 38–9.
173 London: E. Pankhurst, 1913.
174 Ibid., see, in particular, pp. vi, vii, viii, 9, 10, 155.

175 It was not until 2003 that the transmission of a disease through sexual intercourse was to be revisited by the courts and found to constitute a section 20 assault. However, the ailment transmitted here was HIV and the time, place and issues were very different. Indeed, whilst I feel inclined towards the view taken by the minority in *Clarence*, in the very different world of the late twentieth and early twenty-first centuries I would have to side with those who question the wisdom of criminalizing the communication of sexually transmitted infections. In particular, see Matthew Weait's work, including, *Intimacy and Responsibility: The Criminalisation of HIV Transmission*, Abingdon: Routledge-Cavendish, 2007.

Chapter 5

R v Jackson 1891[1]

Dictating dominion

> ... such quaint and absurd dicta as are to be found in the books as to the right of a husband over his wife in respect of personal chastisement are not, I think, now capable of being cited as authorities in a court of justice in this or any civilized country ... no English subject has such a right of his own motion to imprison another English subject, whether his wife or any one else ... [2]

> A series of propositions have been quoted which, if true, make an English wife the slave, the abject slave, of her husband. One proposition that has been referred to is that a husband has a right to beat his wife. I do not believe this ever was the law.[3]

This chapter takes the infamous Clitheroe abduction of 1891 as its focus. Against her relatives' wishes and without their knowledge, Emily Hall, a lady of independent means, had married Edmund Jackson, a man of uncertain wealth, in the autumn of 1887. On the day of the nuptials the couple parted company by agreement and Edmund[4] left the country a few days later. Upon his return, Emily refused to live with him. Having gone to court in an attempt to force her to cohabit, but to no avail, he decided to take matters into his own hands, forcibly seizing Emily and keeping her captive in a Blackburn property owned by his brother. There she remained, whilst her family (the word is used for ease throughout this chapter to refer to her two sisters and brother-in-law – but *not* her husband) sought her release through the courts.

The legal action at the heart of this chapter's story concerned the challenge to this forcible detention which played out in the civil courts. This means that, unlike the other chapters in this volume, although the subject matter here remains men and violence, the case forming the focus of this tale-telling is not one involving a prosecution in the criminal law courts. That said, the issues raised implicated both civil and criminal law, with matrimonial law being the focus of the case and the possibility of criminal charges being pursued against a violent husband forming a backdrop to it.

The *Jackson* case involved an application for a writ of *habeas corpus* seeking Emily's release, the argument being not only that Emily wanted and had a right to her freedom, but also that Edmund had no right to have seized and imprisoned her. This strategy was initially unsuccessful in the High Court, where the two judges viewed Edmund's action as morally and legally justified and defended the supremacy of husbands in marriage. That decision, however, was appealed to the Court of Appeal, where, just a few days later, the three judges adopted a very different perspective and Emily's liberty was restored. In so deciding, they ruled in no uncertain terms that, in both morality and law, a husband's physical control over his wife was limited. More specifically, the decision meant that a husband could neither attempt to bend his spouse to his will through coercion nor enforce conjugality through confinement.

Jackson has been written about before, not least in the context of historical work on marriage, women's rights and feminism, as well as in the field of literary studies.[5] There is also scholarship on issues of gender, law and marriage during the period.[6] This work is drawn upon and forms a backdrop to the story-telling and argument in this chapter. However, the approach adopted here is distinct, as not only is more detail included than in previous accounts of the case, but also the focus is on law and ideas about men and, more specifically, English manliness, with the text recalling contemporary concerns about the male of the species which resonated with the *Jackson* litigation.

In terms of this book's 'binding men' narrative, the tale told about the case focuses on efforts to end, or at least restrict, a husband's dominion in marriage. In particular, the Court of Appeal decision is cast in the context of other late nineteenth-century attempts (both within and beyond legal spheres) to address what we would now call 'domestic violence'. In doing so, such abuse is taken to encompass financial, emotional, psychological and physical ill-treatment as well as the overarching idea of coercive control (whilst sexual violence is also a form of such behaviour it is not specifically considered in this chapter as it did not figure in *Jackson*[7] and men's sexual conduct towards women – including husbands and wives – is the focus of Chapter 4). This definition reflects both late nineteenth-century and early twenty-first-century understandings of spousal (or, in the modern context, partner) ill-usage, as these conceptions are by no means as distinct as might perhaps be supposed, although in the earlier period they were not all categorized as 'violence' but were seen as cruelty and mistreatment.[8] Indeed, this chapter catalogues Victorian concerns about each of these kinds of misuse.

In this context, the wealth and social standing of the Jacksons (and, in particular, of Emily) becomes an important consideration as, although the legal decision in the case would be binding on all husbands, the discussions and pronouncements were very much tempered by the identity of the particular husband and wife at its centre. Thus, for the Court of Appeal judges who met Emily, she was a 'lady' who had been very much wronged by the very man who should have been her companion and protector. In contrast, Edmund's character, actions and motives were at least a matter of some doubt – particularly when it came to money.

The text below begins by looking at the events which led to the case being brought, traces its progress through the courts, briefly considers the legal issues and arguments involved and the decisions taken by the High Court and Court of Appeal. *Jackson* is then re-narrated in the context of pre-existing anxieties about husbands who ill-treated their wives, as well as other attempts to legally limit abusive husbands. Then reactions to *Jackson* are examined, along with continued efforts to rein in male marital violence following the case. At the same time, there is also consideration of contemporary resistance to the idea that men's rights in marriage should be restricted.

Jackson

The basic happenings which led to *Jackson* recounted here, along with the story of the court case, are reconstructed from a range of sources, including the law reports of the Court of Appeal decision, newspaper articles as well as Emily and Edmund's conflicting descriptions of their courtship and marriage. The law reports offer little by way of colour, focusing upon the judicial pronouncements. In terms of the press, the happenings received a good deal of coverage, not only in Britain and Ireland, but also in papers around the world.[9] To those publications which had a tendency towards a sensationalist tone, the Jacksons' story was something of a gift and some of the reporting made the most of this, seemingly revelling in adopting a rather short-breathed and exaggerated air in order to depict the daily developments in 'The Clitheroe Romance'. Indeed, the unfolding events in Lancashire seemed to have more than a little in common with the melodramatic fiction which was so popular in the late nineteenth century and the newspapers often made the most of this.[10]

Accounts of a different order were produced by Edmund and Emily. These were published following her release from captivity[11] and, unsurprisingly, told distinct tales of the history and portrayed their respective author's thinking and emotions very differently. Edmund sought to represent himself as a thoroughly reasonable man, who had conducted himself entirely honestly and, in abducting and holding his wife, had been completely within his moral and legal rights. He had, however, been wronged by his wife's family's determination to first prevent then wreck their union. In contrast, Emily's story provided a poignant description of her time in captivity:

> During all the days I passed much of my time in crying, and that day, when I was told that I had no chance of escape I was more miserable and cried more than ever. I cried all the evening. I begged and implored

> many times every day of all I saw in the house from the day of my being taken to help me to get my release. I never ceased to wish earnestly to be set free.[12]

Keeping in mind this demonstration of the psychological and emotional harm caused by the imprisonment, let alone the stress, upset and physical harm of being forcibly abducted, we turn to the background to the litigation.

The abduction and imprisonment

At the time we take up her tale in 1887, Emily Emma Maude Hall was a woman of means,[13] aged in her early 40s (she was 46 at the time the *Jackson* case reached the courts in 1891).[14] Emily, the youngest of three sisters had

Figure 8 Emily Emma Maude Jackson.

Y Genedl Cymreig, 1 April 1891, p. 6.

not married, and was living with her unmarried sister, Esther Anne Maude Hall, in Clitheroe. Her other sibling, Betsy Alice Maud Baldwin, had wed and lived nearby. Emily's brother-in-law, Hartley Baldwin, was a lawyer – something which was to prove of assistance when the family were called upon to consider how best to release Emily from what they saw as Edmund's far from loving clutches. It is also worth noting that Emily had a weak constitution and suffered from attacks of rheumatic fever.[15]

Edmund Haughton Jackson's antecedents were less clear. Press reports of the abduction and its aftermath described him variously as being in his forties, fifties or early sixties and as 'an elderly man with grey hair and grey moustache'. In his affidavit, however, he stated that in March 1891 he was in his 48th year, making him only slightly older than his wife.[16] He had grown up in Blackburn and came from a military family.[17] Some papers described him as having had great adventures as an irregular in New Zealand, fighting in the Maori Wars, as well as having reputedly had a part in the American Civil War and in 'some of the petty wars in South America'. He was said to have then opted for a less glamorous career, taking up a position with the New Zealand Post Office. This he then 'threw up' in order to return to England,[18] meaning that he had no occupation at the time of his marriage to Emily; thus, the parish register listed him only as 'Gentleman'.[19] As to his financial position, Edmund claimed to have enough by way of income to keep himself, although not a wife, but stated that he also possessed capital with which he planned to buy land in New Zealand, begin farming and thereby make his fortune. He made no secret of the fact that he felt his means were insufficient to support a wife, so that Emily, along with her family, were apparently aware of his professed circumstances by the time of the marriage.[20] However, it is possible, given what happened subsequently, that he had in fact somewhat over-estimated his resources.

On Saturday 5 November 1887, Emily travelled from her home in Clitheroe to St Paul's Church, Blackburn, where she married Edmund in a private ceremony. The two, having known each other for some time,[21] seem to have chosen this course because Emily's family had some reservations about her groom. Indeed, it very much appeared that she herself had initially either gone along or agreed with these misgivings. So, it was not until the evening of their nuptials that the couple went to see her family to communicate the news. At this point, Emily's husband was apparently accepted by her two sisters and brother-in-law, both her parents being deceased.

That night (their wedding night) they went their separate ways. Emily returned to the house which she shared with her unmarried sister in Clitheroe, whilst Edmund went to Blackburn where he spent the night, as he planned to leave for London early the next day in order to set things in motion for their future. He was imminently to depart for New Zealand, where it was intended that Emily would join him once he had established himself. All this had been previously planned by Edmund and accepted by Emily. During the few days before his departure Emily made a settlement in relation to her wealth (by this time the Married Women's Property Acts 1870 and 1882 meant that she was able to retain control of her own property and financial affairs in marriage).[22] According to Emily, this document provided that the whole of her income of about £600 a year was to go to Edmund for the duration of his life, should he outlive her.[23] Edmund, she claimed, 'brought nothing to the settlement.'[24] He, however, was to maintain that the arrangement was 'wholly in [his wife's] favour'.[25] Shortly after this legal document was drawn up, Edmund set sail for New Zealand, leaving on Thursday 10 November, five days after the wedding.[26]

Emily and Edmund communicated by letter during his travels. However, they soon fell out. Their accounts differ as to what was actually written, when it was received and what was going on behind the scenes. Emily's version of events suggested, amongst other things, that he had misled her as to his financial resources and his business abilities – and it seems likely that she came to doubt his motives in marrying her as a result of this. In contrast, Edmund maintained that he had been harshly and wrongly judged by his wife, who he felt was, at this time, under the influence of her relatives. He also offered alternative explanations for his lack of success in the Antipodes and pleaded miscommunication as the cause of what he saw as misunderstandings between himself and his spouse.

Whatever the truth of the matter, and feeling her health prevented her from joining him, Emily requested that Edmund return to England. He agreed to do so but asked that she send money to pay for his and a companion's fares; something which only seems to have heightened Emily's doubts about her husband. He, nevertheless, headed homeward. Meanwhile, at some stage during his absence, Emily decided that she would not live with him.

Having arrived back in England in July 1888 and unsuccessfully sought to persuade his wife to cohabit with him, in the summer of 1889 Edmund applied for a decree of restitution of conjugal rights, which he obtained on 30 July.[27] At this time he could also have applied for a settlement of his wife's property, which might have provided him with an annual income in the form of maintenance payments,[28] but he did not do so.[29] This court order required Emily to cohabit with her husband. Emily refused to comply and, because the 1884 Matrimonial Causes Act had removed the court's power to penalize spouses who refused to obey the decree by imprisoning them, Edmund's options in terms of legal actions were limited.[30] As non-compliance with such a decree constituted desertion, he might have applied for a judicial separation, although not a divorce, meaning that the marriage would continue[31] – moreover, as the marriage does not seem to have been consummated he could have applied for an annulment on the grounds of Emily's refusal or inability to have sexual relations.[32] Edmund, however, pursued neither option.

Instead, after some time had passed, Edmund decided to take matters into his own hands. On Sunday, 8 March 1891 he and two male friends (brothers Dixon Robinson, an articled clerk, and W.H. Robinson, a medic) forcibly abducted Emily when she and her married sister, Betsy, emerged from Clitheroe Parish Church.[33] As they realized what was happening, Emily and her sibling clung to one another, but to no avail. Emily was grabbed, literally manhandled, dragged away and bundled onto the floor of a waiting carriage. Betsy recalled the circumstances of the seizure, describing how, once it was clear what was happening, Emily had asked her to hold on to her so that she could not be taken. Then '[a] struggle ensued' between the men and the two women:

> Eventually [Emily] was dragged backwards into the bottom of the carriage by her husband, I clinging to her all the time. He then bent back with great violence two of the fingers of my right hand, and so loosened my grip round her waist. When my hands were being thus loosened, Dixon Robinson (the articled clerk) pushed me violently on the right shoulder, and I fell back from the carriage. My sister's legs were sticking out of the carriage when she was on the bottom of the carriage, and Dixon Robinson, after pushing me away, got hold of her legs and shoved them into the carriage and jumped in, and immediately drove away with her … She resisted going with him to the utmost of her power, and struggled violently against him, and was only taken away by main force.[34]

Significantly, this account (which appeared in Betsy's sworn statements and was put before both the High and Appeal Court) highlighted the level of violence used against both women.

Once secured, the captive was taken to a house owned by Edmund's brother in Rover Street, Blackburn (see Figure 9). Her family followed and soon the police arrived, with the aim of maintaining a watch over proceedings in order to keep the peace. The press also took an immediate interest, with the first stories about the happenings appearing the day following the abduction.[35]

Some sources reported that, when Emily's brother-in-law arrived on the scene, he was keen to use force to seize her back immediately but that he was dissuaded from this course by the local chief constable.[36] Whatever the truth of this, her family maintained a presence outside the house and it was rumoured that they were either preparing or ready to have the property stormed.[37] In response, Edmund arranged for men to guard the premises and entrance and exit to the house was restricted, with provisions being brought up by means of a rope and basket dropped from a window and communications being maintained with the outside world by telephone.[38] As the story of the abduction spread, the property soon became the centre

THE BLACKBURN COTTAGE TO WHICH MR. JACKSON ESCORTED MRS. JACKSON.

Figure 9 'The Blackburn Cottage to Which Mr Jackson Escorted Mrs Jackson.'

Penny Illustrated Paper and Illustrated Times, 28 March 1891, p. 6.

of some attention and at various points curious crowds gathered outside to watch 'the siege of Rover Street'.[39]

Meanwhile, inside the house, Emily was placed in the care of Edmund's sister along with a nurse employed by her husband for this very purpose. She was also seen by a doctor known to her husband (Dr Martin) – although Edmund, who arranged the medic's visit, claimed not to know of her fragile health at this stage.[40] Emily's personal medical advisers were, however, refused entrance. Aside from the violence of her capture and containment, there was evidence of a direct physical assault committed against her by Edmund during the course of her confinement; soon after their arrival at this address her husband had pulled off her bonnet, throwing it into the fire.

As the actions of Emily's relatives following her abduction illustrate, it was abundantly clear that they objected to both this and her captivity and tried to end it or at least watch over her to ensure no additional ill was done to her behind the doors of the Blackburn house, which in their eyes was her prison. In particular, as the hours of the detention turned into days her unmarried sister, Esther, repeatedly tried to gain access to Emily but was thwarted. Instead, she was left to keep watch and wait for a chance to communicate with her sister.

It seems that some words and signs were exchanged between the siblings, with Emily snatching limited opportunities of signalling and speaking from the windows of the house. According to Esther's affidavit, each time they had managed an exchange Emily had 'told me that she was detained against her will' and that she 'wanted to get out'. Moreover, she had 'frequently been in tears, and apparently in great distress.'[41] In addition, during these interactions Emily had apparently suggested that involving a solicitor might be the answer. Emily's lawyer was duly contacted and he attempted to enter the house to consult with her but, like her relatives and her medical advisers, was refused access.[42]

Emily's family's response to all this included initiating a criminal prosecution against Edmund and the Robinson brothers in connection with the violent struggle with Emily and her sister, Betsy, outside the church. Betsy's husband obtained warrants for the three men's arrest for a common assault upon his wife.[43] However, as the central aim of this strategy was most probably not to prosecute and convict Edmund and his coadjutors, but rather to free Emily, it seemed likely to be fruitless. Indeed, such an action allowed for no means to challenge either the abduction or the imprisonment. However, it did involve an attempt to call Emily as the principal prosecution witness and thereby require her to be produced in court in order that she might be heard. Her family may well have hoped that this would create an opportunity for rescuing her – or that the fact her abductors were facing criminal charges might have caused them to rethink their actions and release their prisoner.

At around this point Edmund seems to have made an offer to Emily's family. He was prepared to allow some very limited and probably censored communication by way of letters with his wife on the condition that the two were left alone to become better acquainted and get on with their married life. This was, unsurprisingly, not accepted by her siblings and brother-in-law.[44]

Edmund and the Robinsons were, consequently, summonsed to appear before the magistrates in Clitheroe, but they resisted the execution of these warrants, remaining locked away in 2 Rover Street. Meanwhile, the police continued to keep vigil outside, along with the crowd of onlookers who haunted the address hoping to witness the next stage in the drama. Eventually an agreement was reached whereby the police would leave and the accused men would peaceably hand themselves over to the authorities and appear in Clitheroe Magistrates' Court on Wednesday 11 March. This they did – but only once the security of the address had been redoubled by the arrival of half a dozen men armed with 'picking sticks', presumably to avert the possibility of an attack or to ensure that, were efforts at rescue made, they could be resisted.[45]

In the Court, following some debate, the criminal case was scheduled for 23 March.[46] If matters had been left as they stood Emily would, therefore, have faced at least another 11 days of confinement – assuming that she was summonsed to give evidence and allowed to appear in court on that date. Unsurprisingly, her family looked to other and what they presumably hoped would be speedier and more assured means of effecting her release. The matter was, therefore, next pursued through the civil, rather than the criminal, courts.

The application

An action was commenced in the High Court, challenging the legality of Emily's captivity and calling for her immediate release. In terms of the legal procedure, this was an application for a writ of *habeas corpus* made by her family on her behalf. Here the burden of proof initially lay upon Emily's family and they needed to establish to the satisfaction of the court that the detention was *prima facie* unlawful. If they were successful, the court would then require Edmund both to produce the captive in the courtroom at a specified time and to provide written statements as to the reasons for the restraint, so that the legality of the confinement could be fully assessed. So, at this stage the burden of proof would shift and Edmund would need to establish beyond reasonable doubt[47] that the incarceration was lawful. If it were found to be unlawful, the court would order Emily's release. If the detention was deemed to be lawful, then Emily would be returned to Edmund's control.

The case came before Justices Cave and Jeune on Monday 16 March, eight days after Emily's churchyard capture. In keeping with the level of interest in events in Clitheroe and Blackburn, the case was widely reported in the press. The description of this stage of the proceedings retold here is largely drawn from the version of events reported in *The Times*, supplemented by a number of other accounts.[48]

The application was supported by affidavits from Emily's sisters, one of her doctors and her solicitor. No statement was sworn by Emily as she had had no opportunity to communicate directly with the outside world, so her view was constructed by others. However, her family's affidavits maintained that their adopted course was fully in accordance with their sibling's wishes, gleaned from the limited exchanges between the inside and outside of the house at Blackburn. Edmund was absent from the court and no representations were made on his behalf.

That Monday the affidavits, along with accompanying argument, were presented by Mr Lankester. He focused upon the idea that a husband's dominion over his wife had limits, maintaining that what had happened in the present case had overstepped them. In doing so, Lankester referred to a series of past cases in which an application had been successfully made on the behalf of a wife being held captive by her husband. These were by no means recent advances for wives' rights but rather authorities which had well over a century of standing.[49] For example, in the mid-eighteenth century there was a case involving the detention of the Countess of Ferrers by the fourth Earl Ferrers, Laurence Shirley. In 1757, a writ had been granted commanding the Earl to 'bring up the body of his countess', which he refused to obey; there then followed repeated efforts to get him to comply. Eventually, the freed Countess obtained a separation from her husband on grounds of cruelty.[50] The court was also directed to *R v Lister* (1721),[51] *R v Mead* (1758),[52] an attempt by a husband to regain his wife, and the infamous litigation concerning Lady Strathmore in the 1780s.[53]

Significantly, *Lister*, *Mead* and *Strathmore* involved extremely wealthy wives who were able to maintain control over their 'separate estates', which had been created by way of carefully (and, in the light of these cases, prudently) devised trusts made to set aside property for their 'separate use' during marriage.[54] Thus, in referencing these past cases there was possibly at least the suggestion that financial motives might also have been a factor in relation to *Jackson.*

Lister involved spouses who had separated by consent, the wealthy wife, Lady Rawlinson, making over some of her fortune to her husband, Captain Lister, as part of the agreement. In a marked parallel with *Jackson*, he subsequently seized her as she left church. He then held her in the hope of securing more of her property. She was located by her family who applied for a writ of *habeas corpus*, resulting in the court granting her release and issuing a warning to the husband that, should there be any further attempts to abduct his wife, 'they should bear a heavy hand over him'.[55]

In *Mead*, the husband, John Wilkes, had ill-treated his wealthy wife, Mary Wilkes. She had then given him 'a great sum' from her separate estate as consideration for a separation agreement[56] and went to live with her mother. Despite this, John subsequently successfully applied for a writ of *habeas corpus*, requiring that her mother produce Mary. When the spouses appeared before the court, however, it was decided that because of the separation agreement John had no power over his wife and she was free to live where and with whom she chose.

Money was also an issue in the wealthy Lady Mary Eleanor Strathmore's case. The fact that her property was protected for her own use was a matter of great concern to her second husband, Andrew Robinson Bowes, who had been unaware of this when they married. He sought by various means, both legal and less legitimate, to gain access to his wife's riches. The part of the story that concerns us here happened after Strathmore, who had been viciously treated by Bowes, had managed to escape his clutches. Knowing that her husband had repeatedly threatened to seize her, she wrote a letter stating that she wished to be released if this were to happen. Strathmore also directed that, in such circumstances, any document signed by her which purported to state that she was happy to remain with her husband should be ignored as it was either a forgery or was written under duress. Moreover, she declared that she would never return to her husband 'except by force' and advised that an application for a writ of *habeas corpus* might be the route to her release.[57] Her husband indeed subsequently captured her, a writ was sought and granted and her release ordered.[58] However, along the way, as in the *Ferrers* case, there was some difficulty in getting Bowes to cooperate.[59]

These cases, Lankester argued, all demonstrated that legally a husband could not forcibly seize and hold his wife. He then cited a much more contemporary basis upon which the application should be granted, referring to the fact that, since the Matrimonial Causes Act 1884, the courts had no power to punish a spouse by arresting and imprisoning them where they failed to comply with a decree for restitution of conjugal rights. This, he said, gave more weight to the argument that a husband could not himself seek to enforce such a decree by seizing and keeping his wife captive. In addition, perhaps realizing that he was not getting a sympathetic hearing from the bench, he maintained that Emily should at least be brought to court so that she might be heard, as to date she had had no opportunity either to consult with a lawyer or tell of any ill-treatment which she might have suffered. He also emphasized that, from what had been observed of her within the house, Emily was distressed by her position.

It was clear, however, from the number of interruptions by Justice Cave, as well as their nature, that Lankester's efforts were unlikely to be met with approval from at least one of the two judges; indeed, the application was refused by both of them. Cave took the view that both seizure and confinement were in accordance with law, as there was to his mind no evidence of ill-treatment. Indeed, he rejected the cases argued in support of the application, in particular distinguishing *Lister* and *Mead* because they involved husbands and wives who had previously made separation agreements, relying instead upon Justice Coleridge's[60] view of the relations between husbands and wives in the more recent but by no means contemporaneous *Re Cochrane* (1840).[61] This was a case involving a wife who had lived apart from her husband for four years before she was seized and held captive by him. The case involved a challenge of the holding. Coleridge had decided that the husband had acted legally and then proceeded to make a number of pronouncements upon the power of a husband over his wife. Most significantly, he had opined that '[t]here can be no doubt of the general dominion which the law of England attributes to the husband over the wife', adding that '[t]he husband hath by law power and dominion over his wife and may keep her by force within the bounds of duty, and may beat her, but not in a violent or cruel manner.'[62]

In contrast, Justice Jeune was both briefer and seemingly more hesitant in delivering his decision. In fact, he admitted that he had originally been minded to have Emily brought to court so that she might be heard. However, he explained that he had come to the conclusion that, although the forcible detention of one citizen by another was generally illegal, this was not true of a husband detaining his wife.

The appeal

The very next day (Tuesday 17 March) the case was taken to the still relatively new Civil Court of Appeal[63] where a brief initial hearing was held. This is only obliquely referred to in the legal reports of the decision[64] – so it is again necessary to look to the many newspaper accounts in order to study the proceedings (again the version primarily relied upon here is that provided by *The Times*).[65] The case was heard by the Lord Chancellor, Lord Halsbury, the Master of the Rolls, Lord Esher, along with Lord Justice Fry. Arguments were again presented on behalf of Emily and, still, neither Emily nor Edmund were present. This time though, the judges decided in the former's favour and issued a writ requiring that, on Thursday 19 March, Emily was to be produced in court and Edmund was to justify the captivity.

Hence it was that, on the 12th day of her imprisonment, Emily was brought to court by Edmund (Figures 8 and 10 depict them watching the proceedings that day).[66] The room was crowded and many who had been hoping to observe were left disappointed that there was insufficient space for all. Three important ladies were not to be so unfortunate as to be prevented from attending, however. Just before half-past ten three extra chairs were placed to the right of the judges' seats on the bench and these were soon occupied by two of the judges' wives – Lady Halsbury and Lady Esher – along with another unidentified lady, highlighting perhaps the degree of female interest (and interest on the part of upper class women, in particular) in a case concerned with the way a husband should treat his lady wife. The judges soon followed them and, at the same time, Emily was shown into the court.[67]

At this point in the proceedings, the onus shifted onto Edmund to justify Emily's holding. His arguments were supported by several sworn statements by himself, both Robinson brothers and Dr Martin, as well as the nurse who had been engaged to look after Emily. The construction of the story offered by his lawyer, Henn Collins, told of Emily's will having been overborne by her relatives, who were portrayed as being bent upon ruining her chance at happiness with her husband.[68] There was also a suggestion that her family wanted to keep Emily under their control because she was possessed of a not insignificant annual income[69] – so financial motives were probably at least implied by both sides in the case. In contrast, it was contended that all Edmund wanted was for his wife to be free of her family's influence, so that she could lead a happy life at his side.[70]

Collins claimed that Emily had been well looked after during her time at Blackburn[71] and in his affidavit Edmund maintained that he had treated his wife 'with every kindness and consideration' and that he could 'not remember to have said or done a cruel, unkind, or ungentlemanly word or act to her during the whole time.'[72] Indeed, all the affidavits presented on his behalf sought to argue that he had used no more force than was necessary in order to secure her person.[73]

So, the answer to the writ entailed that Emily was 'restrained only so far as to enable her husband to have a fair opportunity of enlisting her sympathies and winning her affections again.' In short, as his lawyer Collins put it, Edmund 'claimed the right of a husband to the custody of his wife and to social intercourse with her.'[74] However, as did not go unnoticed by the Court of Appeal judges, at points the contents of the affidavits submitted on Edmund's behalf contradicted the overarching story which was being presented to the court. There were, for example, the descriptions of her seizure by the abductors, which highlighted that force was used. Also, Dr Martin's sworn statement included a description of 'an extensive bruise' on her arm which was the result of the events outside St Mary's Church[75] as

Figure 10 Edmund Haughton Jackson.

Y Genedl Cymreig, 1 April 1891, p. 6.

well as an account of Emily having her bonnet ripped off her head and thrown in the fire by Edmund upon her arrival at Rover Street.[76] In addition, the doctor made reference to her initial state of 'excitement and exhaustion' and mentioned that at points during her time at Rover Street she had 'suffered from fits of depression'.[77]

In terms of law, Collins focused upon the idea of the dominion of a husband over his wife, referring to Coleridge's judgment in *Cochrane*, arguing also that, while a wife could not be imprisoned, she could be confined. That these contentions were reportedly met with some laughter in court, was perhaps suggestive of the direction in which the proceedings were heading, as was the line and tone of questioning from Halsbury and Esher, which was far from supportive of what they were hearing.[78] Perhaps more telling, though, was the continued presence of the three ladies to the right of the judges, who observed the proceedings, including in the case of two of them, their husbands' comments, and presumably had views as to Edmund's conduct – views of which their husbands were undoubtedly aware.

As to Emily's part, the Hall/Baldwin position as presented in the High Court was simply reiterated in the course of the appeal proceedings, then, at the close of the case, Emily was asked to withdraw with the judges to their chambers so that they could ascertain her story and views. What passed between the judges and the lady in the hallowed confines of the Court of Appeal remains shrouded in some mystery.[79] However, the effect of the conversation along with counsels' arguments was soon clear.

The decision

Upon the judges' return to the courtroom a unanimous decision was pronounced, rejecting Edmund's contentions and releasing Emily. To varying degrees, all the judges emphasized that a husband no longer (if he ever had) possessed complete dominion over his wife and, in doing so, the three rejected *Cochrane*; Esher declared the case to be wrong, Fry indicated that the correct approach had not been taken and Halsbury simply dismissed it as the only case which suggested that husbands had rights such as were claimed on the part of Edmund. As a result, Emily left the court a free woman and returned to Clitheroe.

Binding men and denouncing domestic violence

Jackson was a controversial case, with clear divisions amongst the judiciary and beyond as to how Emily's refusal and Edmund's actions should be viewed, as well as to what the legal outcome of their case should be. However, integral to all perspectives on the case were ideas concerning the nature of a man's role and duties in wedlock and the powers of a husband over his spouse – and these reflected contemporary thinking. Broadly speaking, those who took Emily's part called for Englishmen's behaviour towards their spouses to be regulated by society and law, so that civilized, chivalrous, gentlemanly and respectful conduct might be encouraged and ill-use punished. In contrast, for those who sided with Edmund, male rights and the dominion of a husband in marriage were stated and defended.

The pre-*Jackson* context

The latter part of the nineteenth century was a period when ideas about marriage were much discussed. Amongst these contemporary debates, there were those who sought to bolster or improve the institution by setting out an idealized image of the state of wedlock. Such authors and commentators tended to propound a particularly middle-class and very English model of domesticity for all, which reflected what were seen as modern Victorian models of manliness. Here, the union was portrayed as being about harmony and companionship, with the need for men to be respectful and chivalrous towards their wives, taking the role of benign and benevolent protector of the family – at its head but not in the role of a dominator, dictator or, indeed, parasite.[80]

For example, the immensely popular self-help books written by Samuel Smiles addressed the marital relationship. These works were aimed at all classes of men (and women) and included discussion of 'Companionship in Marriage'. Here the emphasis was upon the importance of purity, respect, esteem, admiration, gentleness, forbearance, sympathy and affection for both women *and* men in wedlock. More specifically, in Smiles's vision husbands were expected to demonstrate truthfulness, love, sympathy, consideration for others, uprightness and manliness.[81] This then, was an image of civilized respectability which did not contemplate the possibility of ill-use or abuse.

Despite such widely circulating ideals, however, it seemed that wife abuse was extremely common in the late nineteenth century, particularly amongst the poor – or, at least, this was the image presented by sections of the press. Indeed, stories of husbands' misdeeds frequently appeared in the newspapers, not least in the more sensationalist publications. Many of these attacks on wives were brought before the criminal courts, with husbands facing charges of assault, attempted murder and homicide – and the men involved often came in for a good deal of criticism (there were, however, few cases involving sexual offences at this time, it not being deemed possible for such crimes to be committed within marriage, unless 'unnatural' behaviour was involved[82]). For instance, in July 1867 the *Illustrated Police News* provided a dramatic illustration of a case arising from an attack by George Amey upon Isabella Amey. According to the accompanying text, Isabella, who 'appeared to have been knocked about brutally' by George, had been saved from further harm by Topey, a favoured cat. The fearless feline had apparently latched onto her husband's face, thereby halting the abuse. George was convicted of assault and sentenced to one month in prison.[83]

Civil litigation in relation to marriage law also revealed abuse and newspapers carried reports of such cases too. For example, in 1886 the *Daily News* gave an account of *Money v Money*, where the wife sought and obtained a dissolution on the grounds of her husband's cruelty and adultery. The cruelty was described by the paper as being 'almost incredible', but it noted that the wife's story was corroborated. Colonel Money had locked his wife in her room for five days, occasionally providing her with sustenance and, when she tried to escape, he apparently 'took her by the throat.' The paper referred to the Colonel's actions as constituting 'monstrous barbarity' and 'wickedness', calling for him to be prosecuted for aggravated assault in the criminal courts.[84]

Whilst cases of cruelty regularly came before both criminal and civil courts, as the case of the Colonel illustrated, the class of the players in the civil courts tended to be more mixed, including couples from different sections of society, except perhaps for the very poorest.[85] Indeed, matrimonial cases often involved apparently respectable husbands and wives from the higher echelons of society, offering a view of life in the more private world of the better off and demonstrating that wife abuse was by no means an activity entirely confined to the supposedly lesser orders of Englishmen. However, this did not stop the perception, fed by the vast number of often sensationalist press reports of wife assaults and criminal prosecutions amongst the poor, that the problem was a class issue.

Civil litigation also revealed that ill-treatment need not only be physical. For example, cases such as *Strathmore*, *Lister* and *Mead* showed that attempts at controlling a wealthy wife's property could go hand-in-hand with other forms of violence. Moreover, matrimonial cases could involve indirect allegations of sexual as well as other forms of physical abuse, with both used as evidence of the 'legal cruelty' which needed to be proved by wives applying for separation or divorce.[86]

In the context of idealized depictions of what matrimony should be like and these stories of different kinds of abuse, it was not surprising that husbands' cruelty towards their wives, particularly where it involved physical violence, was a matter of concern. This was often reflected in the press, with journalists criticizing what they perceived to be the sometimes overly lenient sentences handed out to abusive husbands – indeed, the *Illustrated Police News* took a dim view of George Amey's one-month imprisonment.[87]

Those who advocated rights for women were unsurprisingly also alarmed about the problem of wife abuse and called for more to be done, not least in terms of law, to rein in cruel husbands. Thus, the likes of Harriet Taylor, John Stuart Mill and Francis Power Cobbe campaigned for legal reforms that would not only afford better protection for wives, but would also seek to punish men and reduce the incidence of violence. Taylor, along with Mill, had first turned their attention to what they saw as the failure of the legal system to deal with male marital violence with sufficient harshness in the 1850s. Their focus was solely upon the poor and their treatment in the law courts, where they argued that even the most severe cruelty tended to be met with leniency and, as a consequence, marriage could become a form of slavery for wives. The solution was equal legal rights for women and men and an idealized model of marriage which was based upon friendship and mutual respect.[88] This was, as Mary L. Shanley has argued, to become an influential approach. Indeed, in the wake of Mill and Taylor, friendship, along with legal and economic rights, were themes which were to become key to Victorian feminists who focused on reforming marriage.[89]

Cobbe's 'Wife-Torture in England', published in 1878,[90] similarly focused upon the issue of marital violence amongst the lowest in society and argued that something needed to be done. In this context, she described Englishmen as being 'proverbial for their unparalleled brutality, till wife-beating, wife-torture, and wife-murder have become the opprobrium of the land'.[91] The article also included her interpretation of the statistics in order to demonstrate what she saw as the extent of the problem and used extreme cases drawn from the pages of the newspapers in order to press her case.[92] In terms of a solution, Cobbe, turned to law, favouring changes in the civil rather than the criminal sphere. In particular, she campaigned for protection orders to be imposed following an assault conviction, for custody of children to be given to the wife and for additional provision to be made for the payment of maintenance to an abused wife by her husband – and, as we shall see, her efforts were to have a degree of success.[93]

Thus, both the idea that wife abuse was a problem and discussions as to how law might best tackle it were common before *Jackson*. However, as already suggested, these concerns were very much classed worries. So, for example, Mill and Taylor focused upon the poor and Cobbe barely acknowledged that violence towards wives might be an issue in the middle and higher reaches of society.[94] Indeed, it often seemed to have been assumed that this was a matter which was largely confined to primitive, less civilized or under-evolved Englishmen who were thought most likely to exist within the lower levels of society, rather than in men of respectability and rank. Such thinking, in part, reflected contemporary ideas about evolution and concerns about the failings of the male of the species to live up to standards of Englishness. Thus, in the context of work by the likes of Edwin Ray Lankester,[95] lower class men who beat their wives could be conceived of as uncivilized brutes and atavistic savages, who were either of barbaric stock or were degenerating into baser types.

Indeed, many of the texts which dealt with male marital violence, whether newspaper reports, the works of campaigners against domestic violence, or even reports of legal cases, tended towards describing husbands who abused their wives using this sort of vocabulary. For instance, Cobbe wrote of the brutality of (lower class) men who beat their wives, seeing them as acting like animals. Moreover, she described wife-beating as an old cruelty 'having its origin in the remotest epochs of barbarian wife-capture and polygamy' which still lingered in 'the dark places of the land.'[96] However, in late Victorian England the fact that an Englishman, even of the supposedly lower orders, could mete out cruelty and violence to his spouse was still a matter of concern, as the English, along with its menfolk, were considered a superior race whom ruled (and were naturally fit to rule) over the savages of Empire (from whom violence towards women would not necessarily be unexpected). So, even if hierarchical evolutionary thinking seemed to offer explanations for male marital violence amongst the lowliest in society, this did not mean that it should be accepted; rather it suggested that something needed to be done to improve the nation's men's behaviour.[97]

More significantly for present purposes, as a result of such thinking, when stories about husbands of the supposedly civilized classes cruelly treating their spouses and seeking to gain control of their money emerged they were, in some respects, arguably more of a concern in terms of ideas about Englishness than tales of such behaviour amongst the poor. After all, men of the 'better classes' were meant to know how to conduct themselves, not least towards their wives – and they were certainly not expected to behave as degenerate brutes and parasites, ill-treating and feeding off the wealth of their spouses like vermin – the parasite, in particular, being a familiar motif in writings on degeneration.[98] What is more, they were breaching not only contemporary conceptions of manliness but also the ideals of companionate marriage, where the role of the husband as protector was key – and these were based upon specifically middle-class ideas of respectability.

Ideas about how all men should behave in marriage, along with the many stories of abuse and campaigns for change, had resulted in a number of legal developments in both the civil and criminal spheres in the years prior to *Jackson*, as well as sparking calls for further reform. These efforts sought by various means to bind men to better behaviour (as well as to provide more protection and better legal remedies for wives who suffered marital misuse) and they targeted a wide range of ill-treatment, rather than merely focusing upon the most extreme instances of physical violence.

In the sphere of criminal law, as the newspaper stories cited above demonstrate, it was well-established that a husband's (non-sexual) violence towards his wife could be held to be a crime – although (as we shall see) there was some confusion as to whether some limited right of physical chastisement existed. However, there had been some developments in this area in the decades prior to *Jackson*. In particular, section 1 of the Aggravated Assaults Act 1853 allowed magistrates to sentence men convicted for assaulting any female (and boys under the age of 14) more severely where bodily harm was caused and, whilst this provision had a more general application, its potential use in cases of wife abuse was clear.[99] Indeed, the discussion of this measure in the House of Commons focused upon graphic accounts of the horrific treatment of wives by their husbands and included strong statements on the behaviour expected of Englishmen in relation to their spouses. Thus, Mr Fitzroy MP, Under Secretary for the Home Department, urged for the Aggravated Assaults Bill to be passed as:

> No one could read the public journals without being constantly struck with horror and amazement at the numerous reports of cases of cruel and brutal assaults perpetrated upon the weaker sex by men who one blushed to think were Englishmen, and yet were capable of such atrocious acts. One's mind actually recoiled when he thought of the dastardly and cowardly assaults which were being constantly perpetrated upon defenceless women by brutes who called themselves men.[100]

Despite this statement, along with Fitzroy's shocking story of a man who attacked his heavily pregnant wife, the debates on the Bill also included some discussion and hilarity as to men's ability to beat their own wives as opposed to women they were not married to[101] – but this was swiftly suppressed by the then Home Secretary, Viscount Palmerston, who stressed that a woman was in fact owed greater protection, rather than more by way of violence, from the man who was her husband.[102] Indeed, it was clear that the legislation would apply regardless of marriage.

The 1853 Act was not the only development on the subject and concerns about wife abuse continued to be expressed. For example, Colonel Egerton Leigh MP, who had experience of dealing with the issue through his work as a magistrate, argued that the current law was inadequate, maintaining that the answer lay in increased punishments for husbands. Thus, in 1874 he appealed in Parliament for the penalty for aggravated assaults on women to be made more severe, in order that the England which had previously been described as 'the Paradise of Women' should not become 'a Hell of Women'.[103] Some members of the judiciary had a similar view and Cobbe reported in 1878 that there were magistrates presiding over the police courts around the country who supported the use of flogging in such cases.[104] So here the focus was upon the criminal justice system as offering the best means of dealing with husband's violence, with sentencing being the focus of attention.

Bridging the terrain between criminal and civil law, Cobbe's work, along with the concerns expressed by others, led to the passing of section 4 of the Matrimonial Causes Act 1878. This included provision for the criminal court in which a husband had been convicted of an aggravated assault against his wife to grant separation, maintenance and child custody to the wife, in circumstances where it was felt that her 'future safety' was 'in peril'.[105]

In terms of legislation in the civil sphere, a notable development of relevance to the *Jackson* case related to property and financial matters. The Married Women's Property Acts 1870 and 1882 meant that wives were much more able to retain control of their own affairs in marriage than previously had been the case and, as a result, were better able to resist financial abuse.[106]

In terms of civil law cases, according to the eighteenth-century authorities like *Lister*, *Ferrers*, *Mead* and *Strathmore*, it had long been decided that husbands could not abduct and hold their wives captive, nor did they have absolute power over their spouses – although Coleridge's early nineteenth-century pronouncements in *Cochrane* had rather confused things in relation to abduction, detention and physical chastisement. However, *Cochrane*'s authority had been undermined by *R v Leggatt* (1852), a case decided, amongst others, by Coleridge – and there seems to have been a feeling that Coleridge had been mistaken in his previous pronouncement, which in no way represented the correct legal position.[107] In *Leggatt* the wife, Anne Maria Sandilands, had been living apart from her husband, Alfred John Sandilands, so he applied for a writ of *habeas corpus* as a means of having her returned to him. His application was denied on the basis that he had no right to her custody. All of the judges who decided the matter found that Anne was living with her son of her own free will – and this was acknowledged by her husband. In this context, the court had no jurisdiction over the matter because they could not compel a wife to return to her husband as she was 'at liberty to go where she chose' – and 'the object of a habeas corpus is to restore to liberty a person who has been unjustly deprived of it', rather than to effectively force cohabitation.[108] More significantly, however, there seemed to be a feeling of unease from the bench about *Cochrane*, including perhaps from Coleridge.

In addition to cases like *Lister*, *Ferrers*, *Mead*, *Strathmore* and *Leggatt*, as we have seen, by the time *Jackson* came before the courts the legal position regarding cruelty in separation and divorce cases was well-established. Indeed, a significant reaffirmation of the idea that cruelty was not limited to physical violence had recently been provided by the case of *Kelly v Kelly* (1869, 1870).[109] Here it was held that 'moral force' could suffice – thus, for example, Baron Channell, one of the judges who presided over the *Kelly* litigation, stated that, whilst 'the most frequent form of ill-usage which amounts to cruelty is that of personal violence ... the courts have never limited their jurisdiction to such cases alone'.[110] The facts of this case related to Reverend James Kelly's behaviour towards his wife, Frances Kelly. Upon discovering that his wife had sought financial advice from her brother and brother-in-law on the effects of his (her husband's) investment and resultant loss of money which she had inherited, the good Reverend seems to have decided not only to chastise her, but also to enforce her obedience. He did so by adopting a variety of forms of ill-treatment and restraints upon her behaviour. Amongst other things, he had his wife followed, instructed their servants not to obey her, stopped her from seeing her friends, opened her post and required that any letters she wrote were subject to his approval before they could be dispatched. As if this was not enough, he subjected her to a stream of reproaches and insults.[111]

Frances went to the Court of Divorce and Matrimonial Causes seeking a separation from her husband. Initially a decree of judicial separation was pronounced,[112] with Lord Penzance, who decided the case, finding that:

> The peculiar and distinguishing feature of this case is the adoption by the respondent of a deliberate system of conduct towards his wife with the view of bending her to his authority … [I]f force, whether physical or moral, is systematically exerted for this purpose, in such a manner, to such a degree, and during such length of time, as to break down her health and render serious malady imminent, the interference of the law cannot be justly withheld by any court which affects to have charge of the wife's personal safety.[113]

So, to his mind, the behaviour in question amounted to force and the extreme forms in which it was expressed meant that it constituted legal cruelty. This decision was then appealed to the full court by the husband.

Penzance reconsidered the case along with two other judges,[114] deciding that the original view had been correct and dismissing the appeal. He stated that there could be no doubt as to the law, which was clear and long-established – it was the extreme nature of the facts of the case which were new and, as far as he could see, unique. Moreover, for him the primary consideration for courts enquiring into the issue of cruelty should be the 'health and safety of the wife'. In this case it was felt by the judges that she had severely suffered and James's conduct came in for a good deal of criticism.[115]

In *Kelly* the courts clearly stated that the 'moral force' by which James sought to bend his wife to his will and punish her was sufficient to entitle Frances to a judicial separation. By doing so, the idea that a man's power over his wife was limited was not only stated but was said to have long been the law, whether this related to physical violence or other forms of oppression and attempts at control. Moreover, the men who sat in judgment of James clearly felt that they were called upon to act as Francis's protector, as the courts had 'charge of the wife's personal safety'.[116] However, in a move that was to be echoed in the Court of Appeal in *Jackson*, the judges then proceeded to limit this justification for judicial intervention to circumstances where 'the troubles of the wife are not owing to her own misconduct.'[117] So the idea of a husband's dominion in marriage was by no means entirely rejected in *Kelly*.

All this demonstrates that ill-treatment, including but not limited to physical violence, was legally unacceptable by the 1890s – and legal developments in the latter part of the nineteenth century had sought to increase both the penalties upon men who abused their spouses and the protection for women. However, at the same time there were those who took a very different view and resisted what was seen as the encroachment of wives' rights into the preserve of husbands, seeking instead, to varying degrees, to defend male dominion in marriage. Such views, for example, could be seen prior to *Jackson* in Coleridge's pronouncements in *Cochrane* as well in the defences of the institution of marriage sparked by (Alice) Mona Caird's radical critique of wedlock in 1888.[118] Taking the part of women, Caird had argued that marriage was a failure. Unsurprisingly there were those who challenged her, with a lively debate taking place within the pages of the *Daily Telegraph*. Indeed, around 27,000 letters were sent to the editor – and a fair number of these contributions focused upon men and their behaviour. Responses included those who argued that the pairing would be more successful if the Church's teachings were followed, with the husband as dominant and the wife as obedient.[119]

Jackson

In this context, the arguments made on Edmund's behalf along with the decision of the High Court and, in particular, the perspective adopted by Cave in *Jackson* were by no means entirely out of step with late nineteenth-century thinking, as there were clearly those who adhered to similar views about husbands, wives and marriage (not least amongst these, of course, was Edmund). Moreover, Cave was able to provide support for his pronouncements about dominion from Coleridge in *Cochrane*. In his view Edmund had done nothing wrong – in fact, he had acted in a manner that was entirely legally justified – and there was no evidence of 'improper treatment, or conduct which is cruel and oppressive' or of 'improper purpose'. Instead, Edmund had been 'compelled to resort to this course by the very mistaken conduct of the lady's sisters'.[120] So, to Cave it was Emily's family who were in the wrong because, rather than immediately using legal means to challenge what had happened or, better still, leaving things alone, thereby 'giving him the opportunity of trying to regain his wife's affections', they '"picketed"' the house 'to such an extent that he thought it desirable to have persons to keep guard'. Moreover, in doing so, her sisters were 'likely to keep up feelings in the mind of the lady which it was most desirable should not be encouraged'.[121] In this context, granting the application and calling for Emily to be produced in court and for her captivity to be justified would be 'the worst thing that could be done', as it would:

> [T]end to unsettle the lady's mind, and make her believe that the Court was going to do what the Court will not do – remove her from her husband's custody – upon no ground whatever, except that she does not like to live with him.[122]

Here, the conception of a man's position in marriage was clear, with neither the wife nor her family having any right to challenge his dominion without evidence of cruelty and oppression – and what had happened to Emily was not seen as coming anywhere near the level of ill-treatment needed for this to be seriously contemplated; indeed, in Cave's mind, Edmund was merely putting matters into their correct order as regards his wilful spouse.

In contrast, by siding with the contentions put on behalf of Emily, the Court of Appeal took a very different view, rejecting the idea of a husband's absolute dominion in marriage and seeking to ensure that in the future men would be legally bound to behave more respectfully towards their wives. Indeed, it was clear from the outset of discussions between the bench and Collins, who presented the arguments for Edmund, that Esher, in particular, was on the side of Emily.[123] His sense of consternation at both the brutish way in which Edmund had treated Emily and what was being argued in terms of the law, was evident even at this stage and prefigured the tenor of his judgment. For example, in response to various suggestions from counsel as to the extent of a man's powers to physically chastise his wife Esher's response was to state that:

> If that were law, and if a wife were always 'under the rod' of her husband, the position of a wife would be worse in this country than that of a dog, and a husband in England would have a right to be a brute. It is not and never was the law of England.

He was similarly vocal as to the facts of the case, asking Edmund's counsel:

> Was it necessary to have those young men in the house with her? What were they there for? And the 'nurse,' too, what was she there for? She wanted no 'nurse.' We cannot shut our eyes to all these circumstances, and we cannot fail to see that they were put there to keep a watch over this lady.

Moreover, here he seemed perhaps to be implying that something darker than mere abduction was involved.[124]

Given such comments and questions, Esher's decision in *Jackson* must have come as no surprise to those present – and there seemed to be indications in the courtroom discussions that his fellow judges took a not wholly dissimilar view of the matter. In general terms, all three judges' construction of the case within their judgments saw Emily as a wife who had been treated insultingly and indefensibly by the very man who should have held her in the highest regard – her husband. Indeed, Edmund's conduct was roundly condemned as savage, uncivilized, unmanly, unEnglish and, at least in the circumstances before the court in this case, indefensible. In addition, lurking behind some of the judicial pronouncements was perhaps again the suspicion that he had not only married for money, but that the abduction was an attempt at gaining more access to Emily's wealth. In this regard, Edmund's behaviour seemed at points to have been cast as having a degenerate, parasitic quality, echoing contemporary concerns about men.

Lord Halsbury delivered the first judgment and took a firm view both as to the legal position and Edmund's conduct. Significantly he began by referring to the interview which the judges had just had with Emily, saying that he was assured that she had not been acting under the pressure or influence of her relatives in refusing to live with her husband, but had rather been exercising her own free will. He then moved on to the contentions made on Edmund's behalf relating to the idea of a husband's legal dominion over his wife. These he rejected in the most definite and condemnatory of terms. For example, the idea of a husband having absolute rights was to him unEnglish, outdated, barbaric and wrong. What is more, he felt that 'some of the propositions' made by Edmund's counsel were 'such as I should be reluctant to suppose ever to have been the law of England.'[125] Besides, the sources which had been cited in support of these statements 'were all tainted with this sort of notion of the absolute dominion of the husband over the wife'[126] and the ideas that had been presented in relation to wife beating were 'outrageous to common feelings of humanity' and 'inconsistent with the rights of free human creatures'.[127] Indeed, echoing the views held by some contemporary campaigners for women's rights, he felt that to make such claims in the late nineteenth century was as ridiculous as to argue that slavery still existed in England. With this, he dismissed the anachronistic authorities which maintained that a husband could physically 'chastise' his wife as 'quaint and absurd dicta' which were no longer 'capable of being cited as authorities in a court of justice in this or any civilized country.'[128]

In terms of the legality of a husband abducting and holding his wife captive, Halsbury stated that he did not believe that any 'such right exists or ever did exist'.[129] Instead, he maintained that 'no English subject has such a right of his own motion to imprison another English subject, whether his wife or any one else'.[130] However, he did not completely rule out some limited power of temporary restraint, saying that, if it were to be found that there was some such authority, this would only be available in instances where a husband had not previously ill-used his spouse or where there was no fear of future ill-usage.[131] Echoing Penzance in *Kelly*, he argued that the circumstances where this 'right of physical interference with the wife's freedom' might be said to be legitimate and legal were limited to situations where a wife's conduct included 'acts of proximate approach to some misconduct'. He went on to give examples of the kinds of wrongdoing that might create a right to restrain, stating that if she 'were on the staircase about to join some person with whom she intended to elope ... there might be to some extent a right to restrain the wife'. In such cases he could 'understand that some authority on the part of the husband of such a nature and so limited might well be justified according to any system of reasonable law.'[132]

So, the Lord Chancellor decided that there were at least limits upon men's rights in marriage. In doing so, significantly, he cited virtually no legal authority. Indeed, beyond dismissing *Cochrane* and other past pronouncements on the extent of a husband's powers, his only reference point was the 1884 Matrimonial Causes Act and its removal of the judicial power to imprison a spouse who refused to obey a degree of restitution of conjugal rights. This again perhaps seemed to suggest the strength of his feeling against the arguments put on Edmund's behalf; so opposed to them was he that he focused upon rejecting them rather than citing support for his own position – and there was, of course, ample support for his position in the successful legal challenges mounted where a husband had abducted his wife and the unsuccessful attempts by husbands to regain their wives.

Next Halsbury turned to the facts of the case before him, finding that, even if some power of detention was found to exist, the happenings in *Jackson* meant that the court would refuse to return Emily to her husband. He then proceeded to run through the treatment meted out to Emily, stressing the degree of 'insult' occasioned to her – and rejecting the idea that judging whether the treatment experienced could be seen as being legally unacceptable was merely a matter of assessing 'the exact amount of force or violence used or pain inflicted.'[133] Moreover, in a similar manner to Penzance in *Kelly*, he made it clear that he thought ill-usage or cruelty by a husband was not limited to physical violence. In doing so, he drew attention to the circumstances of the abduction with a sense of consternation that this should be thought to be acceptable. His sense of outrage was underlined by the fact that he not only repeatedly referred to Emily as 'a lady', implying that a high standard of behaviour should be accorded to a female of such stature, but also by his use of rhetorical questions as a means of emphasizing just how deplorably she had been dealt with. Thus he asked:

> But is it nothing that a lady coming out of church on a Sunday afternoon is to be seized by a number of men and forcibly put into a carriage and carried off? Must not the element of insult involved in such a transaction be considered?[134]

Here then, the fact that the capture was carried out by force and by several men and that it happened on a Sunday as Emily was emerging from a house of worship, were all elements that were highlighted by Halsbury.

The judge was similarly alarmed by Emily's account of having her bonnet pulled off and thrown in the fire by her husband upon her arrival at the Blackburn house. This, taken together with the method of her seizure, was something that Halsbury regarded 'with something like indignation'. In his view there had been an 'absence of a due sense of the delicacy and respect' which was 'due to a wife whom the husband has sworn to cherish and protect.'[135] In these words, in particular, it was clear that the Lord Chancellor had in his mind a view as to how a man should behave towards his wife, especially perhaps when the latter was 'a lady'. Moreover, his reference to respect, delicacy, cherishing and protection recalled contemporary ideals of marriage, with their focus upon companionship and chivalry.

As to his opinion of Edmund in general, Halsbury seemed to doubt his trustworthiness, a view he had most likely formed as a result of the evidence as to Emily's ordeal. Towards the end of his judgment, for example, Halsbury called into question Edmund's depiction of the 'earlier part of the history of the case', refusing to even consider it. Thus, whilst accepting that the husband's statements 'make out a case in his favour' by showing that the marriage was honourably entered into on his part, he clearly had misgivings regarding their accuracy – 'I do not know how far they can be trusted'. Here he also noted that there was no means of enquiring further into the circumstances of the courtship and marriage as Emily had had no opportunity to consult a lawyer and consider contradicting the affidavits made by and in support of her spouse.[136]

So, to the Lord Chancellor, Edmund was cast as a brutish scoundrel for the ill-treatment of his wife and he may well have been suspected of having shadier motives for his actions in marrying and seeking the (enforced) company of Emily. In contrast, Emily was a lady in peril who needed rescue and protection – and these were tasks which, amongst the Court of Appeal judges, Halsbury, in particular, was keen to perform.

Halsbury concluded by summarizing his position, emphasizing that the legal power claimed by Edmund did not exist and, even if it did, Edmund would be prevented from taking his wife back to Blackburn because there was more than enough evidence that Emily might rightly anticipate the use of violence against her in the future.[137] However, this did not quite end the matter for the Lord Chancellor. At the close of the case in the Court of Appeal, he directed a warning at Edmund, stating that any further attempt to seize and hold Emily against her will would 'be a serious contempt of Court.' By the time these words were uttered, however, '[t]he lady … had already left … in the company of her sisters and friends.'[138]

Lord Esher's judgment reflected similar concerns to Halsbury's but, unsurprisingly given his earlier comments, was arguably expressed more vehemently and, as we shall see, was perceived to be more controversial, with his most contentious pronouncement relating to the notion that an *English* husband had, at some point in history, had the right to beat his wife. Here he was, like Halsbury, particularly exercised, but went further stating 'I do not believe this ever was the law'.[139] As to Edmund's view of his rights to take custody of and hold his wife, echoing Mill and Taylor's sentiments, an aghast Esher declared that the propositions upon which these ideas were based would 'make an English wife the slave, the abject slave, of her husband'.[140]

A similar sentiment was reflected when Esher considered the argument that confinement could be distinguished from imprisonment – the former being permissible, according to counsel for Edmund, because 'by the law of England the husband has the custody of his wife'.[141] In this regard, he could neither see the distinction between the two words, nor could he accept that there was a legal right to imprison; indeed, he felt the need to express this in no uncertain terms, stating 'I protest that there is no such law in England'.[142] Consequently, whilst he found that *Cochrane's* case probably did decide that there was a right to custody, he maintained that the 'case was wrong as to the law enunciated in it, and that it ought to be overruled'.[143]

For all this concern about wives being treated as slaves to their husbands, however, Esher, like Halsbury, was reluctant to abandon completely the idea that a husband had marital powers which he could use, in some limited circumstances, in order to protect his honour. Thus, whilst he emphasized that he did 'not believe that an English husband has by law any such rights over his wife's person, as have been suggested', he submitted that there may be 'occasions' when 'he would have a right of restraint, though not of imprisonment'.[144] Restraint he felt could be used but this would be in the form of a temporary intervention and he gave the following example by way of illustration:

> For instance, if a wife were about immediately to do something which would be to the dishonour of her husband, as if the husband saw his wife in the act of going to meet a paramour, I think that he might seize her and pull her back.[145]

However, Esher saw the *Jackson* case as being completely different from this scenario, as it concerned the use of potentially perpetual imprisonment 'by way of punishment' or to prevent a wife from absenting herself from him or for other reasons where she is 'innocent of any moral offence'.[146] Here again he was at pains to stress his view as regards arguments made on Edmund's behalf as to a husband's rights: 'I do not think that this is the law of England'.[147]

In terms of the facts, Esher offered a fairly melodramatic account of the abduction and confinement, which he repeatedly termed 'insulting'. In describing the seizure, for example, he stressed the time, location and manner of the taking in order to demonstrate just how reprehensible it was and, like Halsbury, he emphasized the violence used:

> The seizure was made on a Sunday afternoon when she was coming out of church, in the face of the whole congregation. He takes with him to assist him in making the seizure a young lawyer's clerk and another man. The wife is taken by the shoulders and dragged into a carriage, and falls on the floor of the carriage with her legs hanging out of the door. These

> have to be lifted in by, I believe, the clerk. Her arm is bruised in the struggle. She is then driven off to the husband's house, the lawyer's clerk riding in the carriage with them. Could anything be more insulting?[148]

As this quotation demonstrates, Esher was especially condemnatory of Edmund's and the articled clerk, Dixon Robinson's, actions. He continued in this vein, describing the presence in the Rover Street house of Dixon Robinson along with the nurse 'to keep watch and control her', although she was not ill, 'insulting'. Overall, he thought the happenings both on the Sunday and subsequently were 'of extreme insult' and that the confinement meant that Emily was 'insultingly imprisoned till she undertakes to consort with him'.[149]

Fry, the most junior of the judges, was the last to make his pronouncements. To some degree, his judgment stood apart from the other two. In terms of law, he dismissed the idea of a husband having any right to capture his wife, finding the notion to be without any foundation.[150] He also stated that there was no general right which allowed a husband to confine his wife, *Cochrane* being based upon little authority, being 'directly at variance' with *Lister* and involving, to his mind, a right of confinement rather than capture. Moreover, Coleridge's pronouncements in that case had been weakened by *R v Leggatt* (1852), this case having decided that a husband had no right to the custody of his wife – and, if there had ever been such a right, the 1884 Act had removed it.[151] Beyond this, Fry deliberately distanced himself from Esher's view of the old law as to a husband's right to beat his wife.[152] He also stated that he would 'abstain from expressing an opinion as to the personal conduct of the husband in this transaction' and did not 'make any view of his conduct any part of the grounds of my decision' – his reasoning here being that there was inadequate information as to the antecedents of the case because only part of the story emerged from the affidavits. Moreover, he observed that '[t]here may or may not have been matters which might more or less furnish excuses for what was done on both sides'.[153] In contrast, of course, Esher, in particular, had not held back from commenting as to Edmund's behaviour – and Halsbury's distrust of the man seemed clear from his words.

Overall, in terms of law, the pronouncements of Halsbury, Esher and Fry sought to restrain not only Edmund but also other husbands from ill-treating, capturing and detaining their wives and, significantly, as in *Kelly*, in doing so, the judges all saw themselves as restating the legal position rather than altering it. Nevertheless, their pronouncements amounted to an outright rejection of the High Court decision just a few days previously and, in particular, of Cave's reliance on Coleridge in *Cochrane* and his reinforcement of the notion of a husband's legal dominion in marriage. This swift reversal, in itself, made the case hugely noteworthy and controversial. However, *Jackson* was by no means as radical as it might have been (particularly, of course, when viewed from the early part of the twenty-first century) as, despite their repulsion at Edmund's behaviour, neither Halsbury nor Esher were prepared to completely abandon the idea that a husband might sometimes have the power to temporarily restrain his wife.

Post *Jackson*

Unsurprisingly, the final decision in *Jackson* neither put an end to discussion of the case nor of the rights and wrongs of the laws relating to husbands and wives. In the immediate aftermath in Lancashire the controversy continued, with supporters of Edmund conducting protests in front of Emily's home in Clitheroe.[154] As mentioned previously, both Emily and Edmund also entered the fray, publishing their own accounts of events. Other responses to the outcome of the litigation were similarly divided as to whether it was the correct approach or not and reflected upon its wider implications for husbands and wives.

In all this continued interest in the affairs of the Jacksons and the effects of *Jackson* there were those who applauded the decision and its confirmation that men were legally bound to refrain from wife abuse, which included the abduction and imprisonment of a spouse and attempts to bend wives to their will. Campaigners for women's rights, along with those supportive of their goal, were, unsurprisingly, in favour of the Court of Appeal's approach. For example, Elizabeth Clarke Wolstenholme Elmy saw *Jackson* as 'the grandest victory the women's cause has ever yet gained, greater even than the passing of the Married Women's Property Acts.'[155] Moreover, the decision was 'epoch-making', allowing as it did for 'the establishment of a higher morality of marriage, and the substitution in the relation of husband and wife, of the ethics of justice and equality for the old and worn-out code of master and slave.'[156]

Similar views were expressed in some sections of the press. Thus, the *Blackburn Standard and Weekly Express* felt that the Court of Appeal decision reflected 'the spirit of an age which has witnessed the upgrowth of the woman's rights movement' which 'revolts at the notion of a wife being her husband's "goods, his chattels … his anything."' Instead, this was said to be an era when marriage was regarded as 'a union of willing hearts, into which no element of compulsion can properly enter.'[157]

The *Daily News*'s response to the release of Emily was unsurprising, given that it had previously greatly criticized the High Court decision in the case, which it characterized as having the effect of making marriage into 'lawful slavery' for wives.[158] The paper's editorial on the conclusion of the case, headed 'Out of Prison', supported the pronouncements of the Court of Appeal judges and expressed outrage at some of the arguments which had been put on Edmund's behalf. There was also relief that the judges, 'thank Heaven!', had decided that no ordinary citizen had the power to imprison another. Moreover, the editorial continued, Halsbury, Esher and Fry had reached the correct decision by deciding that 'a man does not own a wife as he owns a dog or a cigar-case, and that his right to her society is governed in its exercise by all sorts of other rights based upon the usages of civilized life.' There was also advice for Edmund as well as criticism for his primitive, anachronistic and under-evolved behaviour. The paper recommended that he should have approached his wife with 'decency, forbearance, moderation and, above all, an open street door.' His interpretation of his role as husband was described as being 'a little too Early British for the taste of this age' and the paper felt that 'his watch surely must have a dial like one of those early chronological pieces with which it was possible to be several centuries behind time.'[159]

In a similar vein, the *Pall Mall Gazette* had described the High Court decision as belonging 'to a period of primitive marriage customs, only to be paralleled in our own times among a few tribes of savages dancing on remote islands'[160] but saw the pronouncements of the Court of Appeal judges very differently. The three judgments, it was felt, had reflected the correct status of the 'modern wife', who was 'exactly as free in law to leave her husband as he is to leave her'.[161]

At the same time as these expressions of approval at the outcome of *Jackson* were being uttered, there were voices of consternation and dissent. These tended to express concerns about men's position in marriage and the worrying increase in women's rights, often also addressing specific worries about men who found themselves in Edmund's situation. For example, a letter to the *North-Eastern Daily Gazette* described Edmund as 'ill-used', criticized Emily, who was a woman old enough to know her own mind, and bemoaned the state in which the case had left the solemn institution of marriage.[162]

The reaction in the *Law Journal* was especially vehement in both its defence of Cave and Jeune and its attack on the Court of Appeal, with the discussion continuing over several issues. As to husbands and the law, the view taken from the outset was that:

> ... it is the law of this country that a husband has the right to all his wife's time, and to direct her manner of life and associates, and, if she refuses to submit to his orders, he can legally confine her to his house, from which she cannot be released by *habeas corpus*.[163]

In the light of this, it was not surprising that Halsbury and Esher's judgments were heavily criticized. They were, for example, described as being 'highly rhetorical, filled with such phrases as "absolute dominion," "abject slave," "imprisonment," "gaoler," "civilised country" and ... display an inability to state fairly the contention raised on Mr. Jackson's behalf'. So here we have not only disapproval of and a sense of anger at the Court of Appeal decision, but also a quite remarkable implication of bias in the direction of Emily and her family.[164] However, what agitated this publication most was Esher's statements as to past law, as the journal felt it impossible to argue that husbands in England had never had the legal right to physically chastise their wives.

Reflecting on the impact of the case more generally, the *Law Journal* felt law reform relating to women had gone too far and that, as a result, men were now the disadvantaged sex in marriage. Thus, in reviewing the legal position post *Jackson*, this publication concluded that by the latter part of 1891 '[t]here are certain particulars in which the position of a husband is distinctly inferior to that of his wife'.[165] Men's rights, rather than those of women were, therefore, very much a matter of concern for some commentators – and the idea of binding men to better behaviour within marriage could not have been further from their thoughts.

Coming from a slightly different perspective, Eliza Lynn Linton, a female journalist hostile to ideas of women's rights, also took serious exception to the Court of Appeal decision, seeing it as amounting to the abolition of marriage and blaming it on the 'wild women' or the 'women's rights women'. What is more, she felt that the result of these females' efforts would be the 'destruction of the family' and the 'absolute supremacy of women over men and justice alike.'[166]

What then of worries about and efforts to address the problem of domestic violence committed by husbands against their wives in the closing years of the nineteenth century? In terms of legislation, the Summary Jurisdiction (Married Women) Act 1895 added to the existing assistance for abused wives in the 1878 Matrimonial Causes Act. In particular, it enabled a wife who left a repeatedly cruel husband or a spouse who wilfully neglected to provide for her and their children to apply for separation, child custody and maintenance.[167]

Campaigners also continued to highlight the problem of domestic abuse as well as the reluctance of some of those within legal spheres to bring down the full force of the law upon men who ill-treated their wives. Thus, an article in the *Westminster Review* in 1898, authored by 'Ignota' (Ignota was just one of Wolstenholme Elmy's pseudonyms),[168] included reflections upon the progress made in *Jackson* but also concerns at the decision reached in the High Court in that case and, in particular, the pronouncements of Cave. The piece focused upon the shifting position of women in different areas of law and highlighted what was described as 'judicial sex bias', warning that this was just one example of judges tending to restrict or take away rights long held by women or refusing to interpret laws in a way favourable to the female of the species. Consequently, the author implied the need for vigilance, called for further law reform – and for men to 'bestir themselves to remove this ignominy from their sex'.[169] Indeed, despite the views of those who felt that *Jackson* had gone too far, or those who, like lawyer Edward Manson, maintained that, as a result of the case, '[t]he advocates of women's rights have really hardly a grievance left',[170] efforts not only to protect women and increase their rights, but also to rein in and bind men (including not only violent husbands but also those defenders of their rights within the judiciary) continued.

Conclusion

This chapter has both constructed a detailed history of *Jackson* and told a story about attempts to bind husbands to better behaviour towards their wives. In doing so, it has focused upon the issue of (non-sexual) domestic abuse. However, as we have seen, it was certainly arguable that *Jackson* did not mark a legal breakthrough in this area but rather that it confirmed the current law, assuming *Cochrane* was wrongly decided. Indeed, this was the view taken by the Attorney General, Sir Richard Webster, when the matter was discussed in the House of Commons. His response to concerns about the effect of the decision upon husbands was to dismiss such worries and point out that the case did not 'make any alteration in the law, but only declared the law'.[171]

In closing the consideration of the fifth and final focal case in this volume it seems only fitting to return to Edmund and Emily's stories and to what happened next. Soon after the Court of Appeal had pronounced its decision, Edmund was rumoured to be planning to appeal the matter to the House of Lords – and some sources suggested that he had wealthy backers keen to support him in this and, in so doing, defend husbands' rights.[172] However, this came to nought. As for Emily and her family, following the success of the civil action, the criminal case against the three abductors was dropped – its purpose presumably having been achieved by other means.[173] *Jackson* was, however, to continue to be something of a cultural reference point. Thus, when Emily died just a few short years after the Court of Appeal had released her, it was reported not only in the British and Irish newspapers but also around the world – and some of the coverage also made mention of the fact that she had made ample provision for the man who had remained her husband.[174]

Notes

1 [1891–4] All ER Rep 61; [1891] 1 QB 671; 60 LJQB 346; 64 LT 679; 55 JP 246; 7 TLR 382. These references refer to the different law reports in which the case was reported. The majority of references to these legal reports of *Jackson* in this chapter are from [1891] 1 QB 671 (the Queen's Bench Division Report) but occasionally, where different information is given or the text differs, another report is referred to instead. As the name suggests, a law report is a published account of courtroom proceedings in a case. It is produced for lawyers and generally includes a summary of the facts which led the parties to come to court and the legal decision as well as the text of the judge's or judges' pronouncements on law.

2 Lord Halsbury, the then Lord Chancellor, in *Jackson* at 679 and 681.

3 Lord Esher in *Jackson* at 682.

4 As with the last chapter, I have opted to refer to the Jacksons by their first names here in order to avoid using Mrs and Mr Jackson or to always use their first and second names, as these options seemed to be overly cumbersome.

5 For example, see: E.C. Wolstenholme Elmy, *The Decision in the Clitheroe Case, and its Consequences: a Series of Five Letters*, Manchester: Guardian Printing Works, 1891; G.H. Knott, 'English Legal Affairs', *American Law Review*, 25, 1891, 400–13, pp. 411–13; M.L. Shanley, *Feminism, Marriage, and the Law in Victorian England, 1850–1895*, London: IB Tauris, 1989, pp. 177–85; D. Rubenstein, *Before the Suffragettes: Women's Emancipation in the 1890s*, Brighton: Harvester, 1986, ch. 5; P. Mallett, '"Smacked and Brought to her Senses": Hardy and the Clitheroe Abduction Case', *Thomas Hardy Journal*, 8(2), 1992, 70–3; A. Robertson, 'The Reform of the Marriage Laws of Great Britain and Ireland, *Law Magazine and Review*, 17(5), 1891, 1–33, pp. 1–13.

6 For example, see: Shanley, *Feminism, Marriage, and the Law*; A.J. Hammerton, *Cruelty and Companionship: Conflict in Nineteenth Century Married Life*, London: Routledge, 1992.

7 *Jackson* involved no references to sexual behaviour. Indeed, the husband and wife appear to have spent no time alone together in private.

8 For present-day definitions of domestic violence see, for example: Women's Aid (2009) Domestic Violence: Frequently Asked Questions Factsheet, http://www.womensaid.org.uk/domestic_violence_topic.asp?section=0001000100220041&sectionTitle=Domestic+violence+%28general%29; Crown Prosecution Service (undated) Policy for Prosecuting Cases of Domestic Violence, http://www.cps.gov.uk/publications/prosecution/domestic/domv.html; Home Office (undated) Domestic Violence https://www.gov.uk/domestic-violence-and-abuse (accessed 30 March 2013).

9 For example, see *Blackburn Standard and Weekly Express*, 14 March 1891, p. 7; *Lancaster Gazette*, 11 March 1891, p. 3; *Lloyd's Weekly Newspaper*, 15 March 1891, p. 9; *Aberdeen Weekly Journal*, 11 March 1891, p. 5; *Belfast News-Letter*, 12 March 1891, p. 5; *Western Mail*, 12 March 1891, p. 5; *New York Times*, 20 March 1891, available at www.nytimes.com (accessed 30 March 2013).

10 An especially noteworthy example of this approach was provided by the 18 March edition of the *Blackburn Standard and Weekly Express* (1891, p. 7). The extravagantly constructed account begins by describing the circumstances at 2 Rover Street, Blackburn, where Emily was being held: 'there was no legal power on earth which would permit one to penetrate the citadel and rescue the forlorn lady, who is at present as jealously and zealously guarded as one OF THE GREEK GODDESSES...' Emily's arrival at that address was in a carriage drawn by a 'brace of fiery steeds … flecked with dazzling foam and bespattered with mud' and the scenes outside the Blackburn address were depicted as being akin to a battlefield. See also the comparisons between Edmund's version of the story and the work of Wilkie Collins in 'The Jackson Case Settled Out of Court', *The Speaker*, 4 April 1891, 399–400, p. 399.

11 Emily's story was published first, appearing in instalments in the *Lancashire Evening Post* in 17 April 1891, p.2, 18 April 1891, p.4, 20 April 1891, p.4, 21 April 1891, p.4, 22 April 1891, p.4. Much of the text of these articles was reproduced in *The Times*. See: 18 April, p. 14, 20 April, p. 12, 21 April, p. 12, 22 April, p. 12, and 23 April, p. 12. Edmund's account, which took the form of a response to Emily's version was published as E.H. Jackson (ed. W.H. Burnet), *The True Story of the Clitheroe Abduction; or, Why I Ran Away with My Wife*, 2nd edn, Blackburn: North-East Lancashire Printing & Publishing Co., 1891. Edmund also

gave interviews to newspapers. See, for example, *Pall Mall Gazette*, 21 March 1891, pp. 4–5.
12 See, for example, *The Times*, 23 April 1891, p. 12.
13 In his Affidavit to the Court of Appeal Edmund himself stated that she was a 'woman of independent means', see, for example, *Jackson* [1891–94] All ER Rep 61 at 62.
14 The application to the High Court gave her age as 46, see *The Times*, 17 March 1891, p. 3.
15 See, for example, *The Times*, 17 March 1891, p. 3.
16 For example, see: *North-Eastern Daily Gazette*, 10 March 1891 (4th edn), p. 3; *Daily News*, 20 March 1891, p. 3.
17 See, for example, the reports as to his family in *Daily News*, 20 March 1891, p. 3.
18 See, in particular, *Blackburn Standard and Weekly Express*, 14 March 1891, p. 7.
19 *Marriages at St Paul in the Parish of Blackburn, Register: Marriages 1884–1892*, p. 115, entry 230, www.lan-opc.org.uk/Blackburn/Blackburn-Central/stpaul/marriages_1884-1892.html#230 (accessed 30 March 2013).
20 This was reflected in both Edmund's and Emily's accounts of the abduction and its antecedents. See *The True Story of the Clitheroe Abduction*, p. 15 and *The Times*, 20 April 1891, p. 12.
21 Both agreed that they had first met in 1881 at a picnic, see *The True Story of the Clitheroe Abduction*, p. 7; *The Times*, 18 April 1891, p. 14.
22 See further below.
23 In some of the press reports it was stated that the settlement included a sum of £5 a week, which had allegedly never been paid to Edmund. See, for example, *Lancaster Gazette*, 11 March 1891, p. 3.
24 *The Times*, 20 April 1891, p. 12.
25 *The True Story of the Clitheroe Abduction*, p. 14.
26 Ibid.
27 See The National Archives PRO J 77/421/2823 (Divorce Court File: 2823. Appellant: Edmund Haughton Jackson. Respondent: Emily Emma Maude Jackson. Type: Husband's petition).
28 See section 3, Matrimonial Causes Act 1884.
29 This was referred in the High Court, see *Lancaster Gazette*, 18 March 1891, p. 3.
30 Section 2. Previously a spouse could have been imprisoned for contempt of court, provided there was no evidence of ill-usage by his or her husband or wife. This all changed as a result of the Weldon litigation regarding the restitution of Georgina Weldon's conjugal rights (see *Weldon v Weldon* (1883) 9 PD 52 and (1885) 10 PD 72). So it was in order to protect a husband from his wife's litigious inclinations, rather than a wife from her husband's ill-use that the so-called 'Weldon Relief Act' was passed. On section 2 see *The Times*, 8 September 1884, p. 2.
31 Section 5, Matrimonial Causes Act 1884.
32 On the state of matrimonial law at this time see further, Frederick Andrew Inderwick's letter about *Jackson*, *The Times*, 20 May 1891, p. 13.
33 A few sources cite her full name, including *Morning Post*, 12 March 1891, p. 3.
34 *Jackson* [1891–94] All ER Rep 61 at 63.
35 For example, see: *North-Eastern Daily Gazette*, 9 March 1891 (4th edn), p. 3.
36 For example, see *Birmingham Daily Post*, 10 March 1891, p. 8.
37 One of the most extravagant claims of a planned rescue was carried by the *Daily News*, 10 March 1891 (4th edn), p. 3.
38 As the great S. Morgenstern (via William Goldman) would have explained, this was after telephones. See further, *The Princess Bride*, San Diego C.A.: Harcourt Brace, 1973, p. 1.
39 See, for example, the report in the *Birmingham Daily Post*, 10 March 1891, p. 8.

40 See *The True Story of the Clitheroe Abduction*, p. 15.
41 *The Times*, 17 March 1891, p. 3.
42 Ibid.
43 See, for example, the reports in: *The Times*, 10 March 1891, p. 8; *The Standard*, 10 March 1891, p. 3; *Northern Echo*, 10 March 1891, p. 3; *Daily News*, 10 March 1891, p. 5.
44 In particular, this was referred to in the High Court, see, for example, *The Times*, 17 March 1891, p. 3.
45 For an account of these events see, for example: *The Times*, 12 March 1891, p. 12; *North-Eastern Daily Gazette*, 12 March 1891 (4th edn), p. 4; *Daily News*, 12 March 1891, p. 2.
46 Reports of the High Court proceedings drawn upon here include: *The Times*, 12 March 1891, p. 12; *North-Eastern Daily Gazette*, 12 March 1891 (4th edn), p. 4; *Daily News*, 12 March 1891, p. 2.
47 At that that time the criminal standard was applied. Today the civil balance of probabilities is used, although a high degree of probability is required. See *Khawaja v Secretary of State for the Home Department* [1984] AC 74; [1983] 1 All ER 765.
48 *The Times*, 17 March 1891, p. 3. See also, for example: *Daily News*, 17 March 1891, pp. 5, 7; *The Standard*, 17 March 1891, p. 3; *Morning Post*, 17 March 1891, p. 2; *Lancaster Gazette*, 18 March 1891, p. 3.
49 That these were not the decisions of courts of appeal or review was of less consequence then than it would be now – and this was the case in both civil and criminal law, as the references to Coleridge's comments about the decisions of single judges in the context of criminal cases in Chapters 1, 2 and 4 demonstrated.
50 See: *R v Earl Ferrers* 97 ER 483; (1758) 1 Burr 631 and *R v Earl Ferrers* 97 ER 522; (1758) 2 Burr 703. The Earl's legal adventures continued. In 1760 he was convicted of the murder of his steward and taken from the Tower of London to Tyburn where he was hung; his body was then exhibited and dissected. See 'The British Aristocracy', *Reynolds's Newspaper*, 1 June 1879, p. 2.
51 (1721) 1 Stra 478; 93 ER 645; sub nom. *Lister's Case*, 8 Mod Rep 22; 27 Digest (Repl) 87, 647.
52 (1758) 2 Keny 279; 1 Burr 541; 96 ER 1182; 27 Digest (Repl) 239, 1918.
53 This matter came before the courts on several occasions. See, for example, *Countess of Strathmore v Bowes* 30 ER 211; (1789) 1 Vesey Junior 22.
54 See further, S.M. Okin, 'Patriarchy and Married Women's Property in England: Questions on Some Current Views', *Eighteenth-Century Studies*, 17(2), Winter, 1983–1984, 121–38, pp. 123–6.
55 (1721) 1 Stra 478 at 478.
56 (1758) 1 Burrow 541 at 542.
57 The letter (dated 27 May 1885) stating her wishes was reproduced in the *London Chronicle*, 16–18 November 1786, p. 487.
58 For an account of her seizure along with a little more of the story see: *A Full, True, and Particular Account of the Manner in which the Right Honourable the Countess of Strathmore was Taken by Force*, London: s.n., 1786.
59 The litigation between the couple and the wider story of their marriage was a lengthy and complex one. See further: M.E. Lyon Bowes, Countess of Strathmore, *Confessions of the Countess of Strathmore, Written by Herself*, London: W. Locke, 1793; W. Moore, *Wedlock: The True Story of the Disastrous Marriage and Remarkable Divorce of Mary Eleanor Bowes, Countess of Strathmore*, London: Weidenfeld and Nicolson, 2009; D. Parker, *The Trampled Wife*, Stroud: Sutton, 2006.
60 This was the father of the Lord Chief Justice Coleridge who had a role in deciding the focal cases of Chapters 2, 3 and 4 respectively.

61 (1840) 8 Dowl 630; 4 Jur 534; 27 Digest (Repl) 86, 642.
62 This was cited in argument by Edmund's lawyers and came from Bacon's Abridgment, the last edition of which was published in 1832. See *Jackson* at 674.
63 The Civil Court of Appeal had been created by the Supreme Court of Judicature Act 1873 and began work in 1875.
64 For example, see [1891] 1 QB 671 at 671–2; [1891–94] All ER Rep 61 at 62.
65 18 March 1891, p. 13. Other accounts which were drawn upon include: *Daily News*, 18 March 1891, p. 5; *Morning Post*, 18 March 1891, p. 4; *The Standard*, 18 March 1891, p. 2.
66 The account of the Court of Appeal proceedings reconstructed here draws on the law reports and is supplemented by press accounts including: *The Times*, 20 March 1891, p. 13; *Daily News*, 20 March 1891, p. 3; *Northern Echo*, 20 March 1891, p. 3; *Morning Post*, 20 March 1891, pp. 4, 6; *Blackburn Standard and Weekly Express*, 21 March 1891, pp. 5, 7.
67 For example, see the account in the *Daily News*, 20 March 20 1891, p. 3. A number of papers noted that 'a large number of ladies' were in court. See, for example, *Morning Post*, 20 March 1891, p. 6. It is perhaps worth noting that it was by no means unheard of at this time for judges to invite guests to sit with them in court.
68 See, for example, *The Times*, 20 March 1891, p. 13.
69 This was, for example, suggested in *The Times*, 20 March 1891, p. 9.
70 See, for example, *The Times*, 20 March 1891, p. 13.
71 See, for example: *Jackson* at 672–4; *Jackson* [1891–94] All ER Rep 61 at 62–3; *The Times*, 20 March, p. 13.
72 See, for example, *The Times*, 20 March 1891, p. 13.
73 For example, see the quotation from Dr Martin's statement in *Jackson* [1891–94] All ER Rep 61 at 63.
74 This wording is taken from *Daily News*, 20 March 1891, p. 3.
75 Again, this was something noted in *The Times*, 20 March, p. 13, along with some of the law reports of *Jackson*; see, for example, [1891–94] All ER Rep 61 at 63. There was also reference to the bruise in Esher's judgment; see *Jackson* at 683.
76 This was noted in *The Times* report of proceedings in the Court of Appeal on 19 March, see 20 March 1891, p. 13 and the bonnet incident along with the violence of the seizure were, for example, commented upon by Halsbury in his judgment; see *Jackson* at 681.
77 See *The Times*, 20 March, p. 13 and the summary of the affidavits in *Jackson* [1891–94] All ER Rep 61 at 63.
78 For example, see the account in the *Daily News*, 20 March 1891, p. 3.
79 For example, in a footnote in the Queen's Bench Reports we are told that '[a]t the close of the arguments the Court saw Mrs. Jackson *in-camera* in order to ascertain whether, in refusing to live with her husband, she was acting as a free agent, and had not been compelled or induced by any external influences.' ([1891] 1 QB 671 at 678, ftn. 4.) Emily's account of her day in court was published in the *Lancashire Evening Post*, 22 April 1891, p.4.
80 For consideration of the idea of companionate marriage see, for example, Hammerton, *Cruelty and Companionship*, ch. 3. On the dominance of the middle class and their values during the latter part of the Victorian era, the associated 'Cult of Respectability' and the depiction of a particular version of domestic manliness at the hearth see, for example, John Tosh *A Man's Place: Masculinity and the Middle-Class Home in Victorian England*, New Haven: Yale University Press, 1999.

81 *Character*, London: John Murray, 1871, ch. 11, especially pp. 308–9.
82 See further Chapter 4.
83 *Illustrated Police News*, 6 July 1867, pp. 1, 2.
84 11 March 1886, p. 4. The wife's name was not given in the report.
85 Indeed, the working class were by no means entirely excluded from this branch of law in the period. For example, see G. Savage, '"The Wilful Communication of a Loathsome Disease": Marital Conflict and Venereal Disease in Victorian England', *Victorian Studies*, 34(1), 1990, 35–54, pp. 45–6.
86 See further Chapter 4.
87 6 July 1867, p. 2.
88 For example, see: Mill and Taylor, *Morning Chronicle*, 28 April 1851, p. 2, 24 August 1851, p. 2, 28 August 1851, p. 4; Taylor, 'The Enfranchisement of Women', *Westminster Review*, 55(2), July 1851, 289–311, p. 299, n.; Mill, *The Subjection of Women*, London: Longmans, Green, Reader and Dyer, 1869 (which is attributed to Mill), pp. 9, 25–6, 57–9, 63, 64, 78, 177.
89 See *Feminism, Marriage and the Law*, pp. 49–78 and 'Marital Slavery and Friendship: John Stuart Mill's *Subjection of Women*', Political Theory, 9(2), 1981, 229–47. See also Hammerton, *Cruelty and Companionship*, pp. 156–8.
90 *Contemporary Review*, 32, April 1878, 55–87.
91 Ibid., p. 56.
92 See, in particular, ibid., pp. 70–2, 73–6.
93 See, for example, ibid., p. 82.
94 See, for example, *Subjection of Women*, p.63 and 'Wife-Torture', p. 58.
95 See, in particular, *Degeneration: A Chapter in Darwinism*, London: Macmillan, 1880.
96 See 'Wife-Torture', pp. 56, 64.
97 Edward Burnett Tylor, for example, arranged the races hierarchically, with the English cast as a superior people, although he also identified examples of inferior types in the lower classes even of England. See further, for example, 'The Science of Culture', in *Primitive Culture: Researches into the Development of Mythology, Philosophy, Religion, Art, and Custom*, London: John Murray, 1871, vol. 1, p. 109, vol. 2, pp. 115–17.
98 See, for example, D. Pick, *Faces of Degeneration: A European Disorder c.1848–c.1918*, Cambridge: Cambridge University Press, 1989, pp. 173–4 and ch. 7.
99 The legislation's full title was 'An Act for the Better Protection and Punishment of Aggravated Assaults upon Women and Children, and for preventing Delay and Expense in the Administration of Certain Parts of the Criminal Law'. It was re-enacted by the consolidating Offences Against the Person Act 1861 (see section 43) and was not repealed until 1988 (see Criminal Justice Act, schedule 16). Despite these measures, sometimes the courts tended to listen to a wife's pleadings for mercy towards her husband or opted to give a man a chance at reform; however, occasionally they were prepared to sentence as severely as they were able. For example, in sentencing John Quick for an aggravated assault on his wife Ann Quick, Sir R.W. Carden felt that 'I must go a little further with a brute like you.' *Daily News*, 14 April 1854, p. 13.
100 3 HC 124, col. 1414, 10 March 1853.
101 For example, see *Daily News*, 7 April 1853, p. 2.
102 See *Morning Post*, 7 April 1853, p. 2.
103 Cited in ibid., p. 78. The Member of Parliament was making his plea in the House of Commons. See 3 HC 219, col. 396, 18 May 1874.
104 See further, 'Wife-Torture', pp. 78–9.

105 For an example of the operation of this statute see the report of the trial at Bristol Police Court of John Bright for assaulting his wife. He was convicted, sentenced to two months' hard labour and, on his unnamed wife's application, the court granted a separation order along with weekly maintenance payments (*Bristol Mercury and Daily Post*, 1 August 1884, p. 3).

106 On these measures and their effect, see, for example: M.B. Combs, '"A Measure of Legal Independence": The 1870 Married Women's Property Act and the Portfolio Allocations of British Wives', *Journal of Economic History*, 65(4), 2005, 1028–57; Shanley, *Feminism, Marriage and the Law*, ch. 4.

107 (1852) 18 QB 781; 16 JP 472; 21 LJQB 342; 17 Jur 317; 118 ER 295; 19 LTOS 201.

108 Lord Chief Justice Campbell (1852) 118 ER 295 at 296 and 295.

109 *Kelly v Kelly* (No.1) (1869–72) LR 2 P & D 31. *Kelly v Kelly* (No.2) (1869–72) LR 2 P & D 59; 39 LJP & M 28; 18 WR 767; [1861–73] All ER Rep 297; 22 LT 308. Among the newspapers which covered the case, the *Daily News* gave a particularly good account of both the facts and the initial decision (8 December 1869, p. 2) and *The Times* included helpful coverage of both decisions (8 December 1869, p. 11, 10 February 1870, p. 11).

110 *Kelly v Kelly* (No.2) (1869–72) LR 2 P & D 59 at 61.

111 There was also evidence that on several occasions he had used some degree of physical force against her but this did not figure in the case.

112 The initial decision of the single judge is reported at (1869–72) LR 2 P & D 31.

113 Ibid., at 31.

114 Aside from Penzance and Channell, the third was Justice Hannen.

115 See, in particular, (1869–72) LR 2 P & D 59, at 76–7.

116 Baron Channell in *Kelly v Kelly* (No.2) (1870) LR 2 P & D 59 at 60.

117 See Channell in *Kelly v Kelly* (No.2) (1870) LR 2 P & D 59 at 60 who was quoting Penzance in *Kelly v Kelly* (No.1) (1869–72) LR 2 P & D 31 at 32.

118 Her articles on the subject were collected together in *The Morality of Marriage and Other Essays on the Status and Destiny of Women*, London: George Redway, 1897. See further, Hammerton, *Cruelty and Companionship*, pp. 159–63.

119 See, for example, H. Quilter, *Is Marriage a Failure*, London: Swan Sonnenschein, 1888, p. 204.

120 *The Times*, 17 March 1891, p. 3.

121 Ibid.

122 Ibid.

123 The quotations of these discussions cited here are taken from *The Times*, 20 March 1891, p. 13.

124 He may have been thinking of factual and fictional stories of husbands who detained their wives as a means of restraining them or acquiring control of wealth. In fiction there was Wilkie Collins's *The Woman in White* (London: Sampson Low, 1860) and a real life example was provided by the infamously litigious Georgina Weldon's husband's unsuccessful attempt to remove her from his life (these were the Weldons of *Weldon v Weldon*, cited above). For her version of the story, see *How I Escaped the Mad Doctors*, London: Mrs. Weldon, 1882.

125 *Jackson* at 678.

126 Ibid., at 678–9.

127 Ibid., at 679.

128 Ibid., at 678.

129 Ibid., at 680.

130 Here he added that 'of course, I am speaking of persons of full age and sui juris' (that is someone competent or with the appropriate capacity to make their own decisions). Ibid., at 681.
131 Ibid., at 681–2.
132 Ibid., at 679–80.
133 Ibid., at 681.
134 Ibid.
135 Ibid.
136 Ibid.
137 Ibid., at 682.
138 *The Times*, 20 March 1891, p. 13.
139 *Jackson* at 682.
140 Ibid.
141 Ibid.
142 Ibid.
143 Ibid., at 683.
144 Ibid.
145 Ibid.
146 Ibid.
147 Ibid.
148 *Jackson* [1891–94] All ER Rep 61 at 67.
149 *Jackson* at 684.
150 Ibid., at 684–5.
151 Ibid., at 685–6.
152 Ibid., at 686.
153 Ibid.
154 See, for example, *Woman's Herald*, 4 April 1891, p. 372.
155 Letter from Wolstenholme Elmy to Harriet M'Ilquham, 21 March 1891, Elmy Collection, British Library, cited by Shanley, *Feminism, Marriage, and the Law*, p. 182.
156 Wolstenholme Elmy, *The Decision in the Clitheroe Case, and its Consequences: A Series of Five Letters*, Manchester: Guardian Printing Works, 1891, 4, pp. 10–11.
157 21 March 1891, p. 7.
158 17 March 1891, p. 5.
159 20 March 1891, p. 5.
160 17 March 1891, p. 2.
161 21 March 1891, p. 1.
162 21 March 1891 (4th edn), p. 3. See also, for example, *The Speaker*, 'The Jackson Case Settled Out of Court', 4 April 1891, pp. 399–400.
163 'Obiter Dicta', 14 March 1891, p. 176.
164 These quotes are drawn from an article that ran over two issues of the journal, see 'Regina v. Jackson', 20 June 1891, pp. 416–17 and 27 June 1892, pp. 433–4, p. 416.
165 21 November 1891, p. 721.
166 'The Judicial Shock to Marriage', *Nineteenth Century*, 29(171), 29 May 1891, pp. 691–700, pp. 700, 691, 692.
167 See sections 4, 5.
168 'Judicial Sexual Bias', *Westminster Review*, 149(3), March 1898, 279–88.
169 Ibid., p. 287.
170 *Law Quarterly Review*, 7, 1891, 244–55, p. 255.
171 3 HC 352, col. 921, 20 April 1891.

172 See, for example: *Pall Mall Gazette*, 23 March 1891, p. 4 (4th edn); *Woman's Herald*, 4 April 1891, p. 372.

173 See, for example: *Pall Mall Gazette*, 23 March 1891, p. 4 (4th edn); *Lloyd's Weekly Newspaper*, 22 March 1891, p. 5; *North-Eastern Daily Gazette* (Middlesbrough, England), 24 March 1891 (4th edn), p. 3.

174 See, for example: *North-Eastern Daily Gazette*, 21 March 1898 (6th edn), p. 3; *Pall Mall Gazette*, 21 March 1898 (4th edn), p. 7; *Lloyd's Weekly Newspaper*, 27 March 1898, p. 6; *The Times*, 23 March 1898, p. 12; *New York Times*, 28 March 1898. The latter article is available at http://www.nytimes.com (accessed 30 March 2013).

Concluding thoughts

> Although history has no beginning and, what is sometimes forgotten, no end, stories are different.[1]

In the five chapters above I have weaved a series of stories about men, violence and law in the late nineteenth century. This has involved telling tales of what brought the cases of *Prince, Coney, Dudley and Stephens, Clarence* and *Jackson*[2] to court as well as the courtroom proceedings and then renarrating these cases in the context of contemporary anxieties concerning the male of the species. In constructing this text, I have had several purposes in mind. These were highlighted within the Introduction and some are briefly revisited below.

Overarchingly, *Binding Men* adopts and seeks to highlight a (to paraphrase historian Alun Munslow)[3] history-as-construction-site model of writing about the past,[4] in the sense that, 'things happen', then they 'get told' and these are two ontologically separate things 'which narrative only *seems* to collapse into a voraciously all-encompassing discourse'.[5] So the tales told in this book are deliberately introduced as self-conscious narrations of the past which are (always) partial – in that there can never be a single definitive or truthful representation of events and because they are my own subjective accounts of happenings as I have chosen to depict them here.

Binding Men's tale-telling also has a conscious gender politics. In focusing upon anxieties about the male of the species, my purpose is to redirect the gaze away from women and, more specifically, from women as being 'the problem'. Thus, *Binding Men*, like my previous work on masculinities, takes men and ideas about maleness as the *subject* and *object* of study. In this context, the stories about *Prince, Coney, Dudley and Stephens, Clarence* and *Jackson* within these pages construct the latter part of the nineteenth century as a period when worries about men resulted in efforts to rein in male behaviour and attempts to legally bind men by delineating the parameters of unacceptable and unlawful violence. In doing so, I am not, of course, suggesting that this is the only way in which this timescape can be conceptualized. Nor am I arguing that this was the only period in which concerns about men or attempts to legally restrain their behaviour can be identified.

Indeed, each of the five chapters, along with their textual notes, delve backwards and forwards in history to varying degrees in order to construct their particular 'binding men' narrative.

At the same time, *Binding Men* is a book about reading and narrating court cases. Following the work of others, it seeks to reconstruct the wider story of five legally binding cases, rather than relying upon the bare facts, judgment and legal decision recorded in the law reports. In order to do this, multiple sources are explored in the pages above, with an eye to what transpired before and within the courtroom as well as after the case. Here the materials consulted vary in relation to the five cases, depending upon what was recorded, what has survived – and what I managed to find. For instance, in relation to *Jackson* the main sources relied upon are law reports, newspaper accounts of what happened and the Jacksons' own versions of events. For *Clarence* there are very few sources, so the law reports are the primary focus, with press reports, commentaries on the case, court as well as census records and parish registers providing a little more by way of detail.

Given all this, in closing it seems appropriate to end, as this project began, with reference to the work of A.W. Brian Simpson and, in particular, to the epigraph to this chapter. As Simpson suggested, whilst history isn't bounded, stories get constructed and, amongst other things, this entails deciding upon a start and a finish. It also requires choices to be made about how far to wander off in a variety of directions in the process of researching and writing a narrative – and there were certainly a number of digressions made and tangents pursued in the process of producing this book. But perhaps the most difficult decision for this author remains when to stop. That place, it seems, is here – at least, for now.

Notes

1 A.W.B. Simpson, *Cannibalism and the Common Law: The Story of the Tragic Last Voyage of the Mignonette and the Strange Legal Proceedings to Which it Gave Rise*, Chicago: University of Chicago Press, 1984, p. 1.

2 (1875) LR 2 CCR 154, 39 JP 676, 44 LJMC 122, 13 Cox CC 138, 24 WR 76, [1874–80] All ER Rep 881, 32 LT 700; (1882) LR 8 QBD 534; 46 JP 404; 51 LJMC 66; 15 Cox CC 46; 30 WR 678, 46 LT 307; (1884) 14 QBD 273, 49 JP 69, 54 LJMC 32, 15 Cox CC 624, 33 WR 347, [1881–5] All ER Rep 61, 52 LT 107, 1 TLR 118; (1888) 22 QBD 23, 53 JP 149, 58 LJMC 10, 16 Cox CC 511, 37 WR 166, [1886–90] All ER Rep 133, 59 LT 780, 5 TLR 61; [1891–94] All ER Rep 61; [1891] 1 QB 671; 60 LJQB 346; 64 LT 679; 55 JP 246; 7 TLR 382.

3 Munslow described the past as 'a building site, not a foreign land to be explored.' See the Preface to K. Jenkins, *Rethinking History*, London: Routledge (Classics Edition), 2003, pp. xii, xiii. In describing the past in this way Munslow is depicting Jenkins's work.

4 Or perhaps more accurately, given my interests, a history-as-blank-canvas-awaiting-vast-quantities-of-paint model.

5 J.E. Young, 'Towards a Received History of the Holocaust', *History and Theory*, 36(4), 1997, 21–43, p. 34.

Select bibliography of published sources

For unpublished sources consulted see the Introduction and Concluding Thoughts, as well as the case specific discussions and detailed referencing in Chapters 1–5.

Addison, A.C., *The Story of the Birkenhead: A Record of British Heroism*, London: Unwin, 1902.

Anderson, J., *The Legality of Boxing: A Punch Drunk Love*, London: Birkbeck Law Press, 2007.

—— 'Pugilistic Prosecutions: Prize Fighting and the Courts in Nineteenth Century Britain', *Sports Historian*, 21(2), 2001, 37–57.

Bailey, V. and Blackburn, S., 'The Punishment of Incest Act 1908: A Study in Law Creation', *Criminal Law Review*, 1979, 708–18.

Baker, J.H., *An Introduction to English Legal History*, 4th edn, London: Butterworths, 2002.

Barnes, J., *Arthur and George*, London: Jonathan Cape, 2005.

Behlmer, G.K., *Child Abuse and Moral Reform in England, 1870–1908*, Stanford: Stanford University Press, 1982.

Bibbings, L.S., 'Men Refusing to be Violent: Conscientious Objectors to Military Service Then and Now (1916–present day)' in A. Carden-Coyne (ed.), *Gender and Conflict Since 1914: Historical and Interdisciplinary Perspectives*, Basingstoke: Palgrave, 2012, pp. 41–54.

—— *Telling Tales About Men: Conceptions of Conscientious Objectors to Military Service During the First World War*, Manchester: Manchester University Press, 2009.

—— 'Images of Manliness: The Portrayal of Soldiers and Conscientious Objectors in the Great War', *Social and Legal Studies*, 12(3), 2003, 335–58.

—— 'Boys Will Be Boys: Masculinity and Offences Against the Person' in D. Nicolson and L. Bibbings (eds), *Feminist Perspectives on Criminal Law*, London: Cavendish, 2000, ch. 9.

Birch, D., 'Untangling Sexual History', *Criminal Law Review*, June 2003, 370–83.

Bland, L., *Banishing the Beast: English Feminism and Sexual Morality* 1885–1914, London: Penguin, 1995.

Bohlander, M., 'The Sexual Offences Act 2003 and the Tyrrell Principle – Criminalising the Victims?', *Criminal Law Review*, September 2005, 701–13.

Bourke, J., 'Sexual Violence, Marital Guidance, and Victorian Bodies: An Aesthesiology', *Victorian Studies*, 50(3), 2008, 419–36.

Brailsford, D., *Bareknuckles: A Social History of Prize-Fighting*, Cambridge: Lutterworth Press, 1988.

Brent, J.J. and Kraska, P.B., 'Fighting is the Most Real and Honest Thing', *British Journal of Criminology*, 53(3), 2013, 357–77.

Butler, J.E., *Some Thoughts on the Present Aspect of the Crusade: Against the State Regulation of Vice*, Liverpool: T. Brakell, 1874.
—— *The Constitution Violated. An Essay [Advocating the Repeal of the Contagious Diseases Acts 1866, 1868 and 1869]*, Edinburgh: Edmonston and Douglas, 1871.
Butter, H., *A Young Man's Questions Answered*, London: W.H. Guest, 1880.
Caird, A.M., *The Morality of Marriage and Other Essays on the Status and Destiny of Women*, London: George Redway, 1897.
Charlesworth, L., 'On Historical Contextualisation: Some Critical Socio-Legal Reflections', *Crimes and Misdemeanours*, 1(1), 2007, 1–40.
Charon, R. and Montello, M. (eds), *Stories Matter: The Role of Narrative in Medical Ethics*, London: Routledge, 2002.
Cobbe, F.P., 'Wife-Torture in England', *Contemporary Review*, 32, April 1878, 55–87.
Collard, G.C., *Up to Scratch: the Story of Bristol's Bareknuckle Champions*, Bristol: Packer, 1992.
Collier, R., *Masculinity, Law and The Family*, London: Routledge, 1995.
Collins, W., *The Woman in White*, London: Sampson Low, 1860.
Combs, M.B., '"A Measure of Legal Independence": The 1870 Married Women's Property Act and the Portfolio Allocations of British Wives', *Journal of Economic History*, 65(4), 2005, 1028–57.
Connell, R.W., *Masculinities*, 2nd edn, Cambridge: Polity, 2005.
Connell, R.W. and Messerschmidt, J.W., 'Hegemonic Masculinity: Rethinking the Concept', *Gender & Society*, 19(6), 2005, 829–59.
Coveney, P., *The Image of Childhood. The Individual and Society: A Study of the Theme in English Literature*, Harmondsworth: Penguin, 1967.
Cowan, D.S., '"Rage at West*sin*ster": Sociolegal reflections on the power of sale', *Social and Legal Studies*, 12(2), 2003, 177–98.
Cross, R., 'Centenary Reflections on Prince's Case', *Law Quarterly Review*, 91, 1975, 540–54.
D'Cruse, S. (ed.), *Everyday Violence in Britain, 1850–1950*, Harlow: Pearson, 2000.
Davidoff, L., 'Class and Gender in Victorian Britain' in J.L. Newton, M.P. Ryan and J. Walkowitz (eds), *Sex and Class in Women's History*, London: Routledge, 1983.
Davidoff, L. and Hall, C., *Family Fortunes*, revised edition, London: Routledge, 2002.
Dyer, A.S., *Safeguards Against Immorality; and Facts that Men Ought to Know*, London: Dyer Brothers, 1884.
—— *The European Slave Trade in English Girls: A Narrative of Facts*, London: Dyer Brothers, 1880.
East, E.H., *A Treatise Of The Pleas Of The Crown*, London: J. Butterworth, 1803, vol. 1.
Egan, P., *Boxiana: Or Sketches of Ancient and Modern Pugilism, From the Days of the Renowned Boughton and Slack to the Championship of Cribb*, London: George Virtue, 1830, vol. I.
Elias, N., *The Civilizing Process*, trans. Edmund Jephcott, Oxford: Blackwell, 1982.
Emsley, C., *Hard Men: Violence in England Since 1750*, London: Hambledon and London, 2005.
Fielden, K., 'Samuel Smiles and Self-help', *Victorian Studies*, 12, 1968, 155–76.
Flegel, M., *Conceptualizing Cruelty to Children in Nineteenth-Century England: Literature, Representation, and the NSPCC*, Aldershot: Ashgate, 2009.
Foster, M., *Crown Law*, 3rd edn, London: E and R Brooke, 1792.
Foucault, M., *Discipline and Punish: The Birth of the Prison*, trans. Alan Sheridan, London: Allen Lane, 1977 (first published in French in 1975).

Garland, D., 'British Criminology before 1935', *British Journal of Criminology*, 28(2), 1988, 1–17.

Gleeson, K., 'Sex, Wives, and Prostitutes: Debating *Clarence*', in J. Rowbotham and K. Stevenson (eds), *Criminal Conversations: Victorian Crimes, Social Panic, and Moral Outrage*, Columbus: Ohio State University Press, 2005, ch. 13.

—— 'The Problem of Clarence, Brutal at His Best: James Fitzjames Stephen and the Doctrine of Sexual Inequality', *Nottingham Law Journal*, 14(1), 2005, 1–16.

Goldman, W., *The Princess Bride*, San Diego C.A: Harcourt Brace, 1973.

Gorham, D., 'The "Maiden Tribute of Modern Babylon" Re-Examined: Child Prostitution and the Idea of Childhood in Late-Victorian England', *Victorian Studies*, 21(3), 1978, 353–79.

Grand, S., *The Heavenly Twins*, London: Heinemann, 1893.

Gray, W.R., 'For Whom the Bell Tolled: The Decline of British Prize Fighting in the Victorian Era', *Journal of Popular Culture*, 21(2), 1987, 53–64.

Greenslade, W., *Degeneracy, Culture and the Novel 1880–1940*, Cambridge: Cambridge University Press, 1994.

Hale, Sir M., *The History of the Pleas of the Crown*, London: Lincoln's Inn, 1736, vol. 1.

Hall, D.E. (ed.), *Muscular Christianity: Embodying the Victorian Age*, Cambridge: Cambridge University Press, 1994.

Hammerton, A.J., *Cruelty and Companionship: Conflict in Nineteenth Century Married Life*, London: Routledge, 1992.

Handler, P., 'The Court for Crown Cases Reserved, 1848–1908', *Law and History Review*, 29(1), 2011, 259–88.

Holland, J.A. and Webb, J.S., *Learning Legal Rules: A Students' Guide to Legal Method and Reasoning*, 7th edn, Oxford: Oxford University Press, 2010.

Hughes, T., *Tom Brown at Oxford*, London: Macmillan, 1883 (the novel was first published in 1861).

Huxtable, R., 'Logical Separation? Conjoined Twins, Slippery Slopes and Resource Allocation', *Journal of Social Welfare and Family Law*, 23(4), 2001, 459–71.

Ignota, 'Judicial Sexual Bias', *Westminster Review*, 149(3), March 1898, 279–88. (Ignota was just one of Elizabeth C. Wolstenholme Elmy's pseudonyms.)

Jackson, E.H. (ed. W.H. Burnett), *The True Story of the Clitheroe Abduction; or, Why I Ran Away with My Wife*, 2nd edn, Blackburn: North-East Lancashire Printing & Publishing Co., 1891.

Jackson, L.A., *Child Sexual Abuse in Victorian England*, London: Routledge, 2000.

Jarvis, A., *Samuel Smiles and the Construction of Victorian Values*, Stroud: Sutton, 1997.

Jenkins, K., *Rethinking History*, London: Routledge, Routledge Classics Edition, 2003.

Kelly, L., Temkin, J. and Griffiths, S., *Section 41: An Evaluation of New Legislation Limiting Sexual History Evidence in Rape Trials*, London: Home Office, 2006.

Kingsley, C., 'The Science of Health' in *Health and Education*, London: Isbister, 1874.

Knott, G.H., 'English Legal Affairs', *American Law Review*, 25, 1891, 400–13.

Lankester, E.R., *Degeneration: A Chapter in Darwinism*, London: Macmillan, 1880.

Linton, E.L., 'The Judicial Shock to Marriage', *Nineteenth Century*, 29(171), 1891, 691–700.

Luckin, B., 'Revisiting the Idea of Degeneration in Urban Britain, 1830–1900', *Urban History*, 33(2), 2006, 234–52.

Lyon Bowes, M.E., Countess of Strathmore, *Confessions of the Countess of Strathmore, Written by Herself, Carefully Copied from the Original Lodged in Doctor's Commons*, London: W. Locke, 1793.

Mallett, P., '"Smacked and Brought to her Senses": Hardy and the Clitheroe Abduction Case', *Thomas Hardy Journal*, 8(2), 1992, 70–3.

Mallin, M.G., 'In Warm Blood: Some Historical and Procedural Aspects of Regina v Dudley and Stephens', *University of Chicago Law Review*, 34, 1967, 377–407.

Mayhew, H., Hemyng, B., Binny, J. and Halliday, A., *London Labour and London Poor*, London: Griffin, Bohn, 1861, vol. 4.

McArdle, D., 'A Few Hard Cases? Sport, Sadomasochism and Public Policy in the English Courts', *Canadian Journal of Law and Society*, 10, 1995, 109–17.

McCormick, D., *Blood on the Sea: The Terrible Story of the Yawl 'Mignonette'*, London: Muller, 1962.

McLaren, A., *The Trials of Masculinity: Policing Sexual Boundaries*, 1870–1930, Chicago: University of Chicago Press, 1997.

Mee, B., *Bare Fists: The History of Bare-Knuckle Prize-Fighting*, New York: Overlook Press, 2001.

Mill, J.S., *The Subjection of Women*, London: Longmans, Green, Reader and Dyer, 1869.

Moore, W., *Wedlock: The True Story of the Disastrous Marriage and Remarkable Divorce of Mary Eleanor Bowes, Countess of Strathmore*, London: Weidenfeld and Nicolson, 2009.

Munslow, A., Preface to K. Jenkins, *Rethinking History*, London: Routledge, Routledge Classics Edition, 2003.

Nicolson, D., 'Telling Tales: Gender Discrimination, Gender Construction and Battered Women Who Kill', *Feminist Legal Studies*, 3(2), 1995, 185–206.

—— 'Truth, Reason and Justice: Epistemology and Politics in Evidence Discourse', *Modern Law Review*, 57(5), 1994, 726–44.

Ormerod, D. and Gunn, M., 'The Legality of Boxing', *Legal Studies*, 15(2), 1995, 181–203.

Pankhurst, C., *The Great Scourge and How to End It*, London: E. Pankhurst, 1913.

Parker, D., *The Trampled Wife*, Stroud: Sutton, 2006.

Pick, D., *Faces of Degeneration: A European Disorder c.1848–c.1918*, Cambridge: Cambridge University Press, 1989.

Quilter, H. (ed.), *Is Marriage a Failure*, London: Swan Sonnenschein, 1888.

Robertson, A., 'The Reform of the Marriage Laws of Great Britain and Ireland', *Law Magazine and Review*, 17(5), 1891, 1–33.

Roper, M. and Tosh, J. (eds), *Manful Assertions: Masculinities in Britain since 1800*, London: Routledge, 1991.

Rowbotham, J. and Stevenson, K., *Criminal Conversations: Victorian Crimes, Social Panic, and Moral Outrage*, Columbus, OH: Ohio State University Press, 2005.

Rubenstein, D., *Before the Suffragettes: Women's Emancipation in the 1890s*, Brighton: Harvester, 1986.

Savage, G., '"The Wilful Communication of a Loathsome Disease": Marital Conflict and Venereal Disease in Victorian England', *Victorian Studies*, 34(1), 1990, 35–54.

Shanley, M.L., *Feminism, Marriage, and the Law in Victorian England*, 1850–1895, London: IB Tauris, 1989.

Shoemaker, R., 'Male Honour and the Decline of Public Violence in Eighteenth Century London', *Social History*, 26(2), 2001, 190–208.

Simpson, A.W.B., *Leading Cases in the Common Law*, Oxford: Oxford University Press, 1995.

—— *Cannibalism and the Common Law: The Story of the Tragic Last Voyage of the Mignonette and the Strange Legal Proceedings to Which It Gave Rise*, Chicago: University of Chicago Press, 1984.

—— 'Regina v Archer and Miller: The Leading Case that Never Was', *Oxford Journal of Legal Studies*, 2(2), 1982, 181–96.

Sithamparanathan, A., 'Noble Art of Self Defence or Unlawful Barbarism?', *Entertainment Law Review*, 13(8), 2002, 183–7.

Smart, C. (ed.), *Regulating Womanhood: Historical Essays on Marriage, Motherhood and Sexuality*, London: Routledge, 1992.

Smiles, S., *Character*, London: John Murray, 1871.

—— *Self-help: With Illustrations of Conduct and Perseverance*, London: John Murray, 1859.

Smith, A., *Victorian Demons: Medicine, Masculinity and the Gothic at the Fin-de-Siècle*, Manchester: Manchester University Press, 2004.

Smith, K.J.M., *James Fitzjames Stephen: Portrait of a Victorian Rationalist*, Cambridge: Cambridge University Press, 1988.

Spierenburg, P., 'Punishment, Power, and History: Foucault and Elias', *Social Science History*, 28(4), 2004, 607–36.

Steedman, C., *Strange Dislocations: Childhood and the Idea of Human Interiority 1780–1930*, London: Virago, 1995.

Stephen, H., 'Murder by Necessity', *Law Quarterly Review*, 1, 1885, 51–61.

Stephen, J.F., *A History of the Criminal Law of England*, London: Macmillan, 1883, vol. I.

Stevenson, K., '"Crimes of Moral Outrage": Victorian Encryptions of Sexual Violence', in J. Rowbotham and K. Stevenson (eds), *Criminal Conversations: Victorian Crimes, Social Panic, and Moral Outrage*, Columbus, OH: Ohio State University Press, 2005, ch. 14.

Stevenson, K., 'Observations on the Law Relating to Sexual Offences: The Historic Scandal of Women's Silence', *Web Journal of Current Legal Issues*, 19, 1999.

Stychin, C.F. and Mulcahy, L., *Legal Methods and Systems: Text and Materials*, 4th edn, London: Sweet & Maxwell, 2010.

Summerscale, K., *The Suspicions of Mr Whicher or The Murder at Road Hill House*, London: Bloomsbury, 2008.

Taylor, H., 'The Enfranchisement of Women', *Westminster Review*, 55(2), July 1851, 289–311.

Temkin, J., 'Sexual History Evidence – Beware the Backlash', *Criminal Law Review*, 2003, 217–42.

Thomas, P.A., *Socio-Legal Studies*, Aldershot: Dartmouth, 1997.

Toczek, L., 'Mistake and age-based sexual offences', *New Law Journal*, 151, 2001, 1328–9.

Tosh, J., *A Man's Place: Masculinity and the Middle-class Home in Victorian England*, New Haven: Yale University Press, 1999 and 2007.

Tylor, E.B., *Primitive Culture: Researches into the Development of Mythology, Philosophy, Religion, Art, and Custom*, London: John Murray, 1871, vol. 2.

Vance, N., *The Sinews of the Spirit: The Ideal of Christian Manliness in Victorian Literature and Religious Thought*, Cambridge: Cambridge University Press, 1985.

Walkowitz, J.R., *City of Dreadful Delight: Narratives of Sexual Danger in Late Victorian England*, Chicago: University of Chicago Press, 1992.

—— *Prostitution and Victorian Society: Women, Class and the State*, Cambridge: Cambridge University Press, 1980.

Watkins, D., 'Recovering the Lost Human Stories of Law: Finding Mrs Burns', *Law and Humanities*, 7(1), 2013, 68–90.

Weait, M., *Intimacy and Responsibility: The Criminalisation of HIV Transmission*, Abingdon: Routledge-Cavendish, 2007.

Weeks, J., *Sex, Politics, and Society: The Regulation of Sexuality Since 1800*, London: Longman, 1981.

Weldon, G., *How I Escaped the Mad Doctors*, London: Mrs. Weldon, 1882.

Wheeler, R.F., 'Organised Sport and Organised Labour: The Workers' Sports Movement', *Journal of Contemporary History*, 13(2), 1978, 191–210.

White, H., 'Historical Emplotment and the Problem of Truth', in S. Friedlander (ed.), *Probing the Limits of Representation: Nazism and the 'Final Solution'*, London: Harvard University Press, 1992.

—— *The Content of Form: Narrative Discourse and Historical Representation*, London: Johns Hopkins University Press, 1987.

—— *Metahistory: The Historical Imagination in Nineteenth-Century Europe*, Baltimore, MA: Johns Hopkins University Press, 1973.

Wiener, M.J., *Men of Blood: Violence, Manliness, and Criminal Justice in Victorian England*, Cambridge: Cambridge University Press, 2004.

—— 'The Victorian Criminalisation of Men', in P. Spierenburg (ed.), *Men and Violence: Gender, Honor, and Rituals in Modern Europe and America*, Ohio, OH: Ohio State University Press, 1998, pp. 197–212.

Williams, G., 'A Commentary on *R v Dudley and Stephens*', *Cambrian Law Review*, 8, 1977, 94–9.

Winter, J., 'The Truth Will Out? The Role of Judicial Advocacy and Gender in Verdict Construction', *Social and Legal Studies*, 11(3), 2002, 343–67.

—— *The Use of Gender in the Trials of Myra Hindley and Rose West*, PhD thesis, University of Bristol, 2001.

Withey, C., 'Biological GBH: overruling Clarence?', *New Law Journal*, 153(7104), 2003, 1698, 1707.

Wolstenholme Elmy, E.C., *The Decision in the Clitheroe Case, and its Consequences: a Series of Five Letters*, Manchester: Guardian Printing Works, 1891.

Wood, J.C., *Violence and Crime in Nineteenth-Century England: The Shadow of Our Refinement*, London: Routledge, 2004.

Young, J.E., 'Towards a Received History of the Holocaust', *History and Theory*, 36(4), 1997, 21–43.

Index

Note: page numbers in italic refer to illustrations

www.ingramcontent.com/pod-product-compliance
Ingram Content Group UK Ltd.
Pitfield, Milton Keynes, MK11 3LW, UK
UKHW011009180926
475701UK00004B/639

* 9 7 8 1 1 3 8 9 5 0 7 9 5 *